FRANCE UNDER THE DIRECTORY

FRANCE
UNDER THE DIRECTORY

MARTYN LYONS

King's College, Cambridge

CAMBRIDGE UNIVERSITY PRESS

CAMBRIDGE

LONDON · NEW YORK · MELBOURNE

Published by the Syndics of the Cambridge University Press
The Pitt Building, Trumpington Street, Cambridge CB2 1RP
Bentley House, 200 Euston Road, London NW1 2DB
32 East 57th Street, New York, NY 10022, USA
296 Beaconsfield Parade, Middle Park, Melbourne 3206, Australia

ISBNs: 0 521 20785 1 hard covers
0 521 09950 1 paperback

First published 1975

Printed in Great Britain
at the
University Printing House, Cambridge
(Euan Phillips, University Printer)

To JACCI and BLAISE

CONTENTS

MAPS

ACKNOWLEDGEMENTS

My first debt is to Richard Cobb, whose teaching and advice have sustained and continually renewed my interest in the French Revolution over the last seven years. His views, or at least some of them, have indirectly but inevitably found their way on to these pages.

A work as dependent on secondary sources as this must owe a considerable obligation to a host of scholars, whose research has made the book possible. Since I cannot mention them all here, I hope they will regard my bibliography as a sufficient indication of the debt I owe them. Of those not included in the bibliography, I should thank Colin Jones, who was kind enough to let me see a copy of his unpublished dissertation on 'Social Aspects of the Treatment of Madness in the Paris Region, 1789–1800'.

I must also thank the Fellows of King's College, Cambridge, where this book was written during the tenure of a fellowship, for supporting my visits to Parisian archives and libraries.

Finally, I must thank Jacci, my wife and sternest critic.

Map 1. France and the annexed departments

x

INTRODUCTION

J'espère que lorsque les passions seront calmées, lorsque les événements et les hommes paraîtront dans tout leur jour et tels qu'ils furent, on ne trouvera pas si méprisable un gouvernement qui fut chargé de l'administration de la France dans un moment où partout régnait le plus affreux désordre et le plus complet dénûment; un gouvernement, qui, à la tête d'une nation sans argent, sans pain, sans revenus, sans police, avait dans son sein deux hommes conspirant chacun de leur côté...un gouvernement qui était environné de pièges, assailli sans relâche par le royalisme et l'anarchie, jalousé par les membres des deux conseils législatifs, qui ne lui accordèrent jamais franchement et loyalement les moyens de faire prospérer le pays; un gouvernement qui, malgré tant d'obstacles, était parvenu à réorganiser l'administration intérieure et à soutenir l'honneur de la république vis-à-vis des puissances étrangères...
– Ce gouvernement, j'ose le croire, s'il ne paraît pas exempt de censures méritées (et qui en est exempt dans ce monde?) obtiendra néanmoins quelque justice de l'impartiale postérité.
–Memoirs of La Revellière, Paris, 1895, vol. i, pp. 308–9

Only recently has La Revellière's modest plea for a balanced consideration of the Directory been answered. There has been no systematic survey of the Directory since the four-volume work of Sciout, published in the 1890s. Although richly documented, Sciout's book is consistently hostile to the régime. Students have for years referred to Lefebvre's short works on the thermidoreans and the Directory, published as long ago as 1937 and 1946 respectively, and only belatedly translated into English. These works, based on Lefebvre's lectures at the Sorbonne, are essentially chronological in structure, and are influenced by the socialist tradition of revolutionary historiography, inherited from Jaurès and Mathiez. In recent years, several publications have rescued the period from 1795 to 1799 from the comparative oblivion to which it had been consigned by post-war revolutionary historians. Soboul's short book in the 'Que sais-je?' series (1967),[1] for example, had the merit of emphasising the links

[1] See Bibliography no. 24 for complete citation.

I

between the Directory and the Consulate. The excellent book produced by Denis Woronoff in 1972 synthesises the findings of recent research in this period.[1]

Critics on the left and the right have joined in relegating the period of thermidor and the Directory to its unenviable status in French history. For the left, the Directory represented a betrayal of the ideal of social equality expressed by the revolutionaries of the Year 2. For the propagandists of Bonapartism, the Directory was a régime paralysed by factional in-fighting, and inherently unstable, a parliamentary system riddled with corruption, in the same way that the Fourth Republic was described by the Gaullists. The drama of the Terror on the one hand, and of the Grand Empire on the other, the great personalities of Robespierre and Napoleon, threw the intervening period into the dark shadows of neglect. The Directory became the 'poor relation of revolutionary historiography', to borrow the phrase of Furet and Richet, an embarrassing hiatus, which happens to separate the fall of Robespierre from the foundation of the Consulate. A whole multitude of books, chapters of books, and articles entitled or subtitled 'From Thermidor to Brumaire' illustrate the enduring nature of this approach.

The balance, however, is being restored. In a well-known article of 1937,[2] Professor Goodwin attacked the myth that the period of the Directory was one of venality and corruption, and asserted that the government's '*politique de bascule*' was a source not of weakness, but of strength. Yet it has taken over two decades for the work of reinterpretation to bear fruit. Many historians would now accept many of Goodwin's arguments, and pay tribute to the importance of, for instance, the Directory's administrative reforms. This book aims at continuing this process of demystification, or of revisionism, as some may have it, and at making the results of recent research available to the English student of French history.

Traditions live on. For committed Jacobin critics of the Directory, the topic which best deserves attention is still perhaps the conspiracy of Babeuf, whose study has now been elevated into a vast academic industry. Nevertheless, the study of the period has been rejuvenated by the research of Cobb and Rudé into the popular movement, and by the work of the American historians

---

[1] Bibliography no. 26.   [2] Bibliography no. 19.

2

Woloch and Mitchell in the study of Jacobinism and the Counter-Revolution. New insights have been provided by Church into the Directorial bureaucracy, and by Suratteau in his scrutiny of the elections of the period. In a period when the powers of the central government were weakened, local studies have also made an important contribution to our understanding of the provinces.

There is no doubt, however, that we still need a full demographic study of the crisis of the Year 3, and full biographies of important Directorial figures like Reubell (although Suratteau has recently stressed the hazards of such an enterprise). Furthermore, local studies of the Midi during the Directory are still lacking. In drawing wherever possible on my own investigations into the history of Toulouse, I hope I shall be forgiven for any geographical imbalance which this might entail.

This book, however, is primarily intended to bring together the diffuse secondary material on the subject for the English reader. It has tried to escape from the strictly narrative form employed by Lefebvre, and it has perhaps given more weight to the intellectual and cultural aspects of the period than Woronoff was able to do. Above all, it is intended to encourage the study of the thermidorean and Directorial régimes in their own right, to emphasise their successes as well as their failures, while placing them firmly inside, rather than outside, the history of the French Revolution as a whole.

The Directorial régime gave France her first experience of representative institutions. This book tries to explain how and why this experiment failed, and why a series of *coups d'état* were necessary to prevent the régime's collapse. The Directory attempted to provide a stable and liberal form of government, which would preserve the moderate social gains of the Revolution, but would avoid a repetition of the repressive violence and tyrannical dictatorship associated with the Terror. Yet the legacy of the past weighed heavily on the régime. Its refusal to compromise with either ex-Terrorists or supporters of the monarchy, and the government's lack of respect for the will of the electorate, stifled the growth of a moderate, centre party on which the Directory could rely.

The Directory's problems, however, were not all political ones. Both the Girondins and the Montagnards had considered the task of social reconstruction, but their schemes had been temporarily set aside, until the nation had been unified to expel the invading armies of Ancien Régime Europe. After the Terror, however, the thermidoreans and the Directory resumed this gigantic task, attempting to renew the liberal ideals of 1790 and 1791, although the rebuilding of the social institutions of France was still vitiated by the financial and military burdens of a continental war. While, for example, the Directory conspicuously failed to heal the religious schism, it introduced important and long-lasting administrative reforms.

The treatment of these problems falls roughly into three sections. The first, narrative section of three chapters is mainly concerned with the political history of the period between 9 thermidor and the *coup* of fructidor Year 5, and discusses the opposition to the Directory on the Left and on the Right. The central, more thematic section begins with a discussion of the victims and beneficiaries of Directorial society, within the framework of the crude contemporary division of society into 'Les Gros' and 'Les Maigres'. The following chapters (6 to 10) examine the Directory's approach to its main social and cultural problems, and discuss the nature of education, religion, science, art, and the army in a Republican society. Chapter 11 deals with the Directory's administrative reforms, and this is followed by chapters on the economy and the war. The political narrative is resumed in the final section of the book, and finally the fall of the Directory in brumaire is analysed.

The revolutionaries of 1789 might have been astounded to learn that within three years France would be a Republic. As far as they were concerned, their task was to provide France with a Constitution, which would give the country political liberty under the monarchy. In modern terms, their view of political liberty was not a generous one. Only men of wealth and property, they considered, had the leisure and sense of responsibility which entitled them to participate in the electoral system. They looked forward to a society in which all men would be equal before the law, and in which justice would be clear, rational, and impartial. Since many of them were lawyers, the provision of a just legal system and a humane penal code were vital preoccupations. They would liberate economic life from the restrictive practices of the guilds, and from the many internal customs barriers, which hindered the growth of trade. They believed in a rational system of government, and in the rights of the individual. While not all men could enjoy equal rights, all could enjoy equal opportunity to pursue the career of their choice. They attempted to create a society whose greatest honours were no longer a privilege of birth or of family connections, but in which individual merit would find its true reward.

Such were the liberal, rational, and individualistic aims of the Constituent Assembly. By 1791, they seemed to have been essentially achieved. In the summer of that year, Barnave declared, 'This revolutionary movement has destroyed all that it set out to destroy, and has brought us to the point where it is necessary to halt...one step further towards liberty must destroy the monarchy, one more towards equality must abolish private property.'

Why did Barnave and the Feuillants fail to stem the revolutionary tide? They failed, firstly, because the monarchy itself did not genuinely accept the limitation of its own powers, and worked to persuade the foreign powers to enforce a full restoration of its authority. They failed because the establishment of a Constitutional Church had already caused a deep rift in French society. The inflation of the *assignats*, the revolutionary paper currency, was to introduce a further element of weakness. The peasant agitation, for the abolition of the seigneurial system without compensation, continued after the Assembly had accepted a very limited reduction in feudal obligations in August 1789. The peasants' demands were not fully satisfied until July 1793. The urban lower classes, who had made an essential contribution to the overthrow of the Ancien Régime, would not passively allow the propertied and professional classes to appropriate the spoils of the Revolution. Barnave failed, too, because the European war catapulted the Revolution into extremism.

The Brissotins had adopted a war policy in order to tear away the veil which disguised the monarchy's real intentions, and to bring themselves to power. The very disparate group of deputies known as the Girondins, however, were ultimately not prepared to take the vigorous measures necessary to win the war. Their rivals, the Montagnards, persuaded the majority of the National Convention that they alone were capable of defeating invading armies, civil war, and the Royalist rebellion in the Vendée. On 31 May 1793, the Montagnards came to power.

The government of the Terror, which they established, was constructed in a spontaneous and piecemeal fashion to meet the particular and immediate threats of invasion and internal subversion. The dictatorial government, centred in the leading Committees of Public Safety and General Security, entered into a tactical alliance with the popular movement. It conceded to the *sans-culottes* the regulation of prices and legislation for the arrest and execution of suspects (September 1793). The demands of the militant sections of Paris were appeased by the admission into the Committee of Public Safety of Collot d'Herbois and Billaud-Varenne. The Revolutionary Government mobilised the entire economic resources of the nation to support the war effort. Carnot, Prieur, and Robert Lindet, in the Committee of Public Safety, worked ceaselessly to supply the army and administer the war machine. In the provinces, the central government delegated the struggle against Counter-Revolution to local revolutionary committees, Jacobin clubs, *armées révolutionnaires*, and its own *Représentants en mission*, whose multifarious activities it found difficult to control.

Gradually, however, the anarchy of the early period of the Terror gave way to a more centralised and bureaucratised system of government. The law of 14 frimaire II attempted to lay down a blueprint for a streamlined administration, which would curtail the local initiatives of *sans-culotte* institutions like the revolutionary committees. The great show-trials of the Dantonists and the Hébertistes, stage-managed by the public prosecutor Fouquier-Tinville, eliminated some of the corrupt parasites who surrounded the Revolutionary Government, and liquidated deviationists to the Right and the Left. Danton was a potential focus for opposition to the Terror, while the proscription of the Hébertistes was the first occasion when the Revolutionary Government crushed militants on its Left. The law of 22 prairial II established a draconian judicial procedure, empowering the Parisian Revolutionary Tribunal to give one of only two sentences: acquittal or death. The moderates in the Convention reluctantly renewed the powers of its executive committees, in the interests of the war effort, and out of fear of purges of its own members. Robespierre, in the Committee of Public Safety, demanded absolute unanimity, loyalty to the new cult of the Supreme Being, and observance of the Republican calendar. Yet the increasing tendency towards dictatorial centralisation in the Year 2 stifled revolutionary inspiration at the grass-roots. 'La Révolution', St-Just could claim, 'est glacée.'

6

Introduction

The late summer of the Year 2 saw the increasing isolation of the men closest to Robespierre: St-Just and Couthon in the Committee of Public Safety, Lebas and David in the Committee of General Security, Hanriot in charge of the Parisian National Guard, and the personnel of the Paris Commune and of the Revolutionary Tribunal. While the country as a whole grew weary of a régime which seemed to have achieved its main military objectives, and thus outlived its usefulness, a group of deputies worked to bring down Robespierre, in the parliamentary coup of 9 thermidor II. On this day, the Republic entered a new phase in its history. The Terrorist dictatorship was at an end; the Convention once more raised its head.

I

'NONANTE-CINQ'

By 3 a.m. on 10 thermidor II, the Place de Grève was littered with the human debris of the Revolutionary Government. In the Hôtel de Ville, Philippe Lebas had shot himself in the head; Robespierre's younger brother, Augustin, who had thrown himself from a top-storey window on the arrival of the forces of the Convention, had broken his thigh, and was not executed till sunset; Couthon, a cripple, had either fallen or thrown himself from his wheelchair down the stone staircase of the Hôtel de Ville, where he lay with a gaping wound in the forehead; the giant Coffinhal of the Revolutionary Tribunal, enraged by the Commune's failure, which he attributed to the drunken incompetence of Hanriot, Commander of the National Guard, seized Hanriot, and threw him bodily out of a third-floor window. Hanriot lay half-dead in an interior courtyard of the Hôtel de Ville, undiscovered for another twelve hours. Coffinhal himself escaped, but after hiding for five days amongst the waste and faecal matter on the Île des Cygnes, returned starving to Paris, and was arrested. St-Just surrendered stoically, but he was now a broken man. Robespierre, who had attempted to blow out his brains but succeeded only in breaking a jaw, lay in great pain, but apparently conscious, on the great table of the Committee of Public Safety, where curious *sans-culottes* taunted him mercilessly, asking, 'Ne v'la-t-il pas un beau roi?', and 'Sire, votre majesté souffre?'

How had the government been reduced to this scene of desolation? The *sections* of Paris had not responded to the call to insurrection issued by the rebel Commune of Paris. Only ten of the forty-eight *sections* supported Robespierre for long enough to compromise themselves. Since the proscription of the Hébertistes, the militants had lost their leading spokesmen. In any case, they had no desire to support an administration which, four days earlier, had introduced a new Wage Maximum scale, which threatened to actually reduce wages in certain trades. There was little popular enthusiasm left for a government of puritanical lawyers, who demanded complete unanimity, dictated the organisation of leisure time and family life, and regarded every form of popular amusement with suspicion.

In the victorious Convention itself, the opposition had been formed by a coalition of different groups of Montagnards, who united with the Plain to defeat Robespierre. This Montagnard defection included old followers of Danton, like Thuriot, and moderates like Bourdon de l'Oise, whose principal concern was to reform the Revolutionary Tribunal; ex-*Représentants en mission*, like Fouché, Barras, Fréron, and Tallien, hated by orthodox Robespierrists for their extreme policies in the provinces, and considered also to be corrupt; and some members of the Committee of General Security, like Vadier, Amar, and Voulland, who resented the way in which the Committee of Public Safety had encroached upon their police powers, and perhaps had serious objections to Robespierre's new policy of religious appeasement, and his own pontifical rôle in it.

These, then, were the thermidoreans, who emerged from weeks of fear and tension to lead France. They had temporarily combined to forestall a purge of the Convention by Robespierre, believing themselves to be the imminent targets for sudden arrest and summary trial, if not, like Collot d'Herbois, of assassination attempts. Yet if they had united to defeat Robespierre, they had little else in common. Some wanted to moderate the Terror, others to maintain it for their own advantage. Some, like Thuriot, were intent on avenging the ghost of Danton; others, like Vadier, had been personally responsible for executing him. Within three months after 9 thermidor, this marriage of convenience ended in divorce. Their different views, however, of the purpose and significance of 9 thermidor, were to alarm patriots and foreshadow the bitter political disputes of the Directory. The Jacobin club of Toulouse prophetically warned the Convention in vendémiaire III, 'Si les Romains n'eussent pas été divisés, Caesar n'eut pas osé passer le Rubicon.'

These thermidorean Montagnards were a minority in the Convention. They had won control on 9 thermidor only with the support of the deputies of the Plain, '*les crapauds du marais*', as they were insultingly known, the great majority of uncommitted deputies in the Convention. In the opinion of the Plain, military victories had destroyed the necessity for the Terror. It was time to relax the hunt for suspects, end the dictatorship of the Committee of Public Safety, and liberate the economy from the restrictions imposed during the emergency. Robespierre himself had persuaded them that extraordinary measures were justified as a means of national defence. Since the military threat was receding, the Republic of Virtue could now be discarded.

After the overthrow of the Jacobin leaders, the Plain found itself responsible for the government of the country. Men who had sat cowed and silent before the rhetorical onslaughts of Robespierre and St-Just now began illustrious careers in the service of the Republic, and later, the Empire. Magistrates and civil servants under the Ancien Régime, expert advisers on the committees of the various revolutionary assemblies, now emerged from relative obscurity to take a leading parliamentary rôle. For a Thibaudeau, a Cambacérès, or a Merlin de Douai, the hour had come. Robespierrist sympathisers regarded these survivors from the Convention's silent majority as pygmies, attempting to shoulder the yoke of the Titans. Even Royalists like Mallet du Pan interpreted 9 thermidor as a victory for mediocrity over talent and character. 'Ce sont des valets', he wrote, 'qui ont pris le sceptre de leurs maîtres après les avoir assassinès.' The long process of denigration of the thermidorean and Directorial régimes had begun. The thermidoreans, however, had no desire to occupy the throne of Robespierre. They intended to end dictatorship and restore parliamentary government and the rule of law. They inaugurated an experiment in representative parliamentary government, which gave the period from 1795 to 1799 its unique importance. It is now time to consider how they carried out these aims.

The Centre exacted a price for its support of the dissident Montagnards on 9 thermidor. It demanded an end to political repression. It was not immediately clear that the Terror was over. Within a month, however, the Convention had started to dismantle the apparatus of the Revolutionary Government of the Year 2. The law of 7 fructidor II weakened the executive committees, and introduced a greater degree of decentralisation into government. The Committee of Public Safety was stripped of its police powers, which even the Montagnards considered illegal, and of its control of the ministries. The powers of the two great committees were dispersed among twelve different government committees, among which the Committee of Legislation began to play a leading rôle, in virtue of its power of appointment of local administrators. The Convention, anxious to keep all its committees accountable to it, insisted on the monthly replacement of a quarter of their membership. The Revolutionary Tribunal was reorganised. With the repeal of the law of 22 prairial II, the Convention restored full legal rights to the defence, which could now call on the services of a lawyer, and summon witnesses. The *sections* of Paris, already emasculated by the Jacobin régime, were brought even more firmly under government control. They were regrouped in twelve *arrondissements*, which each had only one *comité de surveillance*, appointed by the Committee of General Security, and directly accountable to it for the arrest and release of suspects.

The reaction did not get fully under way for at least two months. Vadier, Voulland, and Amar, for instance, were not definitively removed from the Committee of General Security until 15 vendémiaire III. The Jacobin club of Paris continued to function until its closure on 21 brumaire. Meanwhile, the thermidoreans could claim to have restored the Convention to its rightful status. Parliamentary debate, with all its personal animosity, its noise and chaos, had resumed. The assembly, for so long intimidated into a frightened silence, now came to life again. The thermidorean Convention, however, had created problems which were to plague French politics for another five years. There was a danger that the demolition of the Terrorist edifice might encourage scavengers – the right wing, the *émigrés*, and the non-juring priests. There was a danger, too, that by limiting the coercive power of the Revolutionary Government, the Convention had undermined its own capacity to maintain order in the departments.

In the provinces, the implications of 9 thermidor were not immediately grasped. Local Jacobins were quick to send their congratulations to the Convention, just as they had done when the Dantonists and Hébertistes were guillotined. In general, the transition was not abrupt. The provinces had not experienced the spate of executions, 'La Grande Terreur', which had gripped the capital in the late summer of the Year 2. Repressive activities had already been relaxed in many areas as early as floréal II, when the military situation started to ease, but there were no immediate signs that the Terror had come to an end. In many departments, local *Représentants* were suddenly freed from Robespierrist supervision, and adopted extreme policies. In Toulouse, for example, Mallarmé brought the clerical repression to a climax after 9 thermidor.

The reaction was naturally most violent where the Terror itself had caused most upheaval. In Marseille, for instance, thermidor was followed by widespread purges of local authorities, and releases of suspects. In areas which had escaped the traumas of civil war and savage repression, that is in most of France, local authorities awaited developments before committing themselves. For this reason, large-scale releases of suspects did not begin until brumaire III. The power vacuum at the centre gave agents of repression like the *Représentants en mission* a brief and illusory period of independence, and increasing government control of revolutionary committees weakened the local pressure groups, which frequently limited the authority of the *Représentants*.

For a while, therefore, the reaction marked time. Revolutionary *commissaires* could not discover the motives which had induced their predecessors to make this or that arrest; *Représentants* had to be called from all six corners of France to answer charges against them, and then, if necessary, replacements had to be sent out. By the winter, however, the reaction had gathered momentum, and the release of suspects was accelerating in the departments. Local Jacobin clubs, led by that of Dijon, protested in vain that these releases were encouraging counter-revolutionaries to come out into the open. In spite of their demands for the full application of the law of suspects, the exclusion of ex-nobles and priests from public office, and the maintenance of the Revolutionary Government '*jusqu'à la paix*', few local *sociétés populaires* survived into brumaire III.

By this time, Montagnard deputies in Paris were feeling the lash of the thermidorean reaction. Not content with dismembering the Revolutionary Government, the thermidoreans were determined to bring individuals to account for their crimes. Carrier, the executioner of Nantes, was the first sacrificial lamb on the thermidorean altar. On his mission in the West, Carrier had been responsible for the execution of two or three thousand Vendéan rebels, some of whom had been drowned by the boatload in the Loire. On 26 frimaire III, Carrier was guillotined.

The thermidoreans had chosen their first victim shrewdly. If the Montagnards had fallen into the trap of defending Carrier, they would only have discredited themselves. Tallien and Bourdon de l'Oise had already covered their tracks by joining the moderate thermidoreans. They left the remaining rank-and-file Montagnards very apprehensive about further reprisals.

On 12 fructidor II, Lecointre de Versailles made a bold attack on the deposed government, when he presented an indictment of Collot d'Herbois, Billaud-Varenne, and Barère, of the Committee of Public Safety, and Vadier, Amar, Voulland, and David, of the Committee of General Security. Lecointre's attack was premature, and hopelessly misjudged the mood of the Convention. In a dramatic session, at which Vadier appeared at the *tribun* with a pistol held at his head, Lecointre was shouted down. His accusations even threatened to backfire when one deputy called for Lecointre's arrest.

The Conventionnels faced an embarrassing dilemma: how could they convict the Jacobin committees of arbitrary and tyrannical acts, without condemning moderate administrators of immense value, like Carnot and Lindet, without condemning themselves, and indeed the whole Revolution? The Convention had, after all, continually renewed the powers of the Committee of Public Safety. The anti-Jacobin backlash, which followed the risings of germinal and prairial III, helped them to overcome these scruples.

Saladin's report on Barère, Collot, Billaud, and Vadier, presented in ventôse III, avoided the pitfalls in which Lecointre had buried himself. Two months' investigation by a special commission had produced an exhaustive list of arbitrary acts committed by the four accused. Although the defendants argued that the Terror was the collective responsibility of the government and the Convention as a whole, they were condemned, and sentenced to deportation.

These proscriptions were made possible by the support of a large group of right-wing deputies, and by counter-terrorist agitation outside the Convention, which the government failed to bring under control. The minority of die-hard Montagnards had repulsed Lecointre's accusations in fructidor, but were not strong enough to prevent the closure of the Jacobin club, or the execution of Carrier. When the proscribed Girondin deputies were readmitted to the Convention in frimaire III, the Jacobins were faced with an overwhelming majority against them. Renegade Montagnards, ex-Dantonists, and reprieved Girondins now united to dominate the thermidorean Convention.

Outside the Convention, the activities of the counter-terrorist bands offered them unofficial assistance, but threatened to compromise them by reviving the spectre of Royalism. The *jeunesse dorée*, encouraged by Fréron in his journal, *L'Orateur du Peuple*, subjected Jacobins to continual harassment. The greatest of these street-fighting gangs, bent on vengeance, were to be found in the provincial cities. Composed of the younger members of influential Ancien Régime families, draft-dodgers and other supporters, these groups were distinguished by their dress, or coloured ribbons: white for the Bourbons, or green for the Duc d'Artois. The '*collets noirs*' at Lyon, the '*chapeaux cirés*' at Toulon, the '*ganses jaunes*' at Toulouse, all brawled with troops, destroyed the property of eminent Jacobins, and disrupted theatre performances with their anthem, *Le Réveil du Peuple*. Jacobins, their homes and lives in danger, began the flight from their claustrophobic, feuding villages and small towns, to the anonimity of the capital. This was one reason why the risings of the Years 3 and 4 were exclusively Parisian affairs. The release of suspects, and the return to local administration of ex-Federalists and Constitutional Royalists swelled the numbers of the royalist bands, and gave them tacit official protection.

To the Jacobins of the Midi, who could not sleep safely in their beds for fear of the marauding murder gangs, thermidorean claims to have restored the rule of law looked shallow. The reaction, however, only assumed bloody and violent aspects in Lyon and the Rhône valley. Known generically as 'Compagnies de Jésus', or 'Campagnies du Soleil', these murder gangs were not organised. They were engaged rather in isolated acts of personal vengeance. The hills of Provence offered ideal terrain for lonely ambushes. A meeting after Mass, a drinking session and a sinister Sunday outing would decide the fate of an ex-Jacobin official, or a Terrorist awaiting trial. The Rhône River provided a convenient dumping ground for corpses. Even when the victims were numbered in hundreds, as in the Lyon prison massacres of floréal III, the authorities turned a blind eye. Elsewhere, however, the thermidorean authorities attempted to defuse a volatile situation, in which released prisoners might be induced to take vengeance on their denunciators. Even compared to the rest of the Midi, the reaction in Lyon was exceptionally blood-thirsty. The trail of blood which flowed down the Rhône into Provence left few stains, for instance, in the *pays de Garonne*.

'Nonante-Cinq'

The government found the impunity of the murderers less worrying than the ominous resurgence of Royalism. Yet, in spite of the anarchy in the Rhône valley, the government scored important victories over Royalist Counter-Revolution. The *émigrés* looked not to the South-east, but to the West, where the Vendéan rising and the spread of *chouannerie* in Brittany seemed to promise them considerable local support. The Convention secured a temporary respite by concluding an armistice with the Vendéan leaders Charrette and Stofflet. By the terms of this agreement, Charrette laid down his arms in return for exemptions from military service and taxes, and, above all, the restitution of religious freedom, a concession which the thermidoreans were soon forced to grant to the country as a whole. Furthermore, the fatal landing of the *émigrés* at Quiberon Bay played into the hands of the Republic. The Royalists who landed from English ships on 9 messidor III were under the illusion that the towns of Brittany would open their gates to them. Instead they faced Hoche's well-prepared Republican troops, who outnumbered them by eight to one. The invaders were routed, and seven hundred were shot. The expedition succeeded only in uniting the Republicans, and in preparing the way for the acceptance of the new Constitution. It illustrated the appalling timing, the ignorance of public opinion, and the tactical fumbling which characterised the Counter-Revolution as a whole.

For the mass of the French population, however, the Year 3 was remembered not for the reopening of the churches, the activities of the White Terrorist gangs, or the proscription of the Montagnards, but for the terrible physical privations it was forced to endure. The winter of 1795 was the bitterest in recent history, colder even than the winter of 1709, which had passed down in folk memory as the coldest of all. The cold of '*nonante-cinq*' was literally killing. Men and horses were found in the streets of Paris, frozen where they had dropped, exhausted by cold and starvation. The rivers froze, and the roads became impassable, making doubly difficult the transport of what little supplies existed. In a temperature of twelve degrees below zero centigrade, it was hardly surprising if the celebration of the anniversary of the King's execution (2 pluviôse III) aroused little jubilation. Lyon, cut off from the grain area of Mâcon by the ice on the Rhône, lived through the winter on a diet of rice. The desperate plight of the poor drove them to crime in order to provide for their families.

Fuel was especially scarce. Forests were raided, tree-stumps hacked out, and coal-heavers attacked in the street. Local police authorities were overwhelmed by a wave of petty theft, mendicancy, and brigandage.

A bad harvest brought famine conditions, and as the economy was prematurely freed from the controls of the Terror, prices soared. Gradually, the edifice of the controlled economy was eaten away. The thermidomeans skilfully turned demands for higher wages against the idea of economic controls, and the principle of economic regulation was breached when the Convention authorised the importation of foreign grain in a desperate attempt to stave off famine. Eager to appease the commercial classes and the wealthier sections of the peasantry, the thermidoreans only delayed the abolition of the Price Maximum because they feared a rising in Paris. Even the Montagnards, however, did not defend the Maximum. They had introduced economic controls as a temporary expedient forced upon them by the *sans-culotterie*. Finally, Cambon's argument proved decisive: the Maximum should be suspended because it was not enforceable, as the Terror itself had ultimately proved. Action was urgently needed. While the issue was being debated at length, merchants were holding back supplies in anticipation of the relaxation of price controls. On 4 nivôse III, the Maximum was repealed, and steps were taken to denationalise the armaments factories.

Prices immediately rose, and as they rose, the daily bread ration fell to only a quarter pound in some *sections* of Paris. Rice was more plentiful, but without fuel, there was no way to cook it. Galloping inflation completed the catastrophe. By floréal III, the *assignat* was worth only eight and a half per cent of its original value. Farmers and shopkeepers, especially in the provinces, would only accept cash, and there was now no way of coercing them.

In demographic terms, the disaster of the Year 3 has yet to be fully measured. Local monographs suggest that this year saw the highest mortality rate between the beginning of the Revolution and the last years of the Empire. As usual, up to fifty per cent of the victims fell within the one-to-ten age-group. The high rate of suicide, of abandoned children, and of births in *hospices* are some indication of the terrible effects of a bad harvest, intense cold, and astronomic inflation. 'Les Parisiens', commented Mallet du Pan, 'ressemblent aux Hindous pendant la famine du Bengale; ils s'empoisonnent, ils se noient, ils se coupent la gorge.'

This was the bleak background to the last *sans-culotte* risings of germinal and prairial III, as well as of the White Terror. Although rioting broke out in Rouen and Amiens in germinal, there were vast areas of France where the cold, hunger, and inflation provoked no bread riots in the image of the Parisian risings. In Bayeux, the urban poor were just as likely to adopt the slogan 'Quand le Bon Dieu était là, nous avions du pain', and similar views could be heard in many southern cities. In other words, the desperate economic situation drove some to extreme Royalism, others to Jacobinism, depending on their environment.

The risings of germinal and prairial have been described as the last purely popular spasms of the '*sans-culotte* movement'. This is exactly why they proved futile, and produced only martyrs. They were essentially bread riots, without *bourgeois* leadership, and therefore without conscious and effective political direction. The Jacobin leadership had been decimated by purges, imprisonment, and deportation. There was no Hébert, no Chaumette, to channel insurrectionary impulses into constructive political demands. Spontaneous reflexes against hunger and high prices were suicidal now that the Convention, through the Committee of General Security, had control of the revolutionary committees. The Convention was able to isolate the extremist *sections* of the Faubourg St-Antoine, wait for their impetus to fade, and then send in troops from the loyal *sections* of the west of Paris. Except for Léonard Bourdon in the Section des Gravilliers, the Montagnard deputies gave the insurrections little assistance, but the thermidoreans nevertheless took the opportunity of arresting Jacobin Conventionnels like Amar, and they disarmed hundreds of Jacobins in Paris and the provinces. The Parisian National Guard was reorganised. Four arrested deputies, Romme, Duquesnoy, Soubrany, and Goujon, committed suicide, and entered Jacobin mythology as 'the martyrs of prairial'. The Convention's victory cemented the support of the middle classes and property-owners for the thermidorean régime. Those classes who had benefited from the end of economic controls could now rest assured that the threat of social revolution was a remote one.

For the main beneficiaries of the thermidorean régime were the middle classes. They were once again able to buy and sell freely, without government interference. They, too, benefited from inflation if they purchased *biens nationaux* in depreciated *assignats*. They were to prove the backbone of the régime, and of the Directory. By crushing popular revolts, the government protected their newly acquired property against a social revolution; by defeating the Royalist threat, it protected them against possible reappropriation by a restored monarchy. It follows that the régime was socially divisive. While the artisan tried to survive on his diet of uncooked rice, the government contractor sat down to his *bon vin* and lobster thermidor, while in 1793, or at least in 1792, they may have stood side by side in the local *société populaire*. Yet these new landowners had good revolutionary credentials. They were the men of '89, and they included committed regicides. They had a vested interest in the social gains of the Revolution, and thus provided a safe guarantee for the Republic against a restoration of the Ancien Régime.

These thermidorean victories were consolidated by a new Constitution, designed to prevent the return both of full democracy and of the monarchy. The Constitution of 1793, although never promulgated, had never been officially disowned, and could be used as a Jacobin rallying-cry. The Constitution of the Year 3, whose founding father was the constitutional theorist Daunou, reproduced many of the oligarchical features of that of 1791, but it also incorporated several novelties which made it something of a freak. Indirect elections were introduced. Adult males who fulfilled a one-year residence qualification were eligible to vote in the primary assemblies if they paid direct taxes, although relatives of *émigrés* and refractory priests were later deprived of voting rights. The electorate thus enfranchised has been estimated to number five million – slightly more than in 1791. The electors, however, who were directly responsible for the choice of deputies were a small number of about 30,000, eligible through a property qualification. At the second stage of the voting process, therefore, the electorate was restricted to a small group of wealthy property-owners, far more exclusive than their equivalents in 1791.

The dream of the anglophile *monarchiens* of 1790 was realised. For the first time in French history, a bicameral system was introduced. The Conseil des Cinq Cents, whose members had to be twenty-five years old, but need not satisfy any property qualification, held the legislative initiative. The Conseil des

Anciens, as the upper chamber was known, was composed of 250 notabilities over the age of forty, who theoretically approved or rejected, but could not amend, legislation drafted by the Cinq Cents. In practice, the Conseil des Anciens did make its own proposals, but the Constitution had condemned it to a mainly obstructive rôle.

The theorists, however, not content with the introduction of these extraordinary age qualifications, and the bizarre, Biblical connotations of the Conseil des Anciens, produced another surprise. They were afraid that a presidential form of government might be the first step towards dictatorship, or to the restoration of the monarchy. Executive power was therefore to be shared between five men, chosen by the legislature, and known as the Directory. The Directors would be at least forty years old, and one of them would be replaced annually, by lot. The Directors had wide powers over the conduct of foreign affairs, and over the armed forces, and they appointed both ministers and local administrators, the *commissaires du pouvoir exécutif*, who now became the government's agents in every commune, canton, and department. The ministers were responsible to the Directory, and they, too, had to be over the age of twenty-five, a stipulation which was later used as an excuse to disqualify Hoche from the War Ministry, just as a feeble attempt was made to exclude Barras from the Directory, on the grounds that he was under forty.

This Constitution was the creation of abstract theorists, who imagined that the most 'rational' plan would necessarily work best. The scheme had several weaknesses. A Directory of five could easily be paralysed by internal divisions, and as long as replacements were decided by lot, the balance of power might be dictated by blind chance. The Constitution of the Year 3 endured for almost five years, longer than any other revolutionary Constitution, but the frequency of *coups d'état* and *lois exceptionnelles* was to show how unworkable it really was. Above all, the executive arm was fatally and deliberately weakened. The ministers did not sit in the legislature, and the Directory communicated with the deputies by official 'messages'. Most important of all, the Cinq Cents retained financial control, since the Treasury was made completely independent of the Directory. The Constitution therefore enforced a rigid separation of powers. It permitted the legislature, if dominated by a hostile majority, to paralyse the Directory. The Directory, which had no power of dissolution, and no veto, could only reply by unconstitutional methods. The procedure for amending the Constitution was almost Byzantine in its complexity. For the Directory itself, the Constitution which created it was eventually to prove a millstone around its neck.

The Conventionnels, anxious to preserve continuity, stability, and their own seats, decided to perpetuate themselves in office. Instead of retiring, and making way for a completely new legislature, they ruled that only one in three of their number would surrender his seat at each annual election. Thus for one year at least, two-thirds of the remaining Conventionnels would continue to dominate the legislature of the new régime. The law of the two-thirds, as it was called, was rejected at the polls by nineteen departments, as well as Paris, and directly provoked the Royalist rising of vendémiaire IV. The Convention enacted further exceptional legislation in order to moderate right-wing successes at the elections of brumaire. An amnesty was granted to those imprisoned for 'crimes concerning the Revolution'. Although proscribed Montagnards were still ineligible for re-election, this measure brought back into circulation a large number of Jacobins imprisoned after germinal and prairial III. By the laws of 3 brumaire III, full sanctions were maintained against refractory priests and *émigrés*, and relatives of the latter were excluded from public office.

The results of the elections of brumaire IV were not encouraging for the new régime. The electoral system now allowed candidates to be nominated in many constituencies at once (although they chose only one to represent), and suspected Royalists, like Lanjuinais and Henri-Larivière, were both elected in over thirty departments. The new government could perhaps derive some satisfaction from the fact that Boissy d'Anglas, one of the founders of the Constitution, was also elected in thirty-six departments. Of the new third, however, well over one hundred were Royalists of one hue or another. The conservative Republicans still dominated the legislature, but they now had on their right over eighty 'pure' Royalists, and almost as many Constitutional Royalists. The right wing had proved particularly strong in the Seine departments and in the Rhône valley. As long as the franchise was restricted to the urban *bourgeoisie*, the west of France remained Republican. The elections revealed the existence of Republican strongholds in the Sarthe, in the Nord, in Toulouse, and in the Ariège.

The first task of the new legislature was to elect the five men into whose hands the fate of the country was to be entrusted. Their choice was impressive only by its banality. They elected the most unpromising combination of an ex-Feuillant lawyer from the East, an ex-Girondin bourgeois from the West, a Terrorist military engineer from the North, and a thermidorean aristocrat from Provence.

The most popular candidate by far was La Revellière-Lépeaux, the only one to poll an absolute majority in the Cinq Cents, and near unanimity in the Anciens. La Revellière, in his early forties, was born into the rural *bourgeoisie* of the Vendée. He made his reputation in the Jacobin club of Angers, was elected to the Convention for the Maine-et-Loire, and supported the Girondins. He was outlawed after protesting against the Revolution of 2 June 1793, and retained a strong fear of the Jacobins, which was hardly surprising, since they had guillotined his brother. He was a dour, melancholic man, who was proud of his honesty and uprightness, and acknowledged the Calvinist inspiration of his religious beliefs. He was a typical *petit-bourgeois*, whose favourite relaxation was a weekend with his family in their country cottage at Andilly and a Sunday outing to the *guinguette*. His main influence in the Directory was on the side of anti-clericalism.

Reubell, a little older than La Revellière, was a lawyer from Colmar. He had earned a reputation in the Constituent Assembly as a strong anti-Semite, but although opposed to Jewish emancipation in Alsace, he played a leading rôle in the campaign for the freedom of black slaves in the colonies. He too was an enemy of Jacobinism, and had been a member of the Feuillant club. He was accused of speculation in the Year 2, but an inquiry acquitted him. He was an able administrator, although he loved argument, and could be obstinate. His main responsibility was to lie in the field of diplomacy. As an Alsatian, he saw the Rhine as France's natural frontier, and supported policies of annexation.

Siéyès, renowned as the greatest constitutional brain of his time, refused to accept his election, and here the Directory made a dangerous enemy. He had refused any responsibility for the Constitution, and retired in the belief that the executive needed to be weakened still further, nursing his pet scheme for an American-style constitutional jury.

His place as Director was taken by Carnot, who, as an ex-member of the Committee of Public Safety of the Year 2, was still thought of as a Jacobin. He enjoyed, however, immense national prestige as the organiser of Republican victory. He was joined in the Directory by another military engineer, Letourneur. Letourneur was a nonentity with few political ideas. He was easily swayed, and usually adopted Carnot's point of view. But he had served for some time in Cherbourg, and while Carnot took charge of military administration, Letourneur became the Directory's naval expert.

The fifth Director, and the one who lasted longest, was Barras, whose reputation for venality and debauchery has rather unfairly coloured views of the Directory as a whole. Barras was a dissipated aristocrat from Provence, who joined the Revolution at a time when he was swamped by gambling debts, and, he claimed, ostracised by his class. He represented the Var in the Convention, and was responsible for crushing the Federalist revolt in Provence. He was elected because of the important military contributions he had made to the Convention. He had besieged Toulon, and he was given charge of the forces of the Convention on 9 thermidor II. Furthermore, Barras was the victor of vendémiaire, when he was again appointed leader of the Convention's armed forces to crush the Royalist rising in the *sections*. Barras took charge of the Directorial police.

The problems they were to face were already apparent in the thermidorean régime. They faced an empty Treasury. The *assignats* were nearly valueless. Working all through the night, the presses could hardly print enough of them for the government's use the following day. Taxes were unpaid, and speculation was becoming a national pastime. Food had to be provided for the population of Paris and the Army of the Interior, but the government could not guarantee even a ration of two ounces of bread per day, four days a week, to the people of Paris. The hospitals had no income, the roads were impracticable, the forests were being pillaged, education was practically nonexistent.

On the military front, it is true, some successes had been achieved. Holland had been invaded, and Carnot, neglecting the Alps, urged Dugommier to continue his advance into Spanish

Catalonia. By the Treaty of Basle, Prussia had recognised France's possessions on the west bank of the Rhine. These advances, however, remained partial ones. Austria fought on, and her hands were now freed by the conclusion of the final Polish Partition. France was forced to abandon Mainz. The army was melting away, the fleet was blockaded, and Corsica was in the hands of the English.

Popular apathy stared the Directors in the face. After the exhaustion of five years of Revolution, the cold winter had frozen what little enthusiasm for politics remained. The Constitution of the Year 3 had been approved by just over one million votes. In brumaire IV, only one in six of the *corps electoral* had gone to the polls. Elections, Constitutions, and referendums were poor counter-attractions compared to the peace and anonimity of family life, and work on the harvest. The Directory thus inherited a mountain of difficulties. If it could not find a way round this mountain, who could blame it?

There were no fanfares for a régime which was not expected to last out the year. As the Directors rode in their carriage to the Petit-Luxembourg on the morning of 11 brumaire, La Revellière-Lépeaux noticed that their cavalry escort were wearing battered shoes over holed woollen socks. The army could not even afford to buy them boots. In the Petit-Luxembourg itself, the Directors found bare rooms, devoid of furniture. The concierge hurriedly found them a rickety table and four chairs. When he brought a few logs and lit a fire, work could begin. The Directory was installed.

2

THE CONSPIRACY OF
THE EQUALS

Jacobinism under the Directory never fully shook off its recent past. Jacobinism had never been endowed with a consciously formed ideology. Rather, it was made up of a series of *ad hoc* measures to meet a series of emergencies, to defeat the Girondins, and to win the war. It was a creed forged in the heat of crisis, invasion, and civil war. It was hammered out piece by piece to cope with particular circumstances – 'la force des choses', in St-Just's phrase.

It embodied, however, a certain conception of the Revolution. The Constitution of 1793 declared for the first time that the purpose of government was '*le bonheur commun*', the common good. This revolutionary innovation was hailed by St-Just when he dramatically announced that happiness was a new idea in Europe. For the first time, the social responsibilities of the State were recognised. The right to work and to education, and *le droit aux subsistances* were accepted as burdens on society as a whole.

Jacobinism also implied a belief in popular sovereignty, expressed through a representative body, elected by universal suffrage. These ideals were protected by the *civisme*, or *patriotisme*, of the citizens, acting through *sociétés populaires*, and other militant organisations. These political clubs developed the nation's political consciousness, and enabled people to keep a check on their representatives. Each citizen, armed with a pike, had the ultimate sanction of insurrection against the government. In case of tyranny, this was his legitimate resource.

In practice, Jacobinism refused any compromise with the Ancien Régime. Vigorous measures against Royalists, *émigrés*, and the refractory clergy were passed. Jacobins had an individual notion of revolutionary justice, based on the guillotine, terrorisation, and repression of all forms of *aristocratie*, that is, all enemies of the Revolution. Here the individual's instinctive notion of natural justice often made legal form and procedure, and even law itself, superfluous.

For many Jacobins, these ideas were of international

significance. The Constitution of 1793 was a declaration of war on Ancien Régime Europe. Oppressed people were offered fraternal assistance in the struggle against tyrannical monarchs. Jacobinism was an ecumenical creed, which proposed a definition of the rights of citizenship for men of all nations.

In social terms, Jacobin ideas remained essentially *bourgeois* ideas. Property rights were maintained under the Jacobin government. The ventôse decrees, which envisaged the liquidation of suspects' property to provide funds for poor relief, were not implemented. Extreme wealth was condemned by Jacobins, who had a Spartan contempt for luxury and the vices it engendered. Food-hoarders and speculators who lived off the poverty of the lower classes were also repressed. The individual, however, was still entitled to his *lopin de terre*. The Jacobin ideal was a society without paupers or millionaires, a society of small, independent property-owners, each with his own shop, workshop, or parcel of land.

The attitude of Jacobins to the *sans-culotterie* was an ambiguous one. While it rejected the extremism of popular leaders and demagogues like Hébert, the Jacobin government needed the support of the *sans-culotterie* to defeat its opponents, fight the war, and staff the munitions factories. Hence the Jacobins compromised with *sans-culotte* demands. Economic controls like the Price Maximum, as well as the creation of *armées révolutionnaires*, which carried the Terror into the departments, were reluctant concessions extracted under duress.

This very brief summary helps towards the understanding of the Jacobin opposition to the Directory. The Directorial Jacobins operated under a régime which rejected social obligations like the right to work; which rejected direct democracy in favour of indirect elections and limited suffrage; and which dismantled the institutions of Jacobin justice. The thermidoreans had further abolished economic controls, but the Jacobins watched their departure with equanimity, since they had always preferred a liberal economy. The Jacobins continued to attack blatant inequalities of wealth, and pressed for higher taxation of the rich. When they considered that the legislation against *émigrés* and clergy was in danger of being diluted, they pressed for more vigorous measures, and these were always high amongst Jacobin priorities.

Nevertheless, the Directory inherited the Jacobin ideal of the nation in arms, institutionalised in the *levée en masse*. It further-more put into practice the Jacobin offer to liberate the op-pressed people of neighbouring countries, although in practice this often looked like naked conquest. Directorial France was as xenophobic as Jacobin France had been, and feeling against England, in particular, ran as high as in the Year 2.

Above all, the Jacobins were no longer forced to contend with pressure from below. The *sans-culotte* movement had been emas-culated by Robespierre; its impotence was underlined when the thermidoreans brought the revolutionary committees of the Paris *sections* under their control. Many *sans-culotte* leaders had been lost in the execution of the Hébertistes and in the disarmament of the Year 3. After germinal and prairial, the popular movement was effectively silenced.

The relationship between the Jacobin government and the artisans and shopkeepers of the *sans-culotterie* had always been equivocal. The *sans-culottes* shared the Jacobin ideal of the small, independent property-owner, and violently defended the in-terests of the urban consumer against food-hoarders and mono-polists, '*les sangsues du peuple*'. Soboul describes this as an essentially anti-capitalist mentality.[1] The *sans-culottes* looked back to the controlled economy of the Ancien Régime, demanding price-fixing, and control of the exportation of essential goods. In September 1793, they had forced the government to accede to demands for a General Price Maximum and for the formation of *armées révolutionnaires* to guarantee food supplies from the provinces.

Yet although the *sans-culottes* were, in this sense, economically reactionary, they were politically *avant-garde*. Soboul claimed that the class-consciousness of the *sans-culotterie* could be defined by a certain moral unity. This unity was expressed negatively, in hatred of the nobles, and indeed all wealth, and of the merchant classes in particular. The *sans-culotterie* were defined not so much by what they were for, but by what they were against, and the Section du Louvre denounced their enemies as 'the ministerial, financial, and *bourgeois* aristocracy, and above all the aristocracy of refractory priests'.

Furthermore, the *sans-culottes* had their own political ethos, their own techniques and institutions, through which they at-

[1] Bibliography no. 51.

tempted to exercise direct democracy. The Paris *sections* exerted constant vigilance over their elected representatives. Denunciation was a civic duty. The publicity of debates, and voting by *acclamation*, or a show of hands, was a safeguard against intrigue and factional politics. The technique of *fraternisation* with other *sections* was used to put pressure on the moderates.

The Year 2's own myth of the *sans-culotte* emphasised his frugality, patriotism, and the humble virtues of manual labour. He was, for one writer, 'a being who always goes on foot, who has no millions, no châteaux, no valets to serve him, and who is lodged very simply on the fifth or sixth floor. He is useful, for he knows how to till the soil, forge, file, saw, put on a roof, make shoes, and pour out his blood to the last drop for the salvation of the Republic.'

Soboul's magisterial study will remain the starting-point for any discussion of the *sans-culotterie*. Nevertheless, his views, it may be suggested, are not exempt from criticism. There is always a danger of confusing the myth of the *sans-culotterie* with its reality. It is risky, for instance, to rely too heavily on the *sectionnaires'* own descriptions of their professional status, when many wealthy men may have downgraded their own social position. For they may have tried to appear as modest artisans merely in order to gain political respectability in the Year 2. It is the author's personal view that the *sans-culotterie* had never been a truly popular movement. Led by an élite of intellectuals and members of the liberal professions, it included wealthy employers and small businessmen, together with shopkeepers and artisans, and only a smattering of wage-earners. Jacobinism under the Directory also bore this resemblance to a kind of 'popular front'. Now that they were no longer intimidated by the threat of direct action from the streets, the middle-class nature of Jacobinism became fully apparent. Its essence had never changed, but the disguise of a popular movement, maintained by the propaganda of the Year 2, was now dropped. The memories with which Jacobins were associated continued to make them feared by the government. They offered, however, no assistance to the risings of germinal and prairial III. The Jacobins eventually rejected the Babouvist attempt to go beyond the Year 2 towards a complete transformation of property relations.

In the Year 3, the Jacobins found themselves in disarray. The Mountain, which had always been a very loose parliamentary group, disintegrated at thermidor II. Some, like Bourdon de l'Oise, Tallien, and Barras, defected to the moderate majority of thermidoreans. Others had been executed with the Robespierrists, others with the Dantonists, Survivors still maintained a loyalty to Robespierre, and looked back nostalgically to his reign. There were other Montagnard Conventionnels, however, including members of the Jacobin Committee of General Security, who saw the overthrow of Robespierre as their greatest service to the Revolution. Naturally, the Robespierrists found it hard to forgive these colleagues. Both, however, could unite against the régime of the Year 3, and it was the uneasy coalition of these two groups which provided the backbone of the early Jacobin opposition to the Directory.

By the end of the Year 3, the outlook had improved. The crushing of the Royalist revolt of vendémiaire gave them encouragement, for it showed that the government needed their support against the Right. The amnesty of brumaire IV released many Jacobins from prison, and opened up possibilities of regrouping.

The presence of a large number of prominent Jacobins in the capital facilitated a renewal of Jacobin agitation at the highest level. Harassed by their enemies in the provinces, many had fled to Paris in search of peace and anonimity. In a small-town environment, they often found it hard to escape the vengeance of their neighbours, clients, and even kinsmen, whom they had terrorised when in office in the Year 2. Many found refuge from the White Terrorist knives in a modest apartment in Paris.

They met, at first quite publicly, in favourite cafés, and political clubs. The Café Chrétien, near the Comédie Italienne, where gatherings sometimes numbered fifty or sixty, the Café des Bains-Chinois, and the Café Chauvin in the Rue du Bac, were their favourite haunts, although police informers were always likely to be amongst those present. There was little formal discussion at these meetings, although the *habitués* might listen to readings from the Jacobin press, the journals of Lebois or Babeuf. The meeting-place most favoured by police agents of the government was, however, the Café Corrazza, in the more select area of the Palais-Égalité (Palais-Royal). Not only was the company more distinguished, and the conversation wittier here, but informers could easily combine a visit to it with one to the Royalist Café Valois, only a stone's throw away.

In the clubs, on the other hand, and in particular in the Société du Panthéon, it was a different matter. Meetings here were larger, and formally organised. Secretaries and other officials were elected every fifteen days, new members were admitted only if they provided referees, and if they made a donation of at least fifty livres to expenses. This was a high figure which excluded lower-class Jacobins. Nevertheless, government spies succeeded in infiltrating this body, especially after the creation of a Police Ministry in nivôse IV, under Merlin de Douai.

In the Club du Panthéon, or de la Réunion, as it was also known, a very wide range of opinion was represented. The enormous latitude it allowed is illustrated by the choice of co-presidents: the anti-Robespierrist Vadier, and the ex-Dantonist Thuriot. This, no doubt, also accounted for the growth in attendance figures. In early frimaire, an informer reported membership at just under 1,000; by nivôse, this had risen to about 1,500. Amongst those present were past members of the government like Vadier, Barère, and Cambon, as well as Robespierrists like Bourgeois, Chrétien, and Buonarroti. Discussions would centre on attacks on the Royalist press, the *chouans*, and on defence of Robespierre and of the Constitution of 1793. The government, which had envisaged the club as a way of rallying Jacobins to the Directory, regarded its vociferous criticisms with increasing alarm. When speakers began to attack the Constitution of the Year 3, it was time to take action. On 10 ventôse IV, the Panthéon was closed, although the government discreetly shut several Royalist- and clerical-inspired assemblies at the same time.

By this time, however, many members had become dissatisfied with the way in which the Panthéon gatherings expressed indiscriminately the full spectrum of left-wing thought. A small group wanted to depart from the moderate tone of the club, and took steps to form their own, more secret assemblies. This was the origin of the Amar committee, out of which were to grow plans for an insurrection. Besides Amar, member of the Terrorist Committee of General Security, this group included the Italian Buonarroti, who had been employed on several missions by the Robespierrist government, Félix Lepelletier, journalist and brother of the assassinated Jacobin deputy, and Darthé, once public prosecutor of the Arras revolutionary tribunal and brother-in-law of the Jacobin extremist Joseph Lebon. Even here, however, there was disagreement, since many distrusted Amar's claim that he had repented of his rôle in the overthrow of Robespierre in thermidor II. Further meetings were held, at which an important rôle was played by the journalist and ex-noble Antonelle, the deputy Drouet, famous for his arrest of the King at Varenne, and Babeuf himself. By germinal IV, these meetings led to the formation of an insurrectionary committee.

Babeuf's ideas, based on intimate knowledge of the workings of the Ancien Régime, were formed during years of revolutionary action, and matured during an enforced period of contemplation in thermidorean prisons. Born in Picardy, the son of a salt-tax collector (*brigadier des gabelles*), Babeuf was himself a *feudiste*, that is a legal expert in the seigneurial obligations of the peasantry. His early revolutionary activity was on behalf of the pauperised peasantry of Picardy against the payment of duties on salt, tobacco, and drink, and against the wealthy tax-farmers who collected these taxes. During this agitation on behalf of peasant grievances, Babeuf, influenced by the thinking of Mably and Morelly, evolved his ideal of the *fermes collectives*, where the land would be cultivated collectively by communities of up to fifty. Seeing that Robespierre offered no hope for any redistribution of property, he supported the Revolution of 9 thermidor, only to find that the new régime was even less inclined towards a reorganisation of property relations. In the course of discussions in prison after prairial III, his circle grew, and his ideas developed.

Babeuf criticised the Constitution of the Year 3, both because it was based on social oppression, and because it failed to meet his ideal of direct democracy. In his view, popular sovereignty would be a reality only when deputies were brought to account for every decision, and when they were under the permanent surveillance of the electorate, which could withdraw their mandate at any time. An insurrection was needed to restore true democracy and social equality. Such an insurrection was to be achieved by a small élite of dedicated activists, who, by means of agitation and propaganda in key sectors like the army, would prepare the way for a sudden seizure of power. Here was Babeuf's greatest innovation in the field of revolutionary theory. The insurrection he envisaged would not be brought about by a spontaneous rising, but by a cell of revolutionaries ready to capture the centre of power and establish a temporary dictatorship until revolutionary legislation had been decreed and approved.

In spite of this modernity, however, Babeuf's ideas had some extraordinary, primitive aspects. He was, for example, almost uniquely concerned with agrarian reform. In his ignorance of the problems of the urban worker and of industrial labour, he remained a pre-industrial socialist. As elaborated by Buonarroti, the ideas of the Babouvists appear hostile to urban life altogether. Towns are described by Buonarroti as places of low morality where the wealth produced by the peasantry is dissipated in useless pleasures. Towns are accused of drawing valuable manpower from the countryside, and of constituting a threat to public order. Although imbued with a fanatical belief in equality, these ideas also show a Spartan view of morality and education, akin to that of several eighteenth-century philosophers.

Historians and Marxists argue whether or not Babeuf was opposed simply to the feudal organisation of property or to private property in any form. While the Soviet historian Daline argues that Babeuf was a true communist in attacking property *per se*, Lefebvre maintained that Babeuf later moderated his support of the *fermes collectives*, and advocated only a redistribution of property.[1] What is important here is that these questions played no part in the 'Babouvist movement'. They were not disseminated to the grass-roots of the conspiracy. The Conspiracy of the Equals was only a communist conspiracy in Babeuf's own imagination.

The ideas of the Equals were diffused to a very mixed audience. In the press, the Babouvist group could rely on Babeuf's own newspaper, *Le Tribun du Peuple*, which had five hundred subscribers. Judging by the readers of the *Tribun*, Babeuf's audience was predominantly Parisian, for over half lived in the capital. In the provinces most readers were to be found in the Nord and the Pas-de-Calais, where the connections of Robespierre and Lebon were strong, and in the southern towns, like Toulon and Avignon, where Jacobins took refuge from the White Terror. But it would be wrong to assume from this that Babeuf commanded a network of supporters all over France. Many of the readers were themselves men in local office, trying to inform themselves of developments in Paris, or else booksellers or hotel-keepers who automatically held a stock of current

[1] Bibliography no. 47.

journals. The proletarian element was entirely absent from the provincial readership of *Le Tribun du Peuple*. There is nothing here to suggest a movement in support of Babeuf's social ideals. Babeuf may have hoped for support, for instance, in the Jacobin city of Toulouse, but there was not one subscriber to *Le Tribun du Peuple* in the Haute-Garonne.

In Paris, Babeuf's readership was drawn from a wider social base. It included wives of guillotined Jacobins like Marat and Ronsin, as well as thirty-two ex-Conventionnels like Fouché, Javogues, and David. Some continuity has been observed between the sectional leaders of the Year 2 and the men Babeuf listed as potential agents. It is probable, however, that all these categories were more interested in a return to the revolutionary government of 1793 than in any form of Babouvist communism. In other words, the Babouvist movement, as such, did not exist.

The Babouvist cell was aware of these weaknesses. They realised, too, the impossibility of conducting a successful insurrection on their own. For the *sections* of Paris were unlikely to flock to the banner of unknown conspirators like Babeuf, Germain, Maréchal, Darthé, names which meant nothing to the average *sectionnaire*. For, whether the Babouvists liked it or not, the only Jacobins who had this kind of public influence were national figures like Robert Lindet, Amar, and Vadier – the ex-Conventionnels. Pressed by Drouet, the Babouvist committee decided to make overtures to the ex-Conventionnels.

Difficulties were in store. The Babouvists had not forgiven these ex-Conventionnels for overthrowing Robespierre in thermidor, and letting in the thermidoreans. While the government of the Year 2, which they represented, was preferable in Babouvist eyes to that of the Year 3, they hoped to establish an even greater degree of social equality when their turn came. Furthermore, if the projected insurrection should be successful, ex-Conventionnels like Amar demanded that the old Convention of the Year 2 should be recalled. Such an arrangement would exclude the Babouvists from power. Negotiations stumbled over this point. There were some Babouvists, like Debon, who would never in their hearts accept co-operation with Robespierre's assassins.

A further tactical concession was necessary. If, as was thought, the people of Paris were not ready for the advanced social programme of Babeuf, an interim programme should be devised, capable of attracting the widest popular support. The Constitution of 1793 was therefore accepted, for strategic reasons, as the rallying-point for Jacobins of all shades of opinion. The Babouvists naturally had very serious qualifications about this Constitution. It did not incorporate the Rousseauist ideal of direct democracy, and it fully confirmed property rights. However, it had been accepted by the people, and the Babouvists agreed to use it as a necessary stage in the achievement of their final goal.

By this time, Babeuf had come a long way from his original beliefs. In order to organise an insurrection, community of wealth, *l'égalité des jouissances*, the egalitarian division of labour, had been shelved. Instead he appealed to the personnel of the Year 2, the *sectionnaires*, the ex-Conventionnels, and the 1793 Constitution. However he himself interpreted these plans, they looked less and less like a proto-communist plot, and more and more like a simple attempt by the Jacobins to re-establish the Revolutionary Government. The one great propaganda success of the Babouvists' campaign, the mutiny in the Parisian *légion de police*, owed as much to the *légionnaires'* fear of being sent to the front as it did to indoctrination by egalitarian principles.

The *légion de police* was ripe for picking by propagandists of any sort. Its officers, many of whom had served in the various police formations of the Ancien Régime, were moderates. Bonaparte, however, as commander of the Army of the Interior, had introduced many Jacobins into the ranks after vendémiaire. A clash between officers and ranks was probably inevitable. Several barracks were in addition highly unpopular as centres of currency speculation. The *légionnaires*, paid partly in cash, sold their money at a high profit. Whatever the Babouvists' contribution to the mutiny, they were wrong to assume that all 7,000 members of the legion would rally to them; only three battalions were affected by the mutiny. The Babouvists may have directed their attention more profitably to winning over the army. However, not even ex-aristocrats like Antonelle and Lepelletier had enough money for the enormous bribes which were necessary. Lack of finance always hampered the Babouvists.

The mutiny in the *légion de police*, in floréal IV, was the turning-point for the conspiracy. It marked its biggest success, and at the same time doomed it to failure. For, having seen the ease with which the government disbanded the mutinous *légion de*

33

police, shot seventeen of the culprits, and sent the rest to the front, the Judas of the Babeuf conspiracy decided to act. Grisel, a Babouvist agent who apparently had access to the group's private meetings, betrayed the plot to Carnot. Thus informed about the Babouvists' immediate intentions, the government was ready to pounce.

The government feared one thing above all – a defection from within its own ranks. According to Buonarroti, Barras had offered to put himself at the head of the rising, or at least to act as a hostage in the Faubourg St-Antoine. The Directory was also suspicious of Carnot's intentions, although it need not have worried on this score. Carnot may have appointed Jacobins to subordinate posts whenever he could, but he was a stranger to any plan for social democracy, or an attack on property. In particular, he was quite prepared to stamp out any signs of extremism within the army, which was his special responsibility. It could lead to insubordination and mutiny, which might paralyse the war effort. Carnot condemned Babeuf, and was to become a determined opponent of the extreme Left.

The Babouvists continued their preparations, oblivious of the approaching menace. They planned to barricade the Faubourg St-Antoine, seal off the underground passages which led from the Luxembourg, and seize the hill of Montmartre which commands the capital. On the next day, 21 floréal, their leaders were arrested at the house of Dufour in the Faubourg Poissonière. The conspiracy had only existed on paper, and it was the seizure of papers, manifestos, and nominations for a future government which sealed Babeuf's fate.

The arrest of Drouet, who was a Conventionnel, enabled the Directory to remove the trial from the ordinary courts to the special Haute Cour de Vendôme. The government intended to make this a trial of Jacobinism as a whole. Fifty-nine Jacobins were indicted when the trial opened in ventôse V, many of whom did not know Babeuf, or had absolutely no connection with the conspiracy. The government, however, was prepared for a trial of strength with the opposition. It hoped to destroy Jacobinism as a political force.

The government had only a partial success. Five Babouvists were deported, and Babeuf and Darthé were guillotined, after they had stabbed themselves in the prisoners' dock. All the other accused were acquitted of the principal charges. The trial dragged on until prairial V, and this prolonged confrontation gave the Babouvists more publicity than they could ever have achieved on their own. Furthermore, Jacobins like Vadier took the opportunity to make an impassioned defence of the Revolutionary Government of the Year 2. Babeuf's communist ideas were hardly discussed at the trial. The main charge against him was not so much his defence of the *loi agraire*, but the capital offence of conspiring to overthrow the Constitution of the Year 3. Babeuf expounded at length his argument that, since only one million had voted for this Constitution, whereas the Constitution of 1793 had been accepted by eight thousand representatives of the primary electoral assemblies, the existing Constitution was illegitimate, and the Robespierrist Constitution should be promulgated. None of this did the government any good.

Just as it is hard to accept the wide diffusion of communist ideas of property among Babeuf's associates, so it is hard to take the Babouvists seriously at all as revolutionaries. The government's attempts to conjure up a 'red peril' looked pathetic when applied to this handful of incompetent dreamers. Germain, accused of being the conspirators' candidate for the War Ministry, protested: 'Si tout jusqu'ici ne prouvait que la conspiration n'est qu'un rêve creux de ceux qui ont intérêt à sacrifier les Républicains, on en serait pleinement convaincu par ce seul fait. Un blanc-bec comme moi Ministre de la Guerre!' Réal, the leading defence lawyer, later disarmingly admitted, 'Dans la Conspiration des Égaux, il n'y avait ni liaisons avec les départements, ni ensemble, ni argent, ni hommes, ni moyens, ni possibilité d'éxécution.'

The government had more success in the affair of the camp of Grenelle, an artillery camp to the south-west of Paris. A group of Jacobins, together with some members of the 21st dragoons, made an attack on the camp on the night of 23 thermidor. If the Babouvists had been tried quicker and sooner, possibly this desperate and futile attack would not have materialised. The government, however, did not prevent the Jacobins from courting disaster. Information reached Carnot of the impending attack, but neither he, nor the Police Minister, Cochon, took steps to prevent it. Egged on by *agents provocateurs* like the notorious Romainville, the Jacobins met heavy fire, and were sabred as they fled, betrayed again. Thirty were executed, including the ex-

Conventionnel Javogues, by order of the Conseil Militaire du Temple, from which there was no appeal.

The Directory had succeeded in defeating the Jacobins by its skilful use of informers and *agents provocateurs*. It had succeeded, too, because of the divisions within the Jacobin camp, between those who looked back nostalgically to the days of Robespierre, those who looked forward to a new Utopia, and those, the most influential, who had been responsible for Robespierre's fall. It had traded on the inexperience of the conspirators, and claimed the existence of a gigantic 'red plot', which, as we have seen, was a figment of official propaganda.

The Directory had destroyed Jacobinism as a subversive force; it had not destroyed it as a political force. For Jacobinism survived by rejecting the explosive ingredient of Babouvism. It continued to act through clubs, local authorities, and newspapers like its mouthpiece, *Le Journal des Hommes Libres*. Jacobins campaigned for more equitable taxation, for the maintenance of laws against the *émigrés*, and for the Republican *culte décadaire*. For a brief period in the Year 6, with the Jacobin sympathiser Sotin at the Police Ministry, they enjoyed welcome and unexpected patronage. They had rejected their revolutionary aims, and become reformists, working within the political framework. The Jacobins survived as a political force by accepting the Constitution of the Year 3, and by assuming the rôle of a parliamentary opposition.

They were never immune from persecution. At every crisis, the government would automatically arrest certain categories of Jacobins. Members of the Terrorist Parisian revolutionary committees, members of the *armées révolutionnaires*, old supporters of the Paris Commune, and well-known local Jacobins frequently found themselves under police surveillance. At any time of crisis, the automatic reflex of the authorities was to arrest a hard core of about two hundred of these men, whatever their offence. Nevertheless, Jacobinism tried to work through respectable constitutional methods, until floréal suggested that the Directory would not tolerate even this. The Directory had easily disposed of the Babouvists; it was not again troubled by any serious attempt from the left to overthrow the system by conspiratorial means.

3

ROYALIST DELUSIONS

Studying the Revolution without considering the Counter-Revolution is like watching somebody shadow-boxing. He seems to be punching air, defending himself against a hallucination. Only when he is matched against his opponent can one judge the strength and accuracy of his blows. This is equally true of the period of the Directory, when the government cultivated the support, first of the Jacobins against the Royalists, then of the Royalists against the Jacobins. So rapid was this see-saw motion of the government, that the student of the Directory may be excused if he suffers from a little seasickness.

The Royalists were potentially stronger than the Jacobins. They could command considerable latent support within the country. Yet the story of their attempts to seize power is one of consistent self-delusion and failure. The Directory's successes against Royalism were amongst its greatest achievements in the revolutionary cause. This chapter examines the reasons both for the latent strength of the Counter-Revolution, and for its inability to capitalise on its advantages. The divisions amongst the Royalists played an important part in their failure. The restoration of the monarchy was a mirage, which looked very different to the peasant of the West and to the *émigré seigneur*, as it did to the royal family itself, the right-wing deputies, and the English Secret Service. To explain these divisions, however, one must refer to the earlier history of the Revolution.

Perhaps the Counter-Revolution began after 14 July 1789, when the King's brother, the Comte d'Artois, decided to become the first of the *émigrés*. But the small army of *émigrés*, who subsequently gathered at Koblenz, was a considerable embarrassment to those it claimed to support. For the monarchy itself, and for Marie Antoinette in particular, the *émigrés* were guilty of deserting their King when he most needed help, and their openly aggressive intentions only made his position worse. Both the royal family and the *émigrés* wanted to restore the monarchy to its full authority, but a restoration engineered by the King's brothers

37

would put the King in their debt, and limit his freedom. Neither Louis XVI nor Marie Antoinette trusted the ambitions of Artois and Provence. They preferred to rely on the foreign powers.

The emigration itself was not homogeneous. Just as the revolutionaries expressed suspicion of 'patriotes de fraiche date', and put their confidence rather in those who had participated in the revolutionary struggles right from the beginning, so, too, there was a hierarchy of counter-revolutionary zeal. Here the Comte d'Artois could claim to be the purest of the pure, since he had emigrated after the fall of the Bastille. Others, however, who left France in 1790, after the flight of the King, or after 10 August 1792, were likely to find a certain resentment against all those who had, however briefly, compromised with the Revolution. For the King's brothers wished to restore the monarchy to absolute authority, as it had existed under the Ancien Régime, in the cherished image of the paternalistic and benevolent St-Louis, granting gifts and dispensing justice to his assembled people in person. Their refusal to recognise that anything had changed since 1789, and their unwillingness, in a well-worn phrase, to learn anything or forget anything, was a stumbling-block for more realistic Royalists.

Life in *émigré* society was one of oppressive tedium, rendered bearable only by the illusion that success was around the corner. Days of idleness followed one upon the other, filled with the time-consuming pursuits of the eighteenth-century drawing-room: minuets, embroidery, and the endless quarrels over precedence. For the social framework of the past was jealously preserved. Court etiquette may have been an anachronism, but it gave some bearing to the lives of these uprooted aristocratic families. War had once been their *métier*, but they were no longer equipped to resist the massed bayonet charges and the growing professionalism of the popular revolutionary armies. Daring sallies, chivalrous self-sacrifice, the duel at dawn, or the abduction at midnight were more attractive to them. Hence the disastrous invasion of Quiberon Bay, where bravery could not compensate for muddled thinking and bad preparation.

There were those within the emigration who were partisans of an absolute monarchy. They included ex-ministers like Calonne, who tried to flood Brittany with false *assignats*, and Breteuil, the King's right-hand man in the crises of 1789. These men preferred a strong monarchy, unfettered by obscurantist *parlements*

and over-privileged aristocrats. For the aristocratic revolutionaries of 1787 and 1788, however, these men were the agents
of hated 'ministerial despotism'. They threatened to undermine
the ancient Constitution of France, provincial liberties, and the
privileged position of corporations like the Church and the
judiciary. For these exiles, many of them provincial noblemen
like the Duc d'Antraigues, monarchical centralisation was
anathema.

Whatever their opinions on the future of the monarchy,
however, the *émigrés* were of negligible military importance. The
foreign powers regarded them as chiefly of nuisance value. The
émigrés in their turn, had no wish to return to France in the
baggage-train of the Prussians, for they too had a sense of
patriotisme. The English, however, who ran a fairly expensive
system of counter-revolutionary espionage, thought the *émigrés*
dangerous because they refused to accept reality. If the idea of a
restoration was to win any credibility inside France, the *émigrés*
and the King's brothers would have to make some concessions to
the Revolution. Two things, above all, were demanded of them:
the promise of an amnesty for revolutionary leaders and regicides, and the acceptance of the permanence of the sale of the
biens nationaux.

Within France, Royalism was of a different kind altogether.
Thermidor and the Directory brought back into power first the
Girondins, and then many of the revolutionary leaders of 1790
and 1791. These men had governed France under a constitutional monarchy, which had collapsed because the court, in the
last resort, could not bring itself to abdicate absolute rule. Once
again the monarchy itself was the main obstacle to a return
to constitutional monarchy, but these men hoped that, if the
princes could be persuaded to make concessions, a restoration
was possible. The Constitutional Royalists were heartily despised
by the *purs*, the *émigrés* and the princes. Many of them were of
(comparatively) low birth, lawyers and *bourgeois;* others, like
Lafayette, were demagogues who had betrayed the aristocracy.
The *monarchiens* of 1789, and the 'Constituents' of 1791, were
beneath the contempt of Koblenz. They, too, were guilty of
self-delusion in thinking that a compromise by the court party
was possible. Nevertheless, the Constitutional Royalists were
prepared to negotiate with the *émigrés* and the foreign powers,
but they demanded first, as a sign of good faith, the release of

Lafayette from his prison in Austria. Soon Madame de Staël began to canvass the possibility of the return of the Lameths, once, with Lafayette, leaders of the Feuillant group in the Constituent Assembly.

There was, finally, another group of Royalists, often neglected because difficult to identify and assess: the partisans of an Orléanist monarchy. There is little doubt that contemporaries imagined them to be strong and numerous. La Revellière, in his memoirs, uses the term 'Orléanist' rather indiscriminately to include men like Talleyrand and Merlin de Douai, and Tallien and Barras were also considered by many to have Orléanist sympathies. A group of deputies dined regularly with the Duchesse d'Orléans, and police reports of the Year 5 describe Orléanism as the most dangerous brand of Royalism for the government. Orléanism was dangerous because it was attractive not only to moderate Royalists who wanted to save their skins and protect their property, but also to ex-Jacobins of 1793, who remembered that Philippe-Égalité had been a Montagnard. In fact, one may speculate that an Orléanist monarchy may have stood a good chance of survival in the late 1790s. However, the Duc d'Orléans himself refused any political rôle, and his departure for America in 1796 made his accession doubly remote.

The vendémiaire rising illustrates the divisions between these Royalist factions. The rising originated in the primary electoral assemblies, which were dominated by Royalists. The Jacobins, disarmed after germinal and prairial III, had been expelled from the sectional assemblies. The Royalists were provoked by the decree of the two-thirds, which stipulated that two-thirds of the membership of the Convention must be re-elected to the new Corps Législatif. This meant that the Right would need three election years before it could oust the ex-Conventionnels and secure a majority. The decree had in fact been rejected by every *section* in Paris, except that of the Quinze-Vingts, in the Faubourg St-Antoine. When the Convention invited the Jacobins of prairial to attend the primary assemblies, and assembled troops to ensure a favourable outcome, the Royalists decided on armed resistance.

The centre of the insurrection was the Section Lepelletier, populated largely by bankers and businessmen, as well as *rentiers* impoverished by inflation. This was the wealthy area around the Stock Exchange, and the heart of the moderate west of Paris.

Several *sections* sent delegates to a central committee in the Théâtre Français (now the Odéon). Government troops fought on two fronts. Their cannon-fire dispersed the rebels who advanced from the Faubourg St-Germain to the Quai Voltaire, on the Left Bank opposite the Tuileries. Thus the rebels in the Section Lepelletier were isolated, and bitter fighting ensued around the Church of St-Roch. General Menou, trapped in the Rue Vivienne, fraternised and beat a retreat. Barras was immediately appointed to lead the Convention's forces, and called on Bonaparte to command them. By the evening of 13 vendémiaire IV, the rebels had been crushed by his artillery. Mallet du Pan estimated the dead at six hundred on the side of the Convention, and eight hundred for the rebels.

The rising had not been adequately prepared. Although it had the sympathy of a few deputies like Boissy d'Anglas, and Le Haye, the rising had no general. The rebels were pitifully short of arms and ammunition, and had no answer to Bonaparte's artillery. The *sections* which took part had accepted the Constitution of the Year 3, and were therefore condemned by the 'pure' Royalists and the emigration. The Paris Agency of the Duc d'Antraigues identified the rising as the work of the Constitutional Royalists, and boycotted it. For the Royalist extremists, the vendémiairists were more concerned simply with reversing the decree of the two-thirds than with an actual monarchical restoration. Hence the *purs* rejoiced in the defeat of the moderate deputies and Constitutionalists in vendémiaire IV, so wide was the gulf which divided them.

Pressures were exerted from several directions to bridge this gulf. Mallet du Pan, the Swiss publicist, whose correspondence with the Court of Vienna remains an important source for the history of the Directory,[1] urged the extreme royalists to work with the Constitutionalists in France. Mallet du Pan was a Calvinist, and an admirer of the British Constitution, who believed the best hope for the accession of Louis XVIII lay in working for a constitutional monarchy. He attacked the *émigrés* for their intransigence, and tried to persuade the courts of Europe to disregard the advice of extremist agents like the Duc d'Antraigues, and to accept the establishment of a reformed monarchy in France.

[1] Bibliography no. 8.

Conciliatory moves also came from England. Grenville posted to Berne his personal friend William Wickham, to whom were entrusted large amounts of Secret Service funds. At first, Wickham naively imagined that the rifts between the King's brothers and the Constitutional Monarchists could soon be mended. This illusion was encouraged by the legitimist Paris Agency, which for a time convinced Wickham that this kind of collaboration was possible. Wickham delighted in his new responsibility of espionage agent extraordinary. Invisible inks, secret codes, and all the paraphernalia of eighteenth-century spies were all brought to bear against the Directory. Wickham, however, was immensely gullible, and his absurd schemes, mounted at vast expense, produced nothing.

His master-plan was to combine an Austrian invasion through Savoy with a rising in south-east France. Austria, however, was not ready, and had no confidence in the *émigré* army, and Wickham's agents in Lyon defected or were captured. Wickham then paid huge sums of money to agents like Précy, to buy arms for a rising in the Cévennes. When this plan, too, proved abortive, Wickham put his money on another losing horse, General Pichegru. Pichegru did not have the nerve or determination to lead a military coup against the government, and after the Directory, correctly suspicious of his loyalty, dismissed Pichegru from his command, he was useless to the Royalists. Wickham's story is one of boundless optimism, a bottomless purse, and fatuous misjudgements.

This confusing picture of Royalist divisions, espionage networks, and self-delusion is not complete without mention of the Paris Agency, and its correspondent, the Duc d'Antraigues. D'Antraigues was a member of the old nobility of the Vivarais, one of the many local Languedocien aristocrats who gave their services to the Counter-Revolution. Snubbed by Marie Antoinette, he was typical of the opposition of the local nobility to the court, their attachment to their family estates, and to their privileges. He was a revolutionary of 1787, who passionately believed in provincial liberties, and attacked attempts to undermine them by ministers like Breteuil and Calonne. He had welcomed the execution of Louis XVI, believing that his martyrdom would force the European powers to take action in defence of the French monarchy. He was in constant correspondence with Royalist groups in the South, old *parlementaires*, and the leaders of the Camp de Jalès, the Royalist gathering in the South-East in 1791.

This Frondeur element was represented in Paris by the Paris Agency, whose chief members included Despomelles, another southern aristocrat, Lemaître, a Norman journalist and ex-member of the Jacobin club, and the naval officer Duverne de Presle. With d'Antraigues, the Paris Agency hated England, which they believed to be more interested in increasing English influence than in restoring the Ancien Régime. D'Antraigues, like Wickham, placed some hope in winning over eminent generals. But documentary evidence of his approaches to Bona-parte, captured by the French in Trieste, helped the Directory to eliminate Royalists like Pichegru after fructidor V. The Paris Agency hatched the Brottier conspiracy, revealed to the govern-ment by an informer in pluviôse V. This time the Royalists apparently envisaged the incredibly rash plan of engineering a rising in the Faubourg St-Antoine, to provoke a counter-rising in the right-wing western *sections* of Paris. The discovery of this scatterbrained plot enabled the Directory to arrest most of the members of the Paris Agency.

One of d'Antraigues's complaints against the English had been that a timely invasion in the Vendée might have brought down the Revolutionary Government. It is to the West that we must now turn, to see how important both La Vendée and *chouannerie* were to the Counter-Revolution. The rising in the Vendée, which broke out in the spring of 1793, had reached its limit with the capture first of Saumur, and then of Angers, in the summer of that year. The defeat of the Royalist army at Cholet in October 1793 was a vital victory for the Republican troops. The severe repression which followed, led by Carrier at Nantes, pacified the area until the Year 3, when fighting resumed. The amnesty concluded with the Vendéan leaders Charette and Stofflet, in the spring of the Year 3, was only temporarily effective.

The rising had been provoked by a multitude of factors, including resistance to conscription, and resentment against the Civil Constitution of the Clergy. It is, however, too simple to regard the Vendéan revolt just as another peasant Church and King rebellion. In Les Sables d'Olonne, for example, sailors refused blessings from Constitutional priests, but still helped to defend the town against the Vendéans. On the coast, at least, the traditional *curé* was not all-powerful, and even in the interior,

43

peasants welcomed the abolition of the tithe. Furthermore, unrest in the region had some purely economic motives. In the area around Cholet, there was considerable unemployment amongst textile artisans on the eve of the Revolution. Priests were equally influential in other parts of France, and it is important to realise that La Vendée was not unique in this. Similar risings occurred during the Revolution, although on a miniature scale, in areas like the Lozère, the Ardèche, and the Ariège, where clashes between Catholics and Protestants may also have played a part.

The grievances of the Vendéans expressed deep-rooted social tensions which had existed long before the Revolution. The Revolution disturbed the age-old framework of peasant communities, and brought these tensions to armed conflict. In the rural area of the Mauges, in southern Anjou, there were no large towns, although Saumur was not far distant. Yet the peasant found himself economically dependent on the townsman. As a part-time weaver, he depended on the textile merchants of towns like Cholet, and, as a farmer, he felt the authority of the landowner's deputy, the steward or estate-manager, usually of *bourgeois* origin. Yet for the isolated and uneducated peasant, these men were virtually the representatives of an alien culture. In the Revolution, all the elements which appeared to disrupt traditional peasant life seemed to come from the towns, and from the middle classes who inhabited them. It was there that the peasant's taxes went; hence the burning of tax records by the Vendéans in the towns they captured. From the town came the National Guardsmen to requisition food, enforce the acceptance of paper currency, and escort the new Constitutional priests, the *intrus*, who were often not installed without bloodshed, and went in fear of their lives. The towns spoke a different language, and they seemed to worship a different faith. The traditional leaders of the remote rural communities of the West, the *curé* and the *seigneur*, had been replaced by a new government bureaucracy which appeared alien and oppressive. Fighting was bitterest where the two worlds of the town and the country met. Conflict frequently occurred in the *bourgs*, small towns or swollen villages, of no more than a few thousand inhabitants, sometimes of very recent growth, where the tensions described were most likely to erupt. La Vendée was not a revolt against capitalism: the most hated members of the *bourgeoisie* were those in the employ of absentee noble landowners. It was rather a revolt against the forces which threatened the bonds of a closed, patriarchal, religious society.

The revolt was favoured by geography. The *bocage* provided ideal terrain for a guerilla war. The high hedges and sunken roads made the movement of large bodies of troops impracticable, and provided good cover for ambushes. There were no large fortified towns, so that the peasant guerillas could melt away easily, dispersing to their tiny hamlets, and becoming part of the civilian population. What is more, the Vendéans knew this difficult terrain, and could draw on the support of the local population, an essential ingredient for the success of what Eric Hobsbawm has called 'social banditry'. There were *bocages*, it is true, in other parts of France (Normandy, for instance), and many of the aspects of Vendéan peasant society we have described could be reproduced from other backward and isolated areas of the Midi. Why the Counter-Revolution was more virulent in the Vendée than anywhere else is a question for which no historian has yet found an adequate answer.

The Vendéan revolt could never have formed the basis for the overthrow of the Republican government. Firstly, d'Antraigues overestimated the rôle of the nobility in the rebellion. There were very few aristocratic leaders in the Vendée, where the rising was led rather by the employees and dependents they left behind. What nobles there were arrived after the rebellion had begun. There was little evidence to suggest any peasant loyalty either to *émigré* landlords or to the English. The Vendée, in any case, was essentially a local revolt. The River Loire was the ultimate limit of the world of the western peasant. He could not be induced to march further, abandoning his family and his fields at harvest time. The Vendéan army was always an irregular one, as far as it existed at all, and there was no military discipline to make him do so. La Vendée could never hope to be more than a running sore to the Republic, which absorbed several thousand troops, but could not aspire to anything more. The execution of Stofflet in ventôse and of Charette in germinal IV made a great impression, and consolidated the authority of the Directory. The government of the Year 2 had never achieved so much against the Vendéans.

The same may be said of *chouannerie*, which, like the revolt in the Vendée, degenerated into acts of banditry carried out by small armed groups. The area of the *chouannerie* was north of the Loire, in Brittany and parts of Normandy. It was a separate movement, although it was joined by some defeated Vendéans. It continued after the defeat of the Vendéans in 1793, and was endemic at least until the Consulate. After the failure of the Quiberon landing, however, it was a movement of hopeless desperation. Leaders like La Rouërie, however, had earlier showed considerable skill in enlisting beggars, deserters, the unemployed, salt-smugglers ruined by the abolition of the *gabelle*, and redundant excise officers. What most impressed Balzac, as he shows in his early novel *Les Chouans*, was their animal ferocity, exploited by demagogic priests. He describes an open-air Mass, held in the wilds of Brittany, as some primitive pagan rite. If Balzac here strayed from the path of realism, his account of Abbé Gudin's sermon may not be exaggerated. The urge to resist conscription, the condemnation of divorce, and the assurance that purchasers of ecclesiastical property were damned to hell were the stock-in-trade of the rhetoric of the counter-revolutionary priesthood, summarised by Abbé Gudin's dictum that 'on peut, sans scrupule, rôtir les apostats'.

The White Terror in the South was similarly brutal, but isolated acts of vengeance in the Rhône valley could never offer much hope for a concerted Royalist movement. The White Terror, unlike the Vendéan rising or the *chouannerie*, was directed not at *les bleus*, the Republican troops, so much as at former Jacobin militants. White Terrorist killings were vengeance killings, of the mayors, leaders of *sociétés populaires* and *armées révolutionnaires*, and members of revolutionary committees of the Year 2, who had not succeeded in escaping after 9 thermidor, or whose hiding place had been discovered. Naturally many private scores were settled, and it is often hard to see a political motive in the killings. Many killings took place on the outskirts of the cities, on the roads leading out of Lyon, Nîmes, Tarascon, Avignon, Marseille, and Aix. Escorts of prisoners were particularly vulnerable, although in Marseille and Lyon, ex-Jacobins were not safe even inside the prisons. One deputy estimated that 1,500 had been killed in the department of the Vaucluse alone during the Directory, and Richard Cobb guesses at a figure of about 2,000 militants of the Year 2 assassinated by White Terrorists in the South-east.[1] Each locality had its own particular category of

[1] Bibliography no. 15.

victims: in Carpentras it might be the Jewish community, while in Nîmes and its environs, the wealthy Protestant silk merchants might fall victim to their Catholic artisans. The purchasers of *biens nationaux* were frequent targets: in the Gard they would be hung from the trees outside their farms, while in the Ariège, their heads would be shaved. As long as local authorities connived at the killings (in Lyon they might even be perpetrated in broad daylight), and as long as the central government remained weak, as it did under the Directory, the series of gruesome assassinations could not be stopped. Even some government officials, the local *commissaires du pouvoir exécutif*, were murdered. Local newspapers, like the *Anti-Terroriste* of Toulouse, assisted the murder gangs by publishing blacklists of ex-terrorists. Weekends, religious festivals, and public holidays rarely went by without an unfortunate *sans-culotte* being sabred, stoned, or dismembered, and his body thrown into the Rhône, the Saône, or the Durance. Memories died hard: in 1815, vengeance resumed against the men of the Year 2 as the old feuds and bloodlusts were resurrected.

'Le Midi', wrote Mallet du Pan, 'fermente, mais d'une agitation vague, sans but ni moyens.' Anarchical and violent expressions of popular Royalism could not in themselves bring the monarchy anywhere nearer to its restoration. They nevertheless testify to the strength of Royalism in the provinces. For Royalism, unlike Jacobinism, did have several thousand men in arms within France. According to Mallet du Pan, about one-third of the population could be described as Royalist. The Directory thus faced a serious threat, as long as Royalism could draw sympathy from Vendéan rebels, many local administrations, and all those who resented the land settlement of the Revolution and the Civil Constitution of the Clergy. Nothing concrete, however, could be achieved without some measure of co-operation between the legitimists and the *émigrés* on the one hand, and the Constitutional Royalist deputies on the other, like Lanjuinais, Dumas, Barbé-Marbois, and Pelet de la Lozère. The death of the young Louis XVII strengthened the King's brothers, but the Declaration of Verona, issued by the Comte de Provence, now Louis XVIII, did him more harm than good. The Declaration made no mention of a political amnesty, and did not recognise the sale of *biens nationaux*.

What brought the factions together was not the efforts of William Wickham and his agents, but fear of their opponents.

The Orléanists seemed to be gaining ground, and there were rumours that Tallien, through his Spanish family connections, was canvassing the possibility of putting a Spanish Bourbon on the throne. The tactics of the *émigrés* had failed. The invasion of Quiberon and the collapse of the Paris Agency had shown the futility of isolated raids and conspiracies. Military action, too, could not bear fruit. The Austrians were reluctant to mount an attack in the East. Hoche was having some success in the West, and Pichegru could no longer bring over his army. A new strategy was needed.

The Royalists, as the Jacobins had done, decided to work through constitutional channels, instead of dissipating their energies in useless adventures which only harmed their cause. William Wickham sent the former Feuillant, d'André, to bring together the Royalist groups in Paris. D'André was well qualified for this task. A former *conseiller* at the Parlement of Aix, he had been a deputy in the Constituent Assembly, but was also an *émigré*. He kept in touch with Wickham, on whom he was dependent for financial backing, but at the same time, he had made his submission to the King in 1796. His connections with the ex-Feuillants, and the members of the moderate Royalist Clichy club enabled him to form a working committee of deputies like Durand-Maillane, Henri-Larivière, and Thibaudeau. Their aim was to secure a victory in the elections of germinal V, and then to impeach and remove the Directors.

Royalist propaganda was diffused through the press, the clergy, Royalist clubs, and associations like the *Instituts philanthropiques* throughout the provinces, and especially Belgium, where popular opposition to anticlericalism was strong. The results, which were disastrous for the government, revealed that the electorate had ignored the Brottier conspiracy. The plains of the middle Loire, large areas of the Mediterranean coastline, and several large cities including Paris and Lyon were won over by the right wing. The Royalist reaction made considerable gains in the newly annexed departments, and in areas of peasant landowner-ship, like Champagne, the Nord, and Picardy. Only eleven retiring Conventionnels were re-admitted, and they now sat with eminent Royalists like Pichegru, Claret de Fleurieu, a minister in 1790, Imbert-Colomès, General Willot, protector of the White Terror in Marseille, and Villaret-Joyeuse, spokesman for the rich plantation owners of San Domingo.

D'André could not claim responsibility for all these successes. In fact, only one of his chief candidates won a seat: Desbonnières, once a legal adviser to the Comte d'Artois. D'André himself failed to get elected, hardly a compliment for the Royalist electoral machine. In fact, even W. R. Fryer, the only historian to make a study of d'André's work, admits that the election results would probably have been much the same even without d'André's efforts.[1]

In a sense, the election results were too favourable for the Royalists. The landslide frightened the moderates among them. So many extremist Royalists had been elected that the Constitutionalists dropped their close ties with d'André, and were ultimately prepared to support the Directory against him. Hence the coalition of legitimists and Constitutional Royalists broke down at the moment of its greatest achievement.

The newly-elected Royalists achieved important successes. Pichegru was elected speaker of the Cinq Cents, and Barthélémy, ex-ambassador to Switzerland, was elected Director in place of Letourneur. Gilbert Desmolières's attacks on financial waste ended in success when a motion was passed to deprive the Directory of control of expenditure. This would have crippled the Directory, and contributed more than any other single factor to its determination not to let the Royalists go any further. The Conseil des Anciens remained loyal to the Directory, and threw out Desmolières's proposals. The weakness of d'André's group in the upper chamber thus proved fatal to the Royalist cause.

The moderate Royalists fought for the relaxation of the legislation against *émigrés* and priests, and argued for the conclusion of peace. For the Directory, these demands could not be conceded without threatening the very fabric of Republicanism. The Republic, in its view, could not compromise with *émigrés* or vendémiairists without weakening its defences against monarchist plots and British gold. Nor could the government pursue a less aggressive foreign policy without losing considerable support on the Left and in the army. For behind the moderate Clichyens stood Koblenz, the *émigré* princes, and the extreme Royalists, whose intransigent pronouncements were beginning to frighten even the Clichyen deputies themselves.

The Directory, as we have seen, had no authority to dissolve a

---

[1] Bibliography no. 57.

hostile legislature. It therefore resolved on a *coup*. The writing was on the wall when Hoche moved troops from the Army of the Sambre-et-Meuse closer to the capital, and both he and Talley-rand were given ministries, although Hoche was disqualified on the grounds of his youth. The Royalists resisted these unconstitutional troop movements, which were withdrawn, but they made no decisive attempt to forestall the *coup* which was clearly imminent. The Royalists enlisted only a few hundred troops in their cause, and resistance in the Cinq Cents was not organised. With d'André on the sidelines, they had no parliamentary leader, and no discipline to win over waverers and absentees. When the Directors Barras and La Revellière had persuaded their colleague Reubell of the need for action, the Royalists were doomed.

To allow the Royalists to exploit their electoral successes to the full might have proved fatal to the Directory. Desmolières threatened to put a stranglehold on government finance, which would bring down the Directory, its armies unpaid, and its coffers empty. The situation had reached deadlock: La Revellière, Reubell, and Barras opposed Carnot and Barthélémy, who had already been excluded from vital decision-making. The Directory was supported by a narrow consensus: it could not survive long periods of paralysis and disequilibrium.

The moderate Clichyens were resigned to waiting for next year's elections, but the Directory was ready to act and to apply the 'dry guillotine' – deportation. On the night of 17 fructidor Year 5, Augereau, commanding the 17th Division, occupied the legislative chambers, and arrested the leading Clichyens. Several, including Pichegru, were deported. Carnot, who had been prepared to compromise with the Royalists, was allowed to flee, but Barthélémy declined to do so, and he too was deported. Fifty-three deputies were deported with him, and elections annulled in forty-nine departments. The laws of brumaire IV stood intact, and full sanctions against *émigrés* and priests maintained.

'Le Directoire', wrote Mallet du Pan, 'ne pouvant gouverner les conseils, doit ou conspirer, ou obéir, ou périr.' The Constitution did not permit the possibility of dissolving the legislature by any other means except force. Fructidor effectively brought to an end the experiment in parliamentary government, and scotched any possibility of compromise between the Republic and the Right. The wishes of the electorate could not be allowed to undermine the Republican system of government. The Directory found that no parliamentary democracy can tolerate the existence of powerful extremists whose aim is to destroy the political system. Ultimately, then, the Directory was not prepared to face the consequences of its own liberalism. Fructidor was a victory for the executive over the elected legislature, as much as it was a victory for the army.

The Royalists, finally, were the victims of their own pusillanimity and internal divisions. The moderate Clichyens took fright and defected at the last moment. Until the King publicly promised an amnesty, they would not risk their necks on his behalf. The remainder were not prepared to defend themselves, even when the *coup* became predictable. The Directory emerged triumphant. Events in the Conseil des Anciens had revealed unexpected support for the régime. The Directory had defeated its enemies to the left and the right. The régime which few predicted would last out the year now lived to fight another day.

4

DIRECTORIAL SOCIETY: 'LES GROS'

L'or change en demi-dieux les hommes inconnus.

The period of the thermidorean reaction and the Directory was one in which glaring contrasts appeared between the extremely wealthy and the destitute. Not only did the rich seem richer, and the poor poorer, but enormous fortunes were amassed in a few months, and some social groups, like the *rentiers*, found themselves fighting for survival for the first time. Contemporaries never tired of pointing out the injustice of growing social inequalities. In brumaire IV, the *Journal du Bonhomme Richard* described 'les fortunes collosales nées comme des champignons; des repas splendides, des indigestions d'un côté, des jeûnes forcés de l'autre...des prisons pleines, des voleurs à foison; des filles publiques agiotant; des défenseurs officieux devenus brocanteurs...beaucoup de bois et de pauvres diables mourant de froid; quantité de charbon, dont on ne peut pas plus s'approcher que s'il était embrasé...voilà une esquisse de notre état actuel'. 'Famine in the midst of plenty' had always been a popular charge against revolutionary governments. Now it appeared to have every justification.

For this reason, the thermidorean and Directorial régimes have been frequently accused of betraying the revolutionary dream of social equality and fraternity. Certainly the *sans-culotte* myth of a society without paupers or millionaires had no application in a period which abounded in both. This is not, however, to say that the Directory betrayed the Revolution as a whole. In fact the acquisition of social and political power by the *bourgeoisie* under the Directory was a direct consequence of the Revolution. For, in spite of direct popular pressure, and in spite of the *sans-culotterie*, the middle classes had never surrendered their control of the revolutionary leadership. The narrowly middle-class basis of the Directorial régime was by no means in contradiction to the revolutionary régime which had institutionalised social discrimination in the distinction between 'active' and 'passive' citizens, and which had always legislated against workers' associations.

It was the Revolution itself which, by destroying a hierarchical system based on birth, and by opening careers to talent, had facilitated the meteoric rise of obscure army corporals, unknown provincial lawyers, doctors, priests, and government officials. It was the Revolution which, by nationalising the property of the religious orders, made possible the rapid enrichment of the propertied *bourgeoisie* of town and countryside. It was the Revolution which, by destroying the charitable institutions of the Ancien Régime, plunged the poorest classes of society deeper into misery. Social developments during the Directory can therefore be seen as the logical consequence of the five years of Revolution which preceded them. The Revolution had undermined or destroyed the old social élites; a period of extreme social fluidity followed, during which new élites emerged. The Revolution had by no means ended on 9 thermidor II; under the Directory, the aspirations of the middle classes who had made the Revolution were only just beginning to come to fruition.

We have borrowed the contemporary classification of the 'Two Nations' of Directorial France, as 'Les Gros' and 'Les Maigres'. Discussion of the second half of the antithesis, the very poor, is reserved for the following chapter. This chapter examines 'The Fat', their composition and the social background in which they moved. In order to make this discussion easier, three paths to wealth and status during this period have been isolated. This chapter will discuss the generals, the purchasers of *biens nationaux*, and the army contractors, for it was in these social groups that the ascent into the new aristocracy of wealth was most spectacular.

The Republican army was a powerful symbol of the new social opportunities opened up by the Revolution. Bonaparte himself, who rose from the ranks of the artillery, incarnated the myth that every corporal carried a marshal's baton in his knapsack. A new generation of young generals exemplified the unlimited chances for promotion created by the introduction of the principle of election of officers.

Although junior officers were nominated by their companies, the government still retained its power of appointment over its generals, and during the Terror, civilian *Représentants en mission* had exercised wide powers of dismissal and appointment in the revolutionary armies. Thus, although military talent would now be rewarded regardless of birth or connections, it did not suffice alone to sweep budding military geniuses into positions of high command. The political opinions of potential generals weighed heavily with the Convention and its representatives. The Directory would not hesitate to dismiss a general like Moreau, if he was suspected of Royalism. Nor is it quite true that contacts in high places were no longer important to aspirants. Bonaparte himself owed something to his connections with Barras, which dated from the siege of Toulon. It was Barras who secured his promotion after appointing him to lead the Convention's forces in vendémiaire IV.

Nevertheless, the revolutionary régimes and the Directory enabled a group of ambitious soldiers, to rise from the humblest origins to positions of power and wealth in the army. Brune, for instance, had been a printer, Lefebvre a notary's clerk, and Hoche, an assistant ostler. Some of the Directory's generals had originally served in the regular army, like Hoche, who had begun as a sergeant. Others, like Kléber, had been a *sous-lieutenant* in the regular army, but then joined the volunteers during the Revolution. Others, like Lannes, Moreau, and Brune, had never served in the regular army, but rose entirely through the ranks of the volunteers.

A galaxy of unknown men were suddenly propelled to the forefront of the army, which they were called on to lead after very little experience, and at a comparatively young age. In 1792, Augereau was thirty-five, Junot twenty-one, and Joubert twenty-three. Bernadotte, who enlisted at the age of seventeen, rose from the rank of sergeant to become a general in four years. In 1796, Lannes, an ostler's son, was *chef de brigade* at the age of twenty-seven. Masséna was by then a veteran of forty.

The promise of power and riches inevitably attracted adventurers of many kinds. One of these was Augereau. The son of a fruiterer in the Rue Mouffetard, Augereau had served in no less than three regiments of the French army, not to mention periods in the armies both of Prussia and Naples. He fought in the Vendée, and then in the Western Pyrenees, to become the strong man of the Directory in the *coup* of fructidor. Augereau ostentatiously advertised his success, and wore a diamond on every finger. Augereau, and perhaps Masséna with him, aspired to play a political rôle, but their candidatures for the post of Director were defeated in the Year 5. The only military man who succeeded in achieving this political honour was the uncontroversial nonentity, General Moulin.

Not only military authority, but also wealth, lay at the feet of military leaders fortunate enough to participate in the general looting which took place on the Italian campaign. By the end of 1796, the French had squeezed forty-five million livres from Italy, and only about a fifth of this reached the Directory. Soldiers were paid in cash, and both they and the generals freely appropriated art treasures and other valuables when the French occupied Rome and Venice. The Pope's ransom alone included the surrender of a hundred works of art and five hundred precious manuscripts, and this does not include the losses suffered through the unofficial seizure of valuables by individuals.

The Revolution, the *carrière ouverte au talent*, and the Italian conquests therefore ensured a strong military contingent amongst the parvenus of Directorial society.

For the commercial classes, public administrators, and the wealthier peasants, the most permanent result of the Revolution and the Directory was, in material terms, the purchase of a *bien national*. The sale of the *biens nationaux* had begun in 1791, but currency depreciation made purchases of the remaining property an extremely profitable investment in the Year 3, and under the Directory. It would be unfair to describe all purchasers of *biens nationaux* as *nouveaux riches*. On the contrary, as we shall see, they tended rather to be established provincial *notables*, already confirmed in a solid and respected social position. By the time of the Directory, however, the *biens nationaux* were attractive bait for different, and rather more predatory animals, like the speculators and the army contractors. The possession of a *bien national* was perhaps something which 'Les Gros' had in common. The major significance of the sales lay in the creation of a class of property-owners with a direct material interest in the survival of the régime, who could be expected to defend the Republic against Royalism. It is therefore important to consider who these purchasers were.

For two main reasons, the conditions of the sales of the *biens nationaux* tended to favour the enrichment of the urban middle classes. Firstly, taking the purchases as a whole since 1791, and

3 55

bearing in mind local variations, the peasantry had a relatively minor share. Secondly, inflation greatly reduced the real value of the purchase price.

The *biens nationaux* fell into two main categories. Firstly, the property of the Church and the religious orders was put up for sale under the Constituent Assembly, as a guarantee for the new paper currency, the *assignats*. Then, after the Revolution of 10 August 1792, the property of the *émigrés* came onto the market, and the government intended that the peasant should benefit from this particular scheme for property redistribution.

This hope, however, was not fulfilled. The property was to be sold by auction in the *chef-lieu du district*, and the *bourgeoisie* were always able to outbid the small peasants. Indeed, the early sales of the *biens nationaux* realised prices far in excess of the official valuations. In the Haute-Garonne, for example, property valued at 10·3 million livres was sold by 1791 for 15 millions. The smaller peasant was only able to secure a reasonable share of the spoils by pooling his resources with those of other peasants, to form a syndicate. This was successful in the Cambrésis, the Laonnais, and the Pyrenéan district of St-Gaudens.

The changing conditions of sales under the Directory did not substantially alter the balance, which always weighed in favour of the propertied *bourgeoisie*. In the Year 4, sale by auction was replaced by the system of '*soumissions*', by which any individual could purchase property at a price fixed at twenty-one times its annual yield in 1790. These '*soumissions*', however, had to be made at the *chef-lieu du département*, and the long journey from remote rural areas may have dissuaded the poorer peasant. Furthermore, the system of purchase by '*soumission*' was secret, and this aroused suspicions of fraud. Secrecy favoured collusion between the bidders, the surveyors, and the departmental administrators, who were themselves able to make very advantageous purchases.

Auctions were re-established in brumaire V, but the urban *bourgeoisie* did not suffer radically from this change, since the auctions were still to be held on their home ground in the *chef-lieu du département*. This time, the purchase price was to be paid half in cash, half in paper currency. This again favoured bankers and businessmen who had a ready supply of cash. Finally, in the Year 7, payments were to be made entirely in metallic currency for the first time.

The inflation of the revolutionary paper currency assured purchasers a large fortune in a very short lapse of time. On 12 prairial III, the price of the *biens nationaux* was to be fixed at seventy-five times the income of the property in 1790; but because the price was payable in vastly depreciated *assignats*, the land could effectively be bought for only a few times its income in 1790, in real terms. The government was desperately short of funds, and was prepared to go to any lengths to raise money quickly. In the process, it suffered severe financial losses in the sales of the *biens nationaux*. In the Year 4, *biens nationaux* could be bought with the new *mandats territoriaux*, at a price fixed at twenty-two times their income in 1790. Once again, however, the government did not account for the rapid depreciation of the *mandats*. If the *mandats* were worth only a tenth of their face value, then it was possible to buy an estate for only two or three times its annual income.

Local variations make it difficult to advance firm conclusions on the significance of the sales. In the district of Cambrai, for example, forty-four per cent of the land changed hands in the sales of the *biens nationaux*, but the sales involved only twenty-five per cent of the department of the Nord, and only three and a half per cent of the Pyrenéan district of St-Gaudens. Moreover, the rhythm of the sales was uneven. A large amount of ecclesiastical property was sold in 1791, and the sales reached another peak in the Year 2, before resuming at a gentler pace under the Directory itself. Thus the bulk of the *biens nationaux* had already been sold before 9 thermidor II. In the district of Strasbourg, one-third of the *biens nationaux* had been sold by 1791; in the Nord, two-thirds of Church property had been sold by 1793; and in Toulouse, over eighty per cent of the *biens nationaux* (measured in terms of value) had been sold by the Year 3.

The local studies so far cited, referring mainly to areas in the North, the East, and the South-west, only describe a few fragments of the national picture. Even with the aid of modern computer techniques, it would take several lifetimes' research to compile sufficient data to justify definite conclusions about the beneficiaries of the sales of the *biens nationaux* in France as a whole. The present state of knowledge authorises only a few tentative remarks.

Once again, local differences make it difficult to estimate the peasants' share of the purchases. In the Nord, taking into account resales of property by speculators, the peasants acquired fifty per cent of the land sold, and up to 1793, their share almost certainly exceeded that of the *bourgeoisie*. In the Toulousain, on the other hand, their share was only about fourteen per cent. The peasant had little interest in buying urban property, unless he was a market gardener on the edge of a city, and in the towns, the *bourgeois* monopoly of purchases was hardly contested. Although for the most part, the peasant purchasers may have been wealthy farmers, there seems little doubt that the sale of the *biens nationaux* multiplied the number of small property-owners in the countryside. Out of about 30,000 purchasers in the Nord, for example, 10,000 became proprietors for the first time.

Although probably very few day-labourers or urban wage-earners bought *biens nationaux*, the small landowning peasants and the urban *petite bourgeoisie* perhaps improved their relative social position. The main beneficiaries, however, seem to have been the *bourgeoisie*, a group which requires more precise definition. Administrative officials were among those who profited from purchases at ridiculously low prices. In the Meurthe, Clémendot found thirty-nine purchases by *commissaires du Directoire*, and another forty-eight by *agents cantonaux*.[1] Members of the liberal professions seem to have bought a relatively minor share of the land offered for sale, compared to that of business-men, who were especially interested in the property of convents, abbeys, and priories. In Toulouse, Sentou found that the commercial *bourgeoisie* made the largest gains.[2] The business community in the town had never been particularly prosperous or numerous. The scale of the *biens nationaux* offered a powerful means of social promotion at the expense of the Church. The hoteliers, already a rich section of the town's community, also made substantial profits.

The *biens nationaux* offered different attractions to different men. For the businessman, a presbytery, consisting of a country house, with a garden, stable, and possibly a small field or barn, provided a second residence, and a place to retire to. For the *petit bourgeois*, however, the priority was rather to buy the apartment he lived in, or the shop he worked in, before he considered property outside his home town.

For others, the *biens nationaux* were bought only to be resold at a profit. There is no doubt that the *biens nationaux* offered ripe

---

[1] Bibliography no. 28.   [2] Bibliography no. 69.

pickings for the enterprising speculator. Large companies like the Compagnie Bodin, many of them based in Paris, made large purchases through intermediaries in the provinces, for instance in the department of the Nord, examined by Lefebvre. The period of '*soumissions*' favoured speculative sales. In some cases, individuals simply held up Church or *émigré* property for ransom by its original owners. The cathedral of Arlesheim, for instance, in the Mont-Terrible, changed hands three times before being sold back to the commune in 1815.

Nothing, however, could be further from the truth than to suggest that the Directory opened up land sales to the rapacity of a few greedy speculators. In many areas, there is very little evidence of speculation in land sales. It seems to have been almost unknown, for instance, in the Haute-Garonne or the Vosges. Secondly, some buyers only resold because they were afraid of the political future: a Royalist restoration might completely reverse the nationalisation of Church property, and buyers of territory in annexed departments might one day be overrun by foreign armies.

Furthermore, speculators from Paris and the large cities had to compete with fierce local resistance. No commune wanted to see outsiders buy the parish church, the presbytery, which they hoped to reserve for the school-teacher, common land, or forest, which the village community had for centuries regarded as its own. In the newly-annexed territory of the Mont-Terrible, for example, the *gens du pays* did their utmost to prevent the attempt at colonisation from the French Rhineland by 'les Belfortains'. They were often successful: a coalition of the *bourgeois* of Montbéliard won a famous victory in saving their Halles from purchase by speculators from outside the department.

The aristocracy, too, began to recover some of its property during the Directory, and this, too, thwarted speculators. In the Meurthe, fifteen per cent of *émigré* property was in fact rebought by *émigrés'* relatives, and their estates were obligingly not sub-divided into small lots by local authorities.

Speculation and corruption therefore had their limits, although existing evidence suggests that the sale of the *biens nationaux* gave scope for the enrichment and social promotion of the *bourgeoisie*. Inflation and the conditions of sale allowed a wide profit margin, and ensured that the peasantry was being increasingly excluded from purchases under the Directory. In financial terms, the Directory itself sold cheaply for the sake of short-term benefits, but the régime had created a large class of landowners with a vested interest in the Republic. We can thus include them in our gallery of 'Les Gros' of Directorial society.

The charge of corruption was most frequently levied against the third example of 'Le Gros', the army contractor. For he appeared to enrich himself at the expense of the State, and his rise to opulence was perhaps the most spectacular of all.

The Convention had nationalised the supply of foodstuffs and other essentials to the army. In brumaire IV, however, after the economic controls of the Terror had been dismantled, these functions were 'hived off' to individual companies. Unable to pay the contractors for their services, the government reimbursed them in *biens nationaux*, or in taxes levied in the conquered territories. Thus the Compagnie Flachat, which supplied the Army of Italy, received the right to collect war taxes, as well as the proceeds of the sale of English goods seized at Livorno. In the Year 7, extensive *biens nationaux* were made over in payment to the Compagnie Bodin. The Compagnie Lamotze, which supplied the Army of the Sambre-et-Meuse, collected war taxes in Frankfurt.

As the wealth of these companies increased, so, too, their reputation worsened. Members of the government were suspected of involvement in corrupt practices in the allocation of contracts. The Compagnie Bodin, for instance, lent money to Joséphine de Beauharnais, who, in return, used her influence over Barras to secure favourable contracts for the company. Laporte, a partner in the Compagnie Flachat, was a personal friend of Reubell. Ouvrard, perhaps the richest man in France, had close personal connections with Barras and Cambacérès, while Michel Simons, who supplied the army in Belgium, was protected by Talleyrand. Most of the large companies were also engaged in banking activities. Their loans to the government, and to well-placed private individuals, helped them to secure the contracts on which their profits were based.

By financial expertise and business drive, astute entrepreneurs were able to amass enormous fortunes. Michel Simons was the son of a carriage-builder in Brussels. He made a fortune supplying the army in Belgium, and in 1798 married the celebrated Mademoiselle Lange. Perhaps the most successful entrepreneur of all, however, was Ouvrard. The outbreak of the Revolution found him sitting at a counter writing out accounts for a grocery firm in Nantes. Anticipating a boom in the revolutionary press, he bought all the paper manufactures in Poitou and the Angoumois, on credit. By the age of nineteen, he had made a fortune of 300,000 francs. Denounced as a profiteer during the Terror, he continued to make large profits in the wholesale grocery trade. He was a frequent visitor to Madame Tallien's salon, and a friend of Barras. He was given responsibility for the food supplies of the entire French navy, with a budget of sixty-four million francs. His annual profit, which cannot be estimated, ran into millions, and when he then secured the contract for the supply of the allied Spanish fleet, he must have increased his total profits by at least another fifteen million francs.

Ouvrard spent lavishly. He bought 18,000 acres of forest, and twenty-four farms in the Gers. He owned estates at Vitry, Marly, Châteauneuf, St-Brice, and Luciennes, as well as several houses in Paris. The most celebrated of all his acquisitions was the château of Raincy, near Paris, extravagantly decorated and luxuriously furnished. Thirty-two Doric pillars lined the vestibule, which led into a salon containing a pool twenty feet in diameter, in which a thousand candles were reflected. The bathroom was built in the shape of a half-moon, with a floor of yellow marble, and two bathtubs hewn out of gray-black granite from the Vosges. In the dining-room, fountains of punch, almond juice, and other exotic drinks played continuously. In 1799, his career was crowned when Madame Tallien became his mistress. He was twenty-nine years old.

Perhaps the fortunes of such pillars of Directorial society were based on graft, corruption, and the embezzlement of public funds. Perhaps, as it has been said, 'les honnêtes gens ne sont pas toujours les gens honnêtes'. Undertaking a government contract, however, was a purely speculative venture, in which the contractor exposed himself to considerable risk. For the few who succeeded on an enormous scale, many failed, and were faced with ruin. Honoré Duveyrier, another acquaintance of Joséphine, and in charge of the military hospitals in Milan, described some of the difficulties in his memoirs.[1] Contractors and generals were often paid in *biens nationaux* in the conquered

---

[1] Bibliography no. 66.

Italian territories. These lands, however, were not easy to sell. Few Italians attended the auctions. The Romans, admits Duveyrier, could hardly be expected to bid for the lands of their own convents. The risks involved in government contracting are further illustrated in the career of Hanet-Cléry, son of a Trianon gardener, and the brother of one of Louis XVI's *valets de chambre*. Hanet-Cléry was essentially a subcontractor, who supplied cattle for the Army of the Rhin-et-Moselle, before winning a similar contract for the Compagnie Petit. This time the government withdrew its order, leaving him 100,000 francs out of pocket, and with one thousand head of cattle on his hands. He incurred further debts as the chief supplier of clothing and equipment to the Armée d'Hélvetie, for the French government could not be relied on to fulfil its side of the contract on time. Hanet-Cléry was again in difficulties when he agreed, in the Year 7, to supply the Compagnie Noé in Nantes, which almost immediately went bankrupt. There were many subcontractors, therefore, who never achieved the status of a *fournisseur* like Ouvrard, who were ruined several times, and died, like Hanet-Cléry, in poverty.

One should therefore not generalise from a few cases of fabulous wealth, like that of Ouvrard, for example. This was speculative business, in which fortunes could be lost as easily as they were made. Mallet du Pan remarked that there was 'À peine une fortune sur cent qui ne soit le prix d'une bassesse ou d'un crime; à peine une fortune sur cent qui ont six mois de solidité.' Since the contractors themselves were naturally reticent about their profits, it is difficult to calculate how far they did, in fact, cheat the Republic. The government contractors have been compared to the *fermiers-généraux* of the eighteenth century; they looked forward as well to the great speculative fortunes built during the Second Empire.

During the Directory, therefore, new élites were formed, and the basis was laid for the fortunes of the mid-nineteenth-century French *bourgeoisie*. The characters of Balzac's novels, those slaves of Mammon like Grandet and Goriot, made their money during this period. Grandet, a barrel-maker, married the daughter of a rich timber merchant, and used the dowry to buy property of the Church: lucrative vineyards and *métairies* around Saumur, on which his fortune and subsequent political career were based. He sold several thousand barrels of wine to the revolutionary armies, and was paid in more land. Under the Consulate, he became mayor of his home town. Goriot was a vermicelli manufacturer, who bought his employer's property, and became president of his *section* during the Revolution. His fortune was made from the sale of grain imports during the food shortage. All these case histories, fictional and real, suggest that the Directory was a formative period in the history of the French *bourgeoisie*, in which it renewed its ranks, and gradually absorbed parvenu elements from the sources mentioned.

The *arrivistes*, whether generals, politicians, or *fournisseurs*, enjoyed very close social contacts with each other. Duveyrier, for instance, lent the dowry for the marriage of General Lannes to his aide-de-camp's daughter, and Ouvrard, too, lent Bernadotte 50,000 francs on the occasion of his marriage. Ouvrard's dinner parties, La Tallien's soirées, and Madame Récamier's salon were the meeting-places for intellectuals like Daunou or La Harpe, statesmen like Talleyrand, generals like Masséna, and bankers like Perrégaux. At a personal and social level, the new élites were intimately interconnected.

The traditional aristocracy, it is true, did not accept these parvenus. Madame de la Tour du Pin relates with obvious satisfaction that, on a visit to Joséphine de Beauharnais, she was deliberately condescending, and thought it proper to keep Joséphine waiting. Within a few months, however, after the *coup* of fructidor, Madame de la Tour du Pin, and her like, once again took the road of the emigration.

The Faubourg St-Germain had been usurped in its rôle as the social centre of Paris. The *hôtels* of the old aristocracy now stood deserted, except for those taken over by government departments, empty of furniture, stripped of curtains and mirrors. Even the lead had been removed from the roofs. Some *hôtels* were bought and sold several times within a few months, without their new owners having even seen them.

The social centre of Paris had shifted to the Right Bank, to the newly developing Chaussée d'Antin, and the area around the Rue de Clichy. The Tivoli, with its dances, waterfalls, and artificial landscapes, and the Bains Vigier, were favourite attractions. New town houses were built on the Chaussée d'Antin, and the Champs-Élysées now became a well-frequented public promenade.

After the puritan régime of the Terror, society now set out to enjoy itself, and the opportunities for public recreation multiplied. The vaudeville, firework displays, *bals publics* resumed. The new social freedom was inaugurated on a macabre note, with the Bal des Victimes, to which were admitted only those who could show a death certificate of a relative killed under the Terror. As official prohibitions on public gatherings and idle leisure pursuits relaxed, Paris, and after Paris the provincial cities, came to life. By 1799, there were 1,500 dance-halls in the capital. The open-air Feydeau concerts enjoyed an enormous vogue. Boxing bouts, and the ascent of air-balloons drew large crowds. Gambling was again popular. Gradually the social fashions and manners of the Ancien Régime, for so long taboo, were re-adopted. In spite of Thibaudeau's protests, 'Monsieur' replaced the Republican form of address, 'Citoyen', in polite circles.

There was no longer any reason to be ashamed of luxury. The relaxation of sexual conventions gave women an important social rôle, which they had lost during a Jacobin régime, which condemned them to devotedly stirring the *marmite*, and breeding recruits for the Republican armies. The way in which the new divorce legislation was welcomed gives some indication of both social permissiveness and the more prominent rôle assumed by women in Directorial society.

The Constituent Assembly had legalised divorce in specific cases like adultery, madness, emigration, and the vaguer *dérèglement des mœurs*. But it also allowed divorce by mutual consent, divorce after six months' separation, and for *incompatibilité d'humeur*. Of all these, separation was the easiest to prove, and became the commonest cause for divorce. There were, according to one visitor, 6,000 divorces in Paris between 1 January 1793 and prairial III, and less than one-tenth of these were by mutual consent.

Attempts have been made to represent this very liberal divorce legislation under the Directory as being responsible for a period of unstable marriages, and a wave of immorality. This was not so. Outside Paris, there was no rush to the *mairie*. In the period between 1792 and 1804, there were more than ten divorces per one hundred marriages in only three provincial towns: Rouen, Versailles, and Marseille. In the newly annexed town of Porrentruy, there were a derisory seven divorces during the Directory.

There were political reasons why divorce should be popular. Many divorces recorded were registered by wives of *émigrés*, who wanted to sever all legal ties with their husbands in order to preserve the family property from confiscation. Other divorcés were priests, who had been bullied into marriage under the Terror, but who divorced as soon as clerical marriage was no longer considered a patriotic duty. Many other men married early to avoid conscription, and later divorced. In a city like Toulouse, which had the tenth highest divorce rate in France in this period, there were a regular twenty divorces a year after the Year 4: a figure which hardly suggests that marriage was being taken any more casually than before.

The Empire was to end this liberal period of the Directory, by suppressing divorce for incompatibility, demanding parental approval for divorce by mutual consent, and by making remarriage more difficult for divorcées. In practice this meant that women were again forced into a dependent rôle, from which, under the Directory, they had been briefly liberated.

This was an age of great hostesses. Intellectuals, soldiers, and statesmen flocked to the salons of Madame Tallien, Joséphine, or Madame de Staël. La Tallien furnished her house on the Champs-Élysées in lavish style, although it was modestly named La Chaumière, while her rival Joséphine lived sumptuously in the Rue Chantereine, off the Chaussée d'Antin, with, inappropriately enough, a bust of Socrates in her bedroom, and standing outside, the magnificent team of black horses with which Barras had provided her.

Around the stars of Directorial society, the politicians, the generals, and the rich contractors, revolved a *demi-monde* of courtesans, who dominated social life at the highest level, maintained by whoever was prepared to reward their sexual attractions with the luxuries and the life of uninhibited pleasure they required. Thérèse Cabarrus, daughter of a Spanish banker, was threatened with poverty when the new King, Charles IV, had her father imprisoned. After mixing in the society of the Federalists of Bordeaux, she threw herself on the mercy of Tallien, who married her, and by whom she had a child named Thermidor. When Tallien's political authority dwindled, Thérèse offered her services to Barras, but only Ouvrard was eventually able to dispel all her anxieties about money.

Joséphine de Beauharnais, her greatest rival, was in similar financial straits. She had a son and daughter to support, her husband had been guillotined, and her only resource was the inaccessible profits from the family estate in Martinique. She, too, was compelled to rely on both the bankers and Barras for support. Barras wrote that her greed was such that she would have drunk gold out of her lover's skull. When he tired of her ageing appeal and her endless demand for money, he arranged for the infatuated Bonaparte to take over her bed and her debts.

All these women, like La Tallien, Joséphine, and Madame Récamier, had similar histories. They had all been victims of an arranged marriage at an early age, usually before they were sixteen years old. They could not find either personal happiness or satisfaction for their political ambitions in a marriage to an older man who was absent or unfaithful or politically uninfluential. They satisfied a current taste for the exotic: La Tallien was a dark-haired Spaniard, Madame Hamelin, the *fournisseur*'s wife, a half-caste, and Joséphine of creole origin. Juliette Récamier, on the other hand, with her milky complexion, was a very French coquette. Her salon was populated by the banking associates of her father and husband, and was to become a focus of opposition under the Consulate.

As under the Second Empire, the courtesans openly offered themselves as the rewards of a successful career in politics, finance, or the army. *Le Miroir* of 13 pluviôse V quoted Rivarol: 'Paris n'est pas une patrie, ce n'est que la guinguette de l'Europe ...l'on sort de Paris comme on sort d'un bal, épuisé d'argent et de fatigue.'

The image of Directorial society as a vice-ridden den of depravity must not be exaggerated. The corruption associated with Barras and his circle must not colour our view of society as a whole. In government and out of it, the typical Directorial was just as likely to be a stolid, upright *bourgeois* like La Revellière, who lived quietly, without ostentation, in his suburban retreat. Reubell, it should be remembered, was acquitted on charges of corruption in 1799. The government was, on occasion, prepared to act against corruption within its midst. In 1798, as the result of a financial scandal, the government dismissed several officials in the Ministry of War, including the brother of Schérer, the minister himself.

If so many businessmen indulged in speculation, this was because it was hard during this period of war, inflation, and economic stagnation, to make a profit honestly. It must be said of Ouvrard in his defence that he had a far more sophisticated concept of the power of credit than anyone in the government. In this sense he was a pioneer, from whom lessons should have been learnt. When the French government approached him for a loan of ten million francs in 1798, he advised the establishment of a sinking fund to pay off the national debt. Ouvrard's ideas, however, were too advanced for his contemporaries, and his advice was in vain.

In the *biens nationaux*, the French *bourgeoisie* could find the fulfilment of the struggle for social recognition which they had waged under the Ancien Régime. To the property of the Church and the *émigrés*, the Directory added the spoils of foreign conquest, and profitable government contracts. Thus, the traditional French *bourgeois* was joined, and in the capital, thrown into the shadows, by parvenu elements, who found a faster way to wealth and success, and were not afraid to show it. Their wealth was paraded ostentatiously, and the mores of high society were liberal to the point of licence, but social life under the Directory avoided the extremes of puritanical repression of the Year 2, and of the tastelessness of the Empire.

5

DIRECTORIAL SOCIETY: 'LES MAIGRES'

Mœurs: il n'y en a plus.
  – *Tableau analytique de la Seine*, fructidor V

One cannot discuss the Directory's liberalism without recognising the wide inequalities of wealth which it tolerated. The deputies, ridiculed for their pretensions, despised for the extravagances of their entourages and kept women, seemed to tolerate with surprising indifference the enormous gulf which separated the château from the *chaumière*. The glaring social contrasts of this period are perhaps reminiscent of Parisian society in the 1840s, under the July Monarchy. Both these régimes were times of urban misery on one hand, and of callous luxury of the ruling classes on the other, of official scandals and of crop failure, of wild financial speculation, and of epidemics, death, hunger, and crime.

One cannot, however, attribute popular misery entirely to the failings of the Directory. Food shortages, high infant mortality, endemic crime, disease, and mendicancy were constant features of the life of the eighteenth-century poor. Not even Barras can be blamed for the exceptionally harsh winter of '*nonante-cinq*'. The Revolution itself had, to a large extent, neglected the poor. The collapse of traditional forms of public charity and poor-relief was the consequence of the middle-class, utilitarian legislation of the Directory's predecessors. Furthermore, this tale of popular misery is only applicable to the early years of the Directory. By the Year 8, a series of good harvests had greatly improved the lot of the poor, and reduced the most blatant discrepancies between extremes of wealth and poverty.

This chapter examines how famine, inflation, and the collapse of public charitable institutions aggravated the miseries of the poor during this period. The techniques of social pathology used by Louis Chevalier in his classic study of Paris in the 1840s may be fruitfully borrowed.[1] At least, the incidence of suicide, crime,

---

[1] Bibliography no. 74.

and prostitution, for example, can be interpreted as symptoms of social dislocation under the Directory. 'Les Maigres' of Directorial society never translated their discontent into political revolution. After the risings of germinal and prairial Year 3, '*les classes laborieuses*' were never '*dangéreuses*'. The very poorest classes and those living on the margins of society were as politically silent as they had been under Robespierre. The weariness of years of Revolution, and the accumulated effects of cold and famine, now kept the poor politically quiescent. As La Revellière wrote, 'À la fièvre chaude succède toujours une entière prostration de forces.'

The Directory must be seen in perspective. One must not anticipate the demographic changes which swelled the ranks of 'Les Misérables' before the Revolution of 1848. It was to take another fifty years before the population of Paris reached one million. In any case, in illustrating various forms of social malaise, we do not have the wealth of statistical data available, for instance, to Chevalier in his dissection of Parisian society in the 1840s. We are forced to supplement our quantitative data with evidence from contemporary newpapers and literary sources.

As in the 1840s, contemporaries of the Directory were aware of an army of the dispossessed, both in the countryside and in the towns, reduced to begging and banditry, robbery and murder, in order to alleviate their misery. For Mercier, the revolutionary crowds had degenerated into *la huaille* (rabble), *la canaille sans nom*. Others expressed the gap between rich and poor more poetically. One ex-friar from Sens complained in messidor Year 3 that 'on laisse le malheureux dans ses fers et au milieu des épines tandis que l'on sème les fleurs sur le passage des riches'. In Paris, at least, the anonymous masses were more an object of fear and abhorrence than of pious sympathy. Rétif de la Bretonne wrote: 'Jette un coup d'œil sur cette multitude de figures presque hideuses qui inondent nos villes; vois la laideur et les tailles petites ou défectueuses.'

Every Parisian apartment block, it has been claimed, was a microcosm of the social strata of the capital, with its poorest members occupying the small, furnished rooms on the fifth or sixth storey, above their social superiors, who lived in descending order of prosperity, with the wealthy *bourgeois* occupying the finest apartment on the first floor. But urban topography did not always follow this pattern. Social divisions emerged not between storey and storey, but between area and area, street and street. In Marseille, for example, the poorest lodging-houses were clustered around the Butte des Carmes, while in Toulouse, there was a world of difference between the residential, parliamentary quarter of St-Barthélémy, and the Faubourg St-Martin, where the poor lived forty to a house. If the idea of a layered division of French society had ever been valid, it was becoming increasingly inappropriate in the Paris of the 1790s. Parisian society was rather divided geographically between the new, fashionable, and residential quarters of the west, and the teeming apartment houses, with their enormous floating population, in the centre, and the small workshops of the faubourgs of St-Antoine and St-Marceau in the east. Here, the low, squat houses of artisans and their employees stretched into the fields and market-gardens of the *jardinage*. The west of Paris had been the centre of the Royalist rising of vendémiaire IV, and it was in the eastern faubourgs that the *Courrier Français* reported 'ces figures hâves, ces teints livides, ces habits déguenillés, ces queues pressées aux portes'.

The poor were often seen as an alien race of barbarians in the midst of a civilised society. The *société populaire* of Marseille talked of 'deux tribus diamètralement opposés', and in the context of the Year 3, this may have been true in social, as well as in political terms. After witnessing a violent scene between a man and his pregnant wife, Rétif's Marquise exclaimed, 'Dans la même ville, au sein d'une capitale policée, nous avons des Hottentots à notre porte.'

Who were these Hottentots, and how is the historian to assess their numbers and composition? He might begin by attempting to define them as the unemployed, the homeless, and the beggars. In 1791, the *comité de mendicité* estimated the number of mendicants in France at at least one-twentieth of the population. Such a classification, however, is vague and self-contradictory. Not all of those who begged were necessarily homeless, and not all vagrants were officially unemployed. The *mendiant*, for the local authorities, was usually someone who begged outside his own parish. He might be an old man or an invalid, following members of his family in their seasonal search for harvest work away from home. The *vagabond*, on the other hand, was a man of no fixed address, but many might have claimed they earned their livings as tinkers, or travelling almanac-sellers, or else they might be pilgrims or deserters.

He might attempt to define the poor as those who earned less than a certain minimum wage, but, as Furet has argued, this method, too, is fraught with difficulties.[1] Wages varied from region to region, and fluctuated with the time of year. Such an approach cannot easily estimate the poverty of those whose income did not come from wages, but was paid in kind, or in rents, or of those who held more than one occupation. Another guide to the extent of indigence is the number of *citoyens passifs*, that is, those who, in 1791, paid less than three days' wages in tax. In the city of Caen, for example, they numbered about twenty-five per cent of the population, although the national average was probably nearer one in three. Alternatively, the historian might assess the level of poverty from possessions declared or transferred in marriage contracts and wills. In Toulouse, Sentou found that eighteen and a half per cent of those who married in the revolutionary years were indigent, although one in every two owned moveable property worth less than 250 francs.

The *comité de mendicité* of the Constituent Assembly described the poor not as wage-earners, taxpayers, brides, or testators, but as consumers. A family was poor, it considered, if it had to feed five mouths with an annual income of 435 livres or less. Almost half of this would have to be spent on rent, clothing, heating, and lighting, leaving only about thirteen sous per day to buy food. In the famine of the Year 3, high prices of essential goods caused many to fall below this threshold. The large floating population of cities like Marseille, described by Vovelle as artisans, *compagnons*, port-workers, and manual labourers, was forced into the hospitals, into the ranks of the criminal population, or alternatively it starved to death in the Year 3.[2] This chapter will consider the poor as contemporary authorities saw them: in the dock in the local courts, in the queues for the distribution of bread rations, in the hospitals, and in the mortuaries.

Perhaps the number of those who received poor-relief provides a basic estimate of 'Les Maigres'. Even in a normal year, they might represent between one-quarter and one-fifth of the population of large cities. In Paris in 1790, for instance, 120,000, about twenty per cent of the total population, received bread rations, although Mercier considered that one-quarter of the capital's inhabitants were not guaranteed the means of survival.

[1] Bibliography no. 77.
[2] Bibliography no. 87.

In Toulouse, about twenty-five per cent of the population received poor-relief in 1790, and a Strasbourg census of 1784 described eighteen per cent of the population as 'poor'. Even in normal times, then, a substantial proportion of the population were the victims of what Braudel, in his *Civilisation matérielle et capitalisme*, has called the 'Ancien Régime biologique', characterised as 'une égalité de la mort et de la vie, une très haute mortalité infantile, des famines, une sous-alimentation chronique, de puissantes épidémies'.

Bearing this in mind, the causes and consequences of poverty and hunger, especially between 1795 and 1797, must now be examined.

Chapter 1 has already suggested some of the reasons for the famine conditions of the Year 3. The relaxation of the Price Maximum by the thermidorean government allowed prices of essential foodstuffs to rise. The difficulties in transportation experienced during the icy winter of 1795 kept grain away from urban markets. Furthermore, the inflation of the revolutionary paper currency, the *assignats*, made it impossible for the very poor to afford soaring prices. By prairial III, the *assignat* was worth only seven and a half per cent of its face value; by vendémiaire IV, its value stood at five per cent, and it was soon to become absolutely worthless. Shops refused to open in the evening until the official parity of the *assignat* (the *cours du soir*) had been published. On 8 brumaire IV, for example, the louis was quoted at 3,700 livres at 2 p.m., but by the evening it stood at 4,800 livres. In the Jardin des Plantes, soldiers played quoits for worthless six-livres pieces.

The situation was not retrieved by the replacement of the *assignats* by the new *mandats territoriaux*. This new currency depreciated as quickly as the *assignat* had done, and by prairial IV, a *mandat* with a face value of one hundred livres was worth only forty sous (20 sous = 1 livre = approximately 1 franc). Property-owners were naturally only too happy to pay their taxes in valueless paper currency, but by the Year 5, shopkeepers would accept only metallic currency. Landlords, too, insisted that rents be paid in cash, and poor tenants who could only pay in paper currency were often evicted.

In vendémiaire IV, the *Gazette Français* published a list of prices which revealed the enormous increase which had taken place since 1790. A sack of firewood, for example, which had cost twenty livres in 1790, cost five hundred livres in 1795, and when the rivers iced over, it was to become even more expensive. In the same five years, the price of a pound of candle-wax had risen from eighteen sous to forty-one livres. In Toulouse, local authorities could only work for a few hours a day, because they could not afford to pay the cost of lighting their offices. Nor could they supply street lamps with oil, with disastrous effects for public security at night. A quarter of a pound of eggs cost twenty-five livres in 1795, compared to its price of just over one livre in 1790. The price of bread remained the most eloquent index of popular misery, and when the price of a pound loaf rose to forty-five francs in brumaire IV, it was not surprising that disturbances broke out at Parisian markets. On the Place du Palais-Égalité, stalls were overturned, and the grain merchants driven off, as customers bought bread at their own fixed price of twenty or thirty livres. Similar examples of popular *taxation du pain* occurred in brumaire and frimaire at the markets of St-Martin, St-Denis, and the Place Maubert.

Under the Terror, bread had been cheap, at least in controlled urban markets, even if it was difficult to obtain other foodstuffs. Under the thermidorean reaction and in the Year 4, the price of bread soared, but a much wider variety of goods was available to those who could afford them. Mercier described the wares offered in the markets of the Palais-Égalité: partridge pâté, cherries, fresh peas, wild boar, and a wide selection of hams. Meanwhile the poor starved. A visitor to the fashionable dances at the Jardin des Capucines, or the Élysée-National, leaving for home late at night, could already see the queues forming outside the bakers' shops. The bread queues began to assemble at about one a.m. Women and children stood all night, in a temperature of twelve or fifteen below zero centigrade, for a meagre ration of one-quarter of a pound of black bread, which was delivered to the lucky ones at seven in the morning. Those who had fought their way to the front of the queue might be fortunate, but others were turned away empty-handed after their long and desperate vigil. 'Le pain', remarked Duval, in his *Souvenirs thermidoriens*, 'n'était plus qu'une affaire de tradition. Quelques personnes se souvenaient d'en avoir vu, mais c'était là tout.'

In the cities, merchants were restrained from taking advantage of the food scarcity by the threat of rioting and by pressure from the local authorities. In the countryside, however, these sanctions did not operate. In the city, the merchant might be coerced into accepting *assignats*. The rural producer, however, who sold grain at his own home, could command his own price, and demand payment in coin. Knowing that the harvest was a bad one, and anticipating inflated prices, the cultivator might withhold his produce until prices soared, as predicted, to new heights. If the people took matters into their own hands, and forcibly imposed their own prices at the town markets, then this was another factor which deterred merchants and cultivators from bringing their produce to market.

Thus even in a well-endowed city like Toulouse, in the fertile plain of the Lauragais, where millet had customarily provided a standby in time of dearth, the markets remained empty. Not only had the canals iced over, but the countryside was unwilling to part with the harvested crop which, because of the bad harvest, barely sufficed for peasant needs. The commune of Toulouse only survived the winter by reducing the daily ration of bread to half a pound per head, and by fixing its price at five sous per pound, although this meant incurring a financial loss of about 15,000 livres per day. After the apparatus of the Terror had been dismantled, local authorities no longer had any means of coercing the peasantry to sell on the urban market.

The scarcity of bread forced the poor to turn to alternative sources of nourishment, like rice and vegetables. The lack of fuel, however, gave them no way of cooking rice. Logs could not be floated down ice-bound rivers. Parisians went out into the woods of Vincennes, St-Cloud, and Meudon to cut wood, while others sawed up their beds for firewood. Some heed was at last paid to the exhortations of many *Représentants en mission* of the Year 2 to start cultivating potatoes. In Paris, some lentils were available, but elsewhere, in the Nièvre, for instance, people scoured the forests for wild berries, nettles, and roots. On the outskirts of Paris, people fed off the carcasses of war-horses, and a flourishing trade in cat and dog meat was conducted in Paris, Châlons-sur-Marne, and other towns. Fish became an important part of the diet of the poor in the Year 4, although fish did not stay fresh very long in the summer months. Wandering tradesmen sold herring in the Norman ports, and on the Pont-au-Change in Paris, Mercier found herring being grilled on the pavement, and sold in plates of three for fifteen sous. In desperation, the poor assuaged their misery with bad cheap wine, drunk in lethal quantities, but adulterated, according to Mercier, with river water, and *eau-de-vie*.

A diet of raw vegetables, fish of uncertain age, and coarse wine could not fail to have disastrous consequences: malnutrition, disease, and death. Until a full statistical survey is completed, it is impossible to give a full account of the demographic effects of the famine and cold of the Year 3. Some conclusions, however, can be drawn from the information available from a few towns and regions. The increase in mortality was the result of accumulated hardship. After two years of near-starvation and malnutrition, the poor lacked sufficient physical strength to resist disease and illness. The bitter winter of 1795 finished the work prepared by malnutrition, exhaustion, and epidemics. The real dimensions of the demographic disaster of the Year 3 can only really be gauged by a consideration of the mortality figures of the Year 4, and by an examination of its effects on conception and fertility in that year. Thus, in Rouen, while the mortality of the Year 3 was about twice that of a normal year, the mortality of the Year 4 was triple the normal rate. Furthermore, the monthly number of births began to fall drastically after pluviôse IV, and normal conditions did not return until after the summer of the Year 4.

Elsewhere, the effects of cold and famine were uneven. In the Meurthe, for example, the mortality of the Year 4 did not exceed that of the crisis year of 1789. In Chartres, however, the number of entries registered to the town's hospital rose from just under 400 in 1793, to 734 in 1796. Here, the mortality of 1795 was more brutal than in any year since 1760. In the South, the effects may have been mitigated by a gentler climate, but in Toulouse, the mortality of the Year 3 was the worst between the outbreak of the Revolution and the crisis of 1813. Unlike Toulouse, Dieppe experienced a higher mortality in the Year 4 than in the Year 3, and the same is true of Paris, where over 27,000 died in 1796. This figure was exceeded in 1814 and in the cholera epidemic of 1832, but it was not regularly surpassed until the 1840s, in spite of the vast increase in the total population of the capital in the intervening period. Death was selective. While adult males had a fair chance of survival, the very old and the very young were struck down. If weak and underfed mothers survived childbirth, their physical exhaustion increased the possibilities of premature births or still-births. In the conditions of the Years 3 and 4, even the birth of a healthy child might be a family tragedy, for few

75

mothers or wet-nurses had sufficient milk to feed their babies. The situation was perhaps worst on the outskirts of the large cities, and in the countryside, where the population was not protected by municipal attempts to control prices and stock the markets.

The fate of young children was perhaps the most horrifying aspect of popular distress. In the last quarter of the eighteenth century in the southern outskirts of Paris, about eighteen out of every hundred children born did not live beyond their first year. In Marseille, the infantile mortality rate was 21 per cent, although even this was below the national average, estimated at 23·3 per cent. In pre-revolutionary Rouen, over 90 per cent of abandoned children died before reaching their first birthday. Some were perhaps killed and buried at birth by desperate mothers, although infanticide is impossible to prove and hence to measure. Others were left by anonymous donors on the steps of churches or hospitals.

The resources of the hospitals had already been decimated by the revolutionary legislation, which nationalised and sold their endowments, and annulled royal charters and grants from local institutions like the defunct Parlements or Provincial Estates. They could not cope with the influx of abandoned children in the Years 3 and 4. An official inquiry of the Year 8 showed that, even in a normal year, departments like the Nord, the Orne, and the Var supported about a thousand abandoned children each every year. Heavily-populated departments, like the Bouches-du-Rhône and the Calvados, received over 2,000 annually. The hospitals could barely afford to feed these children. The wet-nurses they employed demanded higher wages in the years of inflation, and with the food shortage so desperate, they could not be relied on to have enough milk to support the children entrusted to them. Neither they nor the hospitals could afford enough clean linen to guarantee standards of hygiene. The pay of both the *nourrices* and the medical staff was months in arrears. Abandoned babies might lie four to a cot, their bodies emaciated and their faces prematurely wrinkled. In these circumstances, it was not surprising that only one in ten abandoned babies emerged from the hospitals alive.

Even those children who did survive the rigours of 1795 did not enjoy bright prospects. Some were condemned to years of ill-treatment and neglect by their appointed nurses, but they at least had a home of sorts. Others would find it extremely hard to find positions as apprentices in a period of high unemployment like the Directory. For many, begging in the streets became the only means of support. Bongert's study of juvenile delinquence stresses the important rôle of minors in petty theft in eighteenth-century Paris,[1] and in Versailles, arrests for *mendicité* were most common among adolescents from thirteen to seventeen years old. Mercier was amazed at the number of children he saw in Paris in this period, and Meister, a foreign visitor to Paris in 1795, noticed the same phenomenon.

Suicide was always a last resort, but this was by no means a monopoly of the poor. The 'martyrs of prairial', and the deputy Charlier in ventôse V testify to the popularity of suicide amongst higher social levels. In popular mythology, the impoverished *rentier* and unlucky gambler were as likely to blow out their brains as the starving labourer or artisan. The Seine, however, yielded up its grim complement of drowned bodies, the flotsam and jetsam of a society in crisis. The *Sentinelle* of 28 prairial V reported sixty suicides since nivôse in the canton of Paris, an average of twelve per month, and a police report of prairial VI reported thirteen suicides in that month alone in Paris. Readers of these reports 'se reprochaient de n'avoir pas le courage d'imiter ces victimes de la misère'.

No woman need starve or commit suicide, unless she was too old to make a living as a prostitute. Professor Cobb has described prostitution as the largest single form of female employment in this period, although this is an impression rather than a calculated estimate, and probably does not apply outside the capital and a few garrison towns.[2] Here, at least, prostitution might be the ultimate fate of many young girls of eighteen or twenty, arriving in Paris from the countryside. A girl would arrive in the city in search of employment, perhaps as a domestic servant, and would contact her relatives and friends who had already emigrated there. This local network would provide her with the work she needed, but the chances were that amongst her compatriots lurked a would-be seducer. The pregnancy records (*déclarations de grossesse*) are full of girls who attached themselves to someone from their own town or village, perhaps their *patron* or, more often, his son, and who were deceived by promises of marriage

---

[1] Bibliography no. 71.
[2] Bibliography no. 15.

into sleeping with them. Their stories are tragically repetitive: the man, frightened by the news that his mistress is pregnant, declares his intention of returning to his native village to get permission to marry, and to make arrangements for the wedding. He is never seen again. For many a girl, this was the first step on the road to a career as a prostitute.

Garrison towns naturally offered a steady income for prostitutes, in spite of the efforts of conscientious administrators to reduce the debilitating effects of venereal disease amongst the *défenseurs de la patrie*. In Versailles, the officers of the prevotal court arrested 524 women for sexual immorality (*libertinage*) and prostitution in four and a half years in the early 1780s. For local authorities, the first priority was to be rid of the prostitutes. After a brief period of detention in the local *hospice des mœurs*, the girls, hopefully reformed, would be sent back to their village of origin. The barracks were not the only haunts of prostitutes. On the Boulevard du Temple, for instance, girls of twelve or thirteen offered themselves, while in the Palais-Égalité, others catered for a very specialised clientele. If prostitution was abolished, wrote the *Journal du Soir*, the deputies' salaries shoud also be reduced, since this would be one expense the less for them.

The poor became poorer during the early years of the Directory not simply as a result of natural causes, bad harvests, and an exceptionally harsh winter. The failure of charitable institutions and severe unemployment in many traditional trades were direct consequences of the Revolution. In towns which had relied economically on the institutions of the Ancien Régime, the Church and the Parlements, acute distress was caused when these institutions were destroyed, or denuded of their financial assets. Monasteries, which had distributed thousands of livres' worth of bread as poor-relief, paid for out of the proceeds of the tithe, were now forced to curtail their charitable work. In towns like Angers and Bayeux, the Church's loss in income during the Revolution caused destitution for thousands.

Not only were the very poor deprived of public charity, but workers and artisans saw their aristocratic clientele evaporate into prison or the emigration. In Toulouse, for example, the Parlement and its hangers-on had constituted one of the largest employers of labour in the city. With the dissolution of the Parlement, and the closure of the churches, sedan-chair carriers, candlestick-makers, painters and sculptors, robe-makers and bookbinders were deprived of employment, or at any rate lost their wealthiest clients. The city's 4,300 domestic servants, representing almost one in three *chefs de famille*, faced a bleak future. To be sure, dealers in second-hand clothes and furniture temporarily profited from the sale of *émigré* property, but for every one of them, there were tailors and carpenters who suffered from a sudden falling-off of demand. In Bayeux, the hospitals demanded the establishment of municipal lace-making workshops to create work for the destitute, and in Toulouse, similar demands were made for a cotton-weaving factory. The Directory at least helped the employment situation by bringing wigs back into fashion, and by relaxing the Republican austerity, which had aggravated the slump in the cloth industries. The Empire was to improve the situation further by re-establishing a court, which heralded a revival in the luxury trades.

The cities seemed to offer only hunger, high prices, and unemployment. The collapse of the luxury trades and the impoverishment of the Ancien Régime's charitable institutions drove many recent immigrants to the cities back into the countryside, where they hoped bread was more plentiful. This exodus from the cities, however, was based on illusory hopes, and merely provided recruits for the bands of wandering beggars and bandits who roamed France.

Vovelle found that three in eight of the wandering beggars he examined in the Beauce had become vagrants in the Year 3.[1] Many of these beggars spent their lives roaming the countryside, as peddlars, dealers in rabbit-skins, or as second-hand clothes merchants. Often, however, these professions were merely excuses for travelling, and for hiding their real sources of income: begging and crime. Many others, however, were not professional beggars, but rural wage-earners, or artisans, weavers, and spinners, whom poverty had driven from the outskirts of towns like Paris, Orléans, and Chartres. All kinds of uprooted victims of the food shortage and the conditions of the Year 3 came together in the wandering bands: abandoned women, cripples unable to work, unemployed textile artisans, and orphans like the Belle Agnès, a beggar at the age of eighteen, who had been raised at the Foundling Hospital in Paris, and worked as an apple-seller and a prostitute.

[1] Bibliography no. 85.

Violent crime was endemic in the French countryside, whether it took the form of the grain riot or opposition to recruiting, or arose from private quarrels. Feuds over property or grazing rights could lead to violence, incendiarism, or pitched battles between villages. Not only the poor were involved. For violent rural crime was often the expression of the solidarity of the whole community, when the young men of rival villages came to blows, at public gatherings like fairs and wedding-feasts.

The most spectacular form of rural crime in this period, however, was banditry. In the Nord, for instance, where the frontier offered an escape route and plentiful opportunities for smuggling, bandit gangs thrived. This was the stamping-ground of the *chauffeurs*, so called because they roasted the feet of their victims until they disclosed the whereabouts of their valuables. In the Year 4, the *chauffeurs* were active in the area around Roubaix and Tourcoing, while the Cambrésis was terrorised by the Bande de Moneux, until the leader's capture in the Year 5. The mountainous departments of the Massif Central were ideal terrain for bandits who descended from the hills to attack isolated travellers. The Ardèche and the Lozère, for example, had been favourite bandit territory from time immemorial. In the Midi and the South-east, however, it is impossible to distinguish rural crime from the vengeance killings of the White Terror. Simple armed robbery could hide long-standing personal and political feuds. At the same time, it could be deliberately dressed up as political crime, when it became clear that acts of politically motivated terrorism would benefit from a general amnesty. The distinction between crime *per se* and conscious popular protest is a very blurred one, which the historian tries to distinguish at his peril.

In Provence, too, the mountainous roads offered excellent opportunities for ambush and robbery throughout the Directory. The roads between Avignon and Aix, Avignon and Digne, Aix and Toulon, Marseille and Toulon, were never safe, and in 1799, the Var was described in an official report as the worst department in France, as far as public order was concerned. The presence of the prison hulks at nearby Toulon was perhaps connected with the high incidence of crime in this department. In the Vaucluse, too, there were seventy-nine murders in the last six months of the Year 8 alone, and passengers from Avignon on the roads south were advised to carry at least four louis for the bandits, if they wished to reach their destination alive.

The lack of an adequate police force, especially in the country-side, enabled the bandit gangs to continue their activities un-punished. The *gendarmerie* was deficient both in numbers and equipment. It was, like all employees of the government, paid months in arrears, and seldom dared to confront a large band of armed criminals. In the department of the Meurthe, for ex-ample, with a population of 340,000, the *gendarmerie* numbered only 110, and they were concentrated in the towns of Nancy and Lunéville. A Parisian police report of nivôse IV described the ineffectiveness of the *gendarmerie:* 'Rien de plus rare que de recontrer des gendarmes le soir sur la grande route; jamais on n'en voit sur celles de traverse; cependant ils font viser leurs feuilles dans les communes; mais ils s'amusent dans tous les cabarets, ils galopent ensuite à toute bride pour regagner le temps perdu. En général, le service de la gendarmerie se fait d'une manière assez équivoque.' There was no substitute for them. The National Guard was primarily an urban militia; the *gardes cham-pêtres*, who patrolled the forests and protected cornfields from marauders, scarcely had enough horses to go round.

It was in the flat, deserted cornlands of the Beauce that the most spectacular bandit gangs flourished. Using the forests as its bases, and operating amongst the desolate and scattered hamlets of the Eure-et-Loir, the Bande d'Orgères was responsible for at least seventy-five recorded murders, between some time before 1791 and the execution of its leaders in 1800. These murders were occasionally accompanied by rape, almost invariably by heavy drinking, and they usually ended with the theft of clothes, jewels, or other valuables from the houses of prosperous farmers. In the years of inflation, there was little point in stealing money; goods were often used instead of cash in these years, and stolen clothes could be disposed of without arousing suspicion.

Bands like the Bande d'Orgères constituted alternative socie-ties in themselves. They had their own hierarchies, and their own family life. Women played an important rôle as inciters of violence, and children could be used to reconnoitre likely farm-steads. They had their own slang, their own well-known hide-outs, and a network of regular contacts in the surrounding towns, who would help to dispose of stolen goods. They coined their own picturesque (and grotesque) nicknames: Le Borgne Du

Mans, Breton Cul-Sec, le Beau-François. The band had its own code of conduct, recognising above all bravery, cruelty, personal loyalty, and the bravado of its leaders, who dressed themselves proudly in the finery stolen on past raids.

It may be a gross idealisation to portray the members of the Bande d'Orgéres as picturesque folk-heroes. For crime in this period, to use Louis Chevalier's terms, was perhaps already a banal, everyday event, a constant symptom of a diseased society. In spite of the antisocial pose of the band's leaders, and the legend they created, this kind of banditry was one manifestation of the social dislocation caused by the upheaval of the revolutionary years, and the conditions of the Years 3 and 4. For these conditions made famine, suicide, the abandonment of children, and endemic rural crime constant features of the life of the poor in Directorial society.

Crime was perhaps becoming less violent. Assaults, woundings, and murders were on the decrease in eighteenth-century France, while, especially in the cities, thefts were becoming more frequent. While in the Norman *bailliages*, for instance, thefts only accounted for about one-third of crimes committed in the late eighteenth century, eighty-seven per cent of cases heard by the Paris Châtelet concerned thefts. While crimes of violence, and collective crime, involving the complicity of whole communities, were more typical of the countryside, urban crime took a different form, characterised chiefly by isolated petty thefts of clothes or linen, and small-scale pickpocketing at fairs and markets. In cities like Paris, criminals did not have deep roots in their local community. They lived rather on the margins of society, immigrants freed from ties of family or village, living a precarious existence in the miserable lodging-houses, like those in the centre of Paris, or around the Place Maubert.

After the early years of the Directory, however, this picture of rural anarchy and popular misery will not stand. It is true that the suppression of the paper currency in the Year 5 inaugurated a period of deflation, in which money was scarce at first, and in which there was no immediate economic recovery. Nevertheless, prices fell. A series of good harvests in 1796, 1797, and 1798 removed the threat of famine. In the Puy-de-Dôme, and in the Haute-Garonne, for example, the price of grain dropped at the end of the Year 7 to its lowest level during the whole revolutionary period.

Wage increases had never kept pace with soaring prices, but wages had nevertheless risen. Francis d'Ivernois calculated in 1799 that the wages of agricultural labourers had risen by eighty per cent since 1789. Furthermore, when prices fell in the Year 5, wages tended to hold their ground. By the end of the Directory, therefore, the poor were no longer faced with starvation, and Mercier could report a much happier Parisian scene in his *Le Nouveau Paris*. He watched the contented families of Belleville stroll to the Pré St-Gervais, in the fine weather of the spring and early summer, to pick fruit, picnic, rest at the *guinguettes*, and listen to the birds singing. This idyllic pastoral scene was a far cry from the hunger and misery which gripped Paris in the winter of 1795. The shortages of that year, and the hardship on a national scale which ensued, were not repeated for another half-century. The decade which followed the Directory was to be a period of general prosperity, demographic expansion, and a rise in the real value of wages.

6

EDUCATION AND SOCIAL WELFARE

The history of education in France during the Revolution was one of sweeping, imaginative schemes, but very limited achievements. The destruction of Ancien Régime teaching institutions brought in its wake a spurt of proposals for reform, incorporating, in various degrees, the principle of a free, compulsory education for all. Theorists began to defend the need for a specifically Republican education, which would be secular in organisation and scientific in spirit, and which would inculcate ideas of civic responsibility. Naturally, educational disputes were heavily politicised: the liberal-minded Girondins believed that private schools could coexist with state schools; the clerical party opposed secularisation; while some of the Montagnards came closest to a plan for Republican indoctrination in the schools. In a time of military crisis, however, the revolutionary assemblies had more urgent priorities, and the solution of vital educational problems was postponed. It was not until the period of the Directory that the Republicans had time to put into practice some of the ideas which emerged from the Revolution. The extent to which they did put them into practice forms the subject of this chapter.

The hospitals and the schools shared a broadly similar fate. Both were largely dependent on the Church in the Ancien Régime; both lost their financial basis during the Revolution, and suffered the attacks of the dechristianisation campaign. The Ancien Régime institutions of education and social welfare were destroyed. It was not until the Directory that a serious attempt at reconstruction was made. After the schools, this chapter will discuss the fate of the hospitals. First, however, a brief summary of education in France before 1794 is necessary.

Before 1789, education was largely in the hands of the Church. In the primary schools, or *petites écoles*, of the towns and countryside, the appointment of every teacher needed episcopal approval. From the age of seven, children were taught reading, writing, and arithmetic, as well as religious instruction, but the first words they learned to read would traditionally be Latin, and they were taught one by one, and not as a class.

In rural France, education was conceived in the context of the religious life of the community, and its tempo was regulated by the demands of the harvest. Many *vicaires* taught in their villages, and many other schoolmasters acted as sextons, grave-diggers, or as assistants to their *curés*. Classes began and ended with a prayer, and were largely devoted to teaching the catechism, and preparing for the First Communion. Village schools often had only the most rudimentary equipment: benches would be borrowed from the church on Monday morning, and returned on Saturday night.

Country schools were only attended regularly between November and March. During harvest-time, they were deserted. The schoolmaster, unemployed during the harvest months, was frequently obliged to take temporary work as an agricultural labourer.

After leaving the *petite école* at the age of about twelve, pupils might go on to one of the *collèges* or seminaries run by the religious orders. There were about 560 *collèges* on the eve of the Revolution, and about half of the places they offered were free. The expulsion of the Jesuits in 1762 had left a certain void, partly filled by the Frères des Ecoles Chrétiennes, and by the Oratorians, who supplemented the traditional emphasis on classical studies with courses in French history and Cartesian mathematics. Many revolutionary leaders were either taught by the Oratorians, or were themselves members of the order, like Daunou, Lebon, Billaud-Varenne, and Fouché.

Alternatively, the pupil might attend one of the universities, which ran general courses for students between the ages of twelve and eighteen, before they went on to specialise in Law, Medicine, or Theology. There were as many as twenty-one universities in France on the eve of the Revolution, and the University of Paris alone had about five thousand arts students.

The educationalists of the Directory agreed with eighteenth-century critics like Helvétius in condemning the ecclesiastical monopoly of education. A few perhaps wanted a more comprehensive system of education for girls, while others followed Diderot and Rousseau in their prejudice against '*les femmes savantes*'. Like Voltaire, they perhaps feared that increased educational opportunities for the peasantry would create social upheaval, and take manpower away from agriculture. As the Abbé Fleury had advised: 'You are born a peasant, stay a peasant; cultivate the field of your ancestors, or, if they have not bequeathed you one, serve a master and work for your daily wage; leave studying to the rich.' Nevertheless, they looked forward to a kind of education which would develop a sense of *civisme*, which would be more rationalist and vocational than the system prevailing in the Ancien Régime.

Many of the *cahiers de doléances* of 1789, however, envisaged not the destruction, but rather the extension of the existing system, demanding a strengthening of the clergy's rôle, as a defence against the supposed 'moral degeneration' of France. The Revolution, itself, however, dealt a series of damaging blows to the Ancien Régime educational system. Firstly, the financial resources of the schools were reduced by the abolition of the tithe, which hit clerical funds for education, and by suppression of the tolls, or *octrois*, which reduced the educational budgets of local communities. Then the teaching personnel itself was savagely limited by the Civil Constitution of the Clergy, and the oath of fidelity to revolutionary legislation which was imposed. Refractory priests and friars, and the schoolmasters who sided with them, were dismissed. The abolition of religious orders forced the dispersal of teaching congregations like the Christian Brotherhood, and the closure of many primary schools formerly run by the monasteries.

The Revolution thus created an immense vacuum in the educational system, which had depended heavily on the Church for its financial backing and teaching personnel. Several progressive schemes were proposed for a national system of education to fill this vacuum. In 1791, Talleyrand sketched out the first plan for a national system, paid for by the government, but allowing the Church to continue its work in primary education. Then Condorcet put forward a plan which was revolutionary in the sense that it envisaged equal education for women, and for the first time incorporated a scheme for teacher training. But he, too, would have allowed the Church schools to continue, and he did not accept the idea that education should be compulsory. The proposals of Montagnards like Lepelletier de St-Fargeau went further in demanding the complete exclusion of the priesthood from education, which should be not only secular, free, and common to all, but also compulsory. He would have imposed a spartan and rigorously Republican régime, but he was attacked because he threatened to undermine parental influences and antagonise the peasantry.

Very little of these utopian schemes ever left the drawing-board. While the revolutionaries agreed that the establishment of a new, national educational system was of fundamental importance, they were preoccupied with other matters, like winning the war, and uniting the country. Until the military security of France was assured, long-term projects were shelved. Condorcet had to interrupt the reading of his report on 20 April 1792, to allow the Assembly to declare war on Austria. In December 1792, Marat attacked the Girondin educationalists for wasting valuable time: 'Vous ressemblez à un général qui s'amuserait à planter, dé-planter des arbres pour nourrir de leurs fruits des soldats qui mourraient de faim.' Until the war was won, therefore, the Convention's time and money was primarily devoted to military success and political unity.

The thermidoreans thus inherited an educational system in a state of chaos. Vital issues had been stated, but not resolved: Should education be free and compulsory? Should ecclesiastics be excluded from the teaching profession? What constituted a truly Republican education? Where were the buildings, staff, and money for a new system of education to be found? The answers found to these crucial questions by the thermidoreans and the Directory were always conditioned by a chronic lack of money, aggravated by inflation. Nevertheless, this period saw a limited but constructive attempt to solve them along liberal, but staunchly Republican lines. This attempt was perhaps most successful in the fields of secondary education, and advanced specialist schools.

In primary education, the work of the thermidoreans and the Directory was generally unsuccessful. The decree of brumaire Year 3, inspired by Lakanal, did go some way towards a solution of outstanding problems. Lakanal accepted the idea that primary education should be free (that is, not paid for directly by the parents), but he also recognised the Church's right to continue to run independent schools. One school was to exist for every thousand inhabitants, and the teachers were to be chosen by a local *jury d'instruction*, appointed by the district administration.

Teachers were to receive a salary of between 1,200 and 1,500 livres, and would be lodged in the local presbyteries. All teaching was to be carried out in French, and it was to include an explanation of the Declaration of the Rights of Man, the Constitution, and history and geography, as well as the three 'Rs'. An École Normale was set up in Paris to train future teachers.

This realistic scheme was followed by the decree of brumaire Year 4, which again accepted that education should be free (*gratuit*), but not compulsory, and not exclusive of independent Catholic schools. Now, however, the teacher's salary would vary according to the number of his pupils, and he would receive a payment from the parents, known as the '*retribution scolaire*'. The amount was left at the discretion of the local authorities, but one-quarter of the pupils could be exempted from payment on the grounds of poverty.

In spite of these reforms, the shortage of primary schools remained, especially in those areas already under-provided (that is, the West, the Centre, and the South-west). In the department of the Manche, in the Year 8, only 177 primary schools had been organised, although under the provisions of brumaire Year 4, there should have been over 400. In the Year 6, there was only one state primary school teacher working in the Lozère, and only three or four in the Ardèche. In Boulogne (Haute-Garonne), there was only one school for over 10,000 inhabitants, and only 25 pupils attended it in the Year 7.

The moderate plans laid down by the Directory had met insurmountable obstacles. Firstly, the École Normale closed within six months of its inauguration in January 1795. Professors of great distinction had been appointed, like the geometrician Laplace, the mathematicians Lagrange and Monge, and the novelist Bernardin de St-Pierre. Their lectures, however, were only marginally concerned with teaching techniques, and went over the heads of most of the students.

Even with the École Normale, however, there was still a teacher shortage. Some former teachers and Constitutional priests were recruited, but the pay was low, and always in arrears. Furthermore, their meagre pay was always liable to be reduced by absentee pupils. Because of the continuing shortage of personnel, former nuns and *curés* had to be appointed. In Riom, there were only eighteen applicants for thirty-nine posts, and of these, seven were ex-ecclesiastics. Their intellectual qualities often left something to be desired, judging from the story of one sixty-two-year-old *vicaire* from the Puy-de-Dôme, who promised to learn to read if he got the job. At the end of the Year 5, in the Seine department, there were only fifty-six state primary schools functioning, with a total of only 1,200 pupils.

Teachers were further deterred by the difficulty in finding lodgings. The law of brumaire Year 4 had officially put the presbyteries at their disposal, but many local authorities were loth to part with their presbytery, unless it was for a price at auction. Many teachers could not move in because the presbytery had already been sold, because it was still occupied by a *curé*, or because it was the premises of some local government body.

Those teachers who did take up posts sometimes faced the unrelenting hostility of the rural population. The influence of the clergy, and the obstinacy of the villagers could, on occasion, demoralise a new *instituteur*. Priests would hold catechism classes during lessons, as a rival attraction, or refuse to confirm pupils who had attended a Republican school. In Bourges, peasants charged the teachers such high prices for foodstuffs that twenty-one of them gave up the struggle. It was still hopeless to hold classes at harvest-time, or on Catholic holidays. Since the teacher's salary depended partially on his attendance figures, he was forced to compromise with local Catholic opinion.

Many parents objected to the laicisation of the primary schools, and to the blatantly Republican aspects of the syllabus. For Republicans saw education as an 'instrument d'émancipation, un foyer de patriotisme, une pépinière de bons citoyens, une annexe en quelque sorte des clubs', which would 'dégager la génération naissante des chaînes que certains préjugés lui préparent' (Dommanget).[1] One 'Catéchisme français' in the Sarthe read as follows:

–Qu'est-ce que l'âme? –Je n'en sais rien.
–Qu'est-ce que Dieu? –Je ne sais ce qu'il est.

There were always a number of private primary schools available to parents who resented the anticlericalism of the Republican schools. The private schools were often run by former friars, nuns, and priests, who continued to teach the Bible, hold religious services, and ignore the obligatory rest on the *décadi*. Competition from these schools inevitably harmed the

---

[1] Bibliography no. 91.

4-2

prospects of the state primary schools. Private schools were usually very small, but taken as a whole, they attracted the majority of pupils. In the Lot department, for example, there were 64 state schools, with 1,600 pupils, but 152 private schools, with a total of 1,850 pupils. Competition from private schools was particularly intense in urban centres. In the Seine department, at the end of Year 5, 56 state schools had to compete with 2,000 private establishments.

After the anti-Royalist coup of fructidor Year 5, the government did take some measures to limit the spread of private and clerical primary education. After brumaire Year 6, for instance, all civil servants had to show that they sent their children to state schools, and a few months later, a system of inspection was introduced, to ensure that the Declaration of the Rights of Man and the Republican Constitution were being taught in all schools. As a result, a small number of private schoolteachers were dismissed, but the measures had no major effect on the number of children attending state schools. In fact, it might be said that this period saw a gradual 'rechristianisation' of the primary schools, as teachers, once again, took their pupils to Mass on religious holidays.

The Directory did not, therefore, fulfil the promise of the Revolution in primary education. It even abandoned the cherished goal of the Terror, the promotion of the French language. A report of 1806 estimated that there were over two and a quarter million non-French speakers in France. These were mostly made up of about one million German-speaking inhabitants of the eastern departments, and almost the same number of Breton speakers, together with the Flemish population of the North, the Basques, and the Corsicans. On 8 pluviôse Year 2, Barère had lauched a searing attack on linguistic minorities: 'Le fédéralisme et la superstition parlent bas-breton; l'émigration et la haine de la République parlent allemand; la contre-révolution parle italien et le fanatisme parle le basque...Brisons ces instruments de dommage et d'erreur.' The liberal sympathies of the Directory opposed any coercion towards linguistic uniformity. At the same time, the shortage of equipment forced the authorities to recognise that primary school teaching could not everywhere be conducted in French. In the North, no teaching could be done without Flemish textbooks, and in many other areas, the only French texts available were catechisms. In fact, the Revolution did succeed in promoting the diffusion of the French language, through conscription, and the need for local populations to familiarise themselves with the plethora of new laws and decrees, published in French. This, however, was a gradual process. One peasant of the Saône-et-Loire gave this revealing answer to an Imperial questionnaire: 'Depeu la Révolution, je commençou de franciller ésé bein.' The Directory did not adopt linguistic uniformity as a deliberate policy.

The period of the Directory, then, saw no great advance in popular education, although the Jacobins still attached considerable ideological importance to this issue. It has been alleged that the régime was far more concerned with the education of the middle classes in secondary schools than with developing popular education at the lowest level. But there were other reasons, like the lack of funds, which left the teaching profession grossly underpaid, and the lack of school premises. The Directory did attempt to formulate a lay, Republican programme of primary education, but it felt it politically unwise to impose this on France.

The Directory's record in secondary education was a much happier one. The experimental Écoles Centrales were not perfect, but they provided answers to many of the régime's problems. They offered a secular, scientific, and Republican education, in the most constructive spirit of the eighteenth-century philosophers. They were liberal, comparatively independent, but unfortunately short-lived, soon replaced by the *lycées*, and the authoritarian, standardised Napoleonic educational system.

The laws passed by Lakanal and Daunou provided for the establishment of an École Centrale in every department. A wide range of subjects was to be taught to students between the ages of eleven to twelve and seventeen to eighteen. The organisation of the schools was left almost entirely in the hands of local authorities. The departmental councils were entrusted with the tasks of finding premises, teachers, and students. The schools were run by *jurys d'instruction*, usually composed of local notables, administrators, and ex-ecclesiastics, who acted as intermediaries between the schools and the departments, choosing professors, arranging courses, and carrying out inspections. This arrangement allowed every department a wide degree of freedom, and since the professors themselves were to have a voice in the running of the schools, government interference was kept to a minimum.

The syllabus was an ambitious one. Students between the ages of ten and twelve were to study drawing, natural history, and ancient languages, and those over fourteen were to study grammar, belles-lettres, history, and legislation, which included politics and political economy. But this schema only rarely operated. The students were often free to enrol in as many courses as they wished, regardless of their age. In most cases, they showed a taste for the exact sciences, and drawing and mathematics were the most popular courses. They were perhaps considered a good training for entrance to the École Polytechnique. Literature courses, on the other hand, were under-subscribed.

The Écoles Centrales recruited an impressive body of professors, considering that the régime still made no provision for teacher training. Many were Constitutional priests, and many had taught in the *collèges* of the Ancien Régime. They were therefore men of some teaching experience, although the only qualification they needed was a *certificat de civisme*.

The professors had absolute freedom to decide the content of their courses. In general, they were scientific and utilitarian, based on the foundation of the Enlightenment. Consider, for example, the practical nature of some of the courses at Besançon. The chemistry course examined vegetable and animal matter, including, for example, the composition of wine, blood, and milk. Here the professor's audience included medical officers from military hospitals. The grammar course included logic, and theories of sensation expounded by Locke and Condillac. Belles-lettres concentrated on the art of public speaking. History incorporated the writings of Mably, Rousseau, and Condillac, and in true eighteenth-century fashion, considered a study of the ancient republics the proper education for a citizen of France. The professors were comparatively immune from political purges, unlike many other public servants. They could only be suspended by the department, on the recommendation of the *jury d'instruction*. They frequently gave various services to the community, speaking at civic fêtes, or advising local authorities in their capacities as agriculturalists or engineers.

This arrangement, of course, was by no means ideal. Many of the subjects taught were perhaps more appropriate to university faculties, and the poverty of primary education left students inadequately prepared for them. The schools did not spring up overnight; it often took years to organise them. Since so much depended on the individual professor, courses were inevitably of a very uneven quality. Physical education also seems to have been an important omission from the syllabus.

Nevertheless, the Écoles Centrales prospered. They took over the enormous libraries of the seminaries and convents, and if the old Jesuit college also had a botanical garden, this too was incorporated. In Besançon, the botanical garden was started from scratch, and yet had a thousand plants by the Year 7. This was indeed the Directory's model École Centrale. By the Year 8, it had over six hundred annual enrolments. It attracted students from neighbouring departments, and even from Switzerland. The disinterested staff waived the *retribution scolaire*, which undoubtedly contributed to the school's popularity. As in several other schools, attempts were made to accommodate a small number of boarders.

The students of the Écoles Centrales were mostly sons of professional men, public functionaries, businessmen, and a few landowners. Some sons of small traders and artisans also attended, and in Besançon, some parents were *vignerons*.

The Écoles Centrales, therefore, were a limited success. The Empire, however, rejected their essential qualities: the independence of the professors, the students' freedom of choice, and the responsibility of the local authorities. Instead, a streamlined and autocratic system was introduced, in which the government regulated every minute of the timetable. Nevertheless, the Écoles Centrales had gone some way towards providing a national, scientific, and Republican secondary education, incorporating the ideals of eighteenth-century educational theory. Let the historian Vial speak their epitaph: 'Si elles ont disparu, c'est parce qu'elles avaient le tort d'être révolutionnaires dans une société qui ne l'était plus.'[1]

The Directory continued the Convention's policy in the field of higher education. The universities, suppressed by the Convention, were replaced by a series of specialised schools. This fragmentation of disciplines reflected an increasingly vocational

[1] Bibliography no. 98.

emphasis. Certain schools fulfilled specific war needs, like the École des Travaux Publics, founded in the Year 3 to train military engineers. This school was staffed by the chemist Fourcroy, the mathematician Lagrange, and the scientist Guyton-Morveau, responsible for the revolutionary reconnaissance balloons used at the battle of Fleurus. At the end of the Year 3, this school became the modern École Polytechnique. The Convention had also established a Natural History Museum, where courses were given in mineralogy, botany, zoology, and chemistry. Some Ancien Régime institutions were maintained, like the renamed Bibliothèque Nationale, and the Collège de France. The old medical faculties, however, were replaced by new Écoles de Santé in Paris and Montpellier. The Conservatoire des Arts et Métiers, at once a teaching institution and an industrial museum, was intended to replace apprenticeships previously run by the guilds. The Convention, therefore, could claim a considerable record of achievement in specialised, professional education.

At the apex of the education system stood the Institut, created in brumaire Year 4. The Institut took over the rôle of the Ancien Régime academies in awarding prizes and disseminating research findings. Its founder, Daunou, grouped it into three classes; the first comprised mathematics and physical sciences, the second literature and the fine arts, and the third, moral and political science. The Institut's membership was the cream of France's intellectual élite, including chemists like Berthollet, Chaptal, and Fourcroy, mathematicians like Lagrange and Monge, and naturalists like Lamarck. The third class of the Institut included many of the Idéologue group, like Siéyès, Cabanis, Garat, and Volney. In vendémiaire Year 7, the Institut was given the task of supervising the educational system of France, when an educational committee of ten was appointed from its membership. This committee attempted to ensure that religion was kept out of the classrooms, and to coordinate the curricula of the Écoles Centrales. The Institut was thus the supreme oracle of French intellectual life, uniting the best brains of the late Enlightenment. It was, in Condorcet's phrase, 'a living Encyclopaedia'.

The educational ideas of the Revolution thus had only a limited application in the 1790s. Under the Directory, respect for freedom of thought prevented the authorities from giving state schools a monopoly. Lack of money and of a body of trained teaching staff made recruitment difficult. Women's education was left entirely to private educational establishments. Nevertheless, the Directory can claim to have made important educational advances. It continued the specialist schools created in the Year 3. The Écoles Centrales were just reaching the height of their success when Napoleon destroyed them. Above all, the Republic had, in the spirit of the Enlightenment, formulated an educational system which emphasised useful studies and the importance of a civic education, in a scientific and non-religious framework.

Similar problems faced the Directory in the administration of the hospitals. The Revolution had destroyed their financial basis, but at the same time, the Convention had recognised public assistance as the responsibility of the government. Lack of time, however, and the pressures of war had postponed any concrete action towards the realisation of this ideal. The Directory began a process of limited reconstruction. As with the schools, however, problems remained. Funds were never sufficient, and the dechristianisation campaign had dispersed the nursing personnel. Shortage of funds forced the Directory to throw responsibility for the hospitals onto the local authorities, just as it did with the secondary schools, while it allowed a resurgence of private charity, and welcomed the nuns back into the hospitals.

Earlier revolutionary governments had failed in their attempts to suppress begging, which Barère had described as 'the leprosy of monarchies'. The Comité de Mendicité of the Constituent Assembly, under the presidency of the philanthropic aristocrat Rochefoucauld-Liancourt, made constructive proposals which were not implemented. He recommended the extension of public works schemes to create employment, the institution of a skeletal, but free, public medical service at a local level, and the treatment of the aged and the sick in their own homes, in order to reduce expenditure on their accommodation. For the able-bodied poor, the solution was 'assistance par le travail', while the incorrigible 'professional' beggars should still be detained in *maisons de correction.*

The Convention had declared: 'Tout homme a droit à sa subsistence par le travail, s'il est valide; par des secours gratuits, s'il est hors de travailler. Le soin de pourvoir à la subsistance du

95

pauvre est une dette nationale.' Once again, however, the war postponed the implementation of reforms, and the extension of public charity. What funds were available for this purpose were destined primarily for the relatives of soldiers killed. The government's only solution was to make a series of provisional subsidies for poor-relief, on a purely *ad hoc* basis.

At the same time, revolutionary legislation decimated the hospitals' income. The tithes and *octrois* were abolished, as were the gifts the hospitals received from the King and from the defunct Parlements or Provincial Estates. Most drastic of all, the hospitals' property was confiscated for sale as *biens nationaux*. The ecclesiastical basis of poor-relief was thus swept away. The income of the Paris hospitals fell from 7·9 million livres in 1788, to 4·1 million in 1790. In Béziers (Hérault), the hospital's income fell from 20,000 livres to 8,000 livres. Elsewhere, the effect was even more catastrophic. Eighty per cent of the annual income was lost in Besançon and Perpignan, and ninety per cent in Castelnaudary, Nîmes, and Brest. Furthermore, nuns of orders like the *sœurs hospitalières* of St-Vincent de Paul, and of Nevers, were imprisoned or expelled, sometimes violently.

A permanent solution to this problem was now an urgent necessity. As local authorities continued to remind the government, 'la faim ne s'ajourne pas'. The hospitals found it difficult to provide for even their most basic needs. Inflation increased the price of food and new linen, and butchers and tradesmen clamoured for the payment of outstanding bills. In Toulouse, for example, in the Year 7, the hospital reported that it had exhausted its stock of linen and grain, although it had 1,800 invalids and orphans to support. It was impossible to pay wet-nurses, except in valueless *assignats*, and it was by no means rare for ninety per cent of foundlings to die. There was no money to pay the staff, let alone purchase elementary medical supplies, or fuel for heating and lighting.

Only in the Year 5 did the Directory begin to remedy the situation. In vendémiaire, the Terrorist law which had nationalised the hospitals' finances was repealed. Property which had not already been sold was returned to the hospitals, and they were to receive compensation for their other losses. Just as secondary education had been entrusted to the departments, so the administration of the hospitals now became the responsibility of the municipalities. In each commune, a *commission administrative*, appointed by the municipal administration, was to supervise the management of the local hospitals. Later in the Year 5, *bureaux de bienfaisance* were established, to distribute relief to the indigent at their own homes. Apart from private donations, however, the financial resources of both the hospitals and the *bureaux de bienfaisance* were inadequate. They were allowed a contribution from the revived *octrois*, as well as the receipts from a new entertainments tax, equivalent to one-tenth of the price of every theatre ticket sold. According to one estimate, there were 90,000 paupers in Paris alone in the Year 7, and this tax would provide them with only four francs each per year. In brumaire Year 7, the hospitals obtained a further concession, when they were exempted from taxes on doors and windows. Many chapels were reopened in the hospitals, and in the Year 8, the Minister of the Interior, Chaptal, allowed the *sœurs hospitalières* to resume their functions. Chaptal had to recognise that recruitment to the nursing profession still drew more on the inspiration of Christian charity than on any lay alternative. On the whole, in spite of the Directory's attempts to revive a system of public relief, reforming ideals were stifled by the economic depression, and the drain on the personnel of the hospitals.

Nevertheless, the Directory's record was not altogether bleak. In certain spheres, important reforms were realised. Consider, for example, the treatment of the insane. Under the Ancien Régime, lunatics were interned, together with beggars, criminals, the aged and the sick, epileptics, and prostitutes. Like criminals and prostitutes, the mad were a threat to society, and were accordingly isolated in institutions on the remote outskirts of the cities. In Paris, these were, principally, Bicêtre for men, and La Salpetrière for women, which housed a population of over 6,000 in 1790, making it perhaps the largest hospital in Europe at this time. It was not until the period of the Directory that any methodical medical treatment became available in these hospitals. Previously, the grouping together of criminals, prostitutes, and the insane merely removed a social problem without remedying it. In fact, it probably made it worse. As Mirabeau proclaimed in 1788, 'Hospitals have been built to engender disease, and prisons to foster crime.'

The revolutionary wars gave a new generation of doctors an opportunity to improve this situation, when they replaced their fallen colleagues. For by 1794, nine hundred medical officers had been killed at the front. Under the auspices of Cabanis, Pinel was appointed doctor to Bicêtre in 1793, and then to La Salpetrière in 1795. Pinel's interest in the problem of insanity was aroused by the sudden madness of a close friend. Under the Directory, Pinel's pioneering work inspired a new attitude towards the organisation of the hospitals. The insane were no longer treated as prisoners of society, but as patients. Hence Pinel abolished the practice of chaining up all the lunatics in Bicêtre. The insane were still isolated from society, and Sunday afternoon outings to view the lunatics were brought to an end. At the same time, however, they were also isolated from criminals, and the other inmates of their places of detention. Gradually, the insane of the capital were concentrated in the three institutions of Bicêtre, La Salpetrière, and Charenton, which the Directory established as a national institution for the treatment of the insane.

Pinel's ideas owed much to the eighteenth-century Enlightenment, which had always been concerned more with the classification of knowledge than with making new discoveries. Pinel spent little time in analysing the root causes of insanity, but he did classify his patients, for the purposes of treatment, as melancholics, dangerous criminal idiots, curable maniacs, and incurable maniacs. For the first time, the insane were regarded as a proper subject for experimentation and scientific, empirical study.

Like the Comité de Mendicité, Pinel believed in the therapeutic value of work, and his treatment was aimed at the moral improvement of the insane. To this end he devised a series of 'punishments' which to modern eyes may appear brutal. He helped to popularise the straitjacket, and at Charenton, lunatics were sometimes thrown blindfold into a cold swimming-pool, an institution affectionately known as '*bains de surprise*', or hydrotherapy. Pinel's approach was rigidly scientific. He refused to treat religious maniacs, and he insisted on the suppression of anything which might awaken the passions of the inmates, like sexual arousal, for instance. In the light of modern psychiatry, Pinel's approach seems primitive. Yet it marked a revolutionary change from the simple repression of insanity, towards appreciation of insanity as a subject for medical treatment.

Thus, the Directory's achievements in the fields of education and social welfare were constructive ones. The régime inherited enormous difficulties: the ecclesiastical basis of education and poor-relief had been irrevocably undermined, but more pressing problems had led the revolutionary governments to postpone putting anything permanent in its place. Shortage of funds forced the thermidorean régime and the Directory to throw the chief responsibility in these fields onto the local administrations, and to acquiesce in the growth of private charity and private education. Lack of personnel further made the return of ecclesiastics as teachers and nurses imperative, although this provoked accusations of clerical subversion in the schools and hospitals. Although the Directory made only limited progress in primary education, it began important experiments in secondary education, which the Napoleonic régime did not allow to reach fruition. It carried further the process of specialisation in higher education, and in the treatment of the inmates of the hospitals. Both the educationalists of the Directory and men like Pinel were disciples of eighteenth-century rationalism. They believed that both education and medicine could be scientific and secular, and that a rational and Republican alternative could be found to clerical education and ecclesiastical charity. With more money and more time, the Directory might have witnessed a more complete fulfilment of the ideas of the Enlightenment in these spheres.

7

'MONSIEUR DIMANCHE' AND 'CITOYEN DÉCADI'

'Among the passions born of this Revolution', de Tocqueville argued, 'the first to be kindled and the last to be put out was the anti-religious passion.' The schism brought about by the Constituent Assembly, however, did not spring from an attack on Catholicism itself, but from disputes over the Church's rôle as a political institution. Force of circumstance led the thermidorean régime to abandon the Constituents' attempts to build a national Church, and to experiment with a complete separation of Church and State. By the time of the Directory, the Civil Constitution of the Clergy was virtually redundant, but the wounds which it had inflicted on French society had not been healed. The régimes of thermidor and the Directory failed to convince Catholics that Catholicism was compatible with Republicanism, and failed to find any alternative to Catholicism. Reconciliation was not achieved until Napoleon's Concordat of 1801.

Nothing in popular attitudes of the 1780s suggested that schism and separation were imminent. The *cahiers de doléances* of 1789 revealed some resentment against the enormous wealth of the upper clergy, and against their rapacity as landlords. One should not, however, confuse the cynicism of a prelate like de Brienne with a general decline in religious faith. For the *cahiers* also revealed a deep attachment linking the faithful and their parish *curés*, whose low pay was everywhere a source of grievance. The resilience of traditional Catholicism was further expressed in demands for the repeal of the Edict of Toleration of the Protestants of 1787. The *curés*, however, and their congregations, were soon faced not just with a reform of these abuses, but with radical changes in the whole conception of the rôle of the Church.

The Civil Constitution of the Clergy destroyed the Church's status as a privileged corporation within France. Priests were now paid by the State, and subject to an oath of loyalty, just like any other public functionary. Diocesan boundaries were reorganised to coincide with the administrative division of France into departments, and the clergy's salaries were revised. The clergy were now to be elected by active citizens, who included Protestants and Jews, as well as Catholics. Not all of this was unacceptable. There could be few objections to higher pay for the *curés*, or to the end of pluralism and non-residence. The clergy did object, however, to the principle of lay election: this was the only clause which the moderate provincial aristocrat Ferrières found obnoxious. Nor did the clergy easily accept the Constituents' idea of a national Church, or for that matter, the refusal of the Constituents to consult the clergy about the reorganisation of the Church. For the Constituent Assembly, if the Church was no longer a privileged corporation, then there was logically no need to negotiate either with an ecclesiastical synod or with the Pope. The Civil Constitution was thus a unilateral act of legislation.

The schism was consummated by the imposition of an oath of fidelity on the French clergy, which gave them no choice but to accept or reject the package *in toto*. Subtlety and tact, however, are not revolutionary virtues, and the Constituent Assembly recklessly forced many priests into the ranks of the Counter-Revolution. The oath caused heart-searching amongst the parish *curés*. Many may have opposed the settlement in spirit, but did not find it easy to abandon their niche in the local community, and leave a loyal and familiar congregation, by refusing the oath. The Pope's indecision made it even harder to take a stand one way or the other. When the Pope did eventually make up his mind, it was too late, although many did subsequently retract their oath. Perhaps about fifty-five per cent of the clergy took the oath, but regional variations were enormous. In the Bas-Rhin, only about eight per cent took the oath, while in Brittany and the Nord, the proportion was only twenty per cent. Refractories, as the non-juring priests were called, were especially strong in the West, while the Constitution was conspicuously supported in Dauphiné, Provence, and the Var, where ninety-six per cent of the clergy took the oath. The main areas of resistance to the oath were the North, Brittany, parts of the Massif Central, and the East.

The seeds of civil war and religious schism had been sown. The new Constitutional *curés* were often not installed without an armed escort, and many went in fear of their lives. Terrorist legislation was to force refractories either to emigrate, or to continue to administer the sacraments in secret. The traditional Catholic Church was to suffer further blows. Religious congregations were dispersed and their property sequestered. Divorce was legalised, and in the winter of the Year 2, clerical celibacy was condemned. In the war emergency, refractories were interned, deported, or, if engaged in seditious activities, executed. In the Year 2, the Revolutionary Government even tended to abandon its protection of the Constitutional priests. The dechristianisation campaign confiscated bells, silver, and ornaments, abused the worship of saints and relics, and attacked the basis of Catholicism itself with the cult of Reason. The *armées révolutionnaires* deliberately set out to shock the peasantry by heaping blasphemous ridicule on their most cherished assumptions. Meanwhile, *Représentants* like Fouché in the provinces officially denied the existence of a life after death.

The thermidoreans and the Directory were incapable of healing the schism. They could not erase memories of the wild iconoclasm of the *armées révolutionnaires*, or of the September massacres, or of imprisonment and the threat of execution in the Terror. Attempts to replace the worship of the Goddess of Reason, and Robespierre's cult of the Supreme Being, with other formulas for a Republican Church, foundered against the deep-rooted Catholic faith of the rural population. Missionaries in the Pyrenees, for instance, who denied the possibility of miracles, destroyed relics, and turned the Immaculate Conception into a salacious tale, were greeted with bewilderment and a sense of moral outrage. As one report had it, 'Le peuple de cette commune, encore simple, est peu capable de s'élever tout à coup à la hauteur de la philosophie et de la Raison où le citoyen Picot a tenté de le porter...à force de tendre l'arc, dit-on, il casse.' So too, institutionalised forms of Deism and natural religion struck few responsive chords amongst the peasant masses. In other chapters, I have argued that the Directory made a praiseworthy, if modest attempt at reconstruction after the Terror. In the religious sphere, however, reconstruction was forced to await the arrival of Bonaparte. The symbolic campaign to enforce observance of the Republican *décadi* never overcame the obstinacy of 'Monsieur Dimanche'.

The coup of 9 thermidor did not bring immediate relief to the Catholic clergy. The coalition of dissident Montagnards who overthrew Robespierre included dechristianisers like Fouché, and men like Vadier, who saw the religion of the Supreme Being as the beginning of a compromise with the clerical Counter-

Revolution. It was often a full three months before priests were released from prison. Individual *Représentants en mission*, freed from Robespierrist supervision, were still able to pursue their own policies in the departments. In Toulouse, for example, Mallarmé brought the dechristianisation campaign to a new level of intensity after thermidor, continuing the internment of priests, effacing all crucifixes from buildings and gravestones, and ordering the strict observance of the *décadi*.

After the winter of the Year 3, however, churches began to reopen, and refractories emerged from hiding. The religious revival was given a special impetus by the terms of the armistice with the Vendéan rebels, in pluviôse, which included a recognition of their freedom of worship. Having made this concession to the Vendéans, the thermidoreans could not refuse it to the rest of France. The law of 11 prairial Year 3 again offered churches to both Constitutional and refractory priests, and this seemed to inaugurate a period of religious appeasement.

The thermidorean régime was forced to make further admissions that the Revolution's religious policy had failed. In the last few days of the Year 2, the Convention stopped all salaries to priests. In fact, these salaries had not been paid for several months, but although this was apparently a financial measure, the decision had wider implications. For it seemed a denial of the Civil Constitution of the Clergy, an admission that the attempt to establish a national Church had failed. The Convention went further towards recognising its own impotence with the law of 3 ventôse Year 3, which officially inaugurated the brief experiment of the complete separation of Church and State. The State no longer recognised any religion. Freedom of worship was guaranteed, but all exterior signs of any religion were prohibited. Priests, for example, were not allowed to appear in public wearing clerical vestments. Religious processions and the ringing of church bells were equally forbidden. The Republic had thus abandoned its support for the Constitutional Church, and now professed complete religious neutrality. This was, in Mathiez's phrase, 'la politique de résignation'.

Nevertheless, the Convention could never totally detach itself from the religious problem. It continued to show hostility to the traditional Catholic Church, and new oaths were imposed on the clergy in order to guarantee their political loyalty. The possibility of clerical, anti-Republican subversion was always likely to provoke a renewal of Terrorist legislation against the priesthood.

So indeed it proved. The régime blew hot and cold according to political fluctuations. After the defeat of the Babouvists, the régime looked for support to its right, and a period of reconciliation followed. Then, with the attempted invasion of Quiberon Bay, Royalism seemed the greater threat, and the government reinforced legislation condemning returning *émigrés* to death, and ordering the deportation of refractory priests. This was not the only abrupt reversal of policy during this period. The Royalist victories at the elections of the Year 5 again heralded a period of leniency towards the clergy. In the aftermath of the *coup* of fructidor, however, the deportation laws were again reinvigorated.

It is now time to consider how the refractory and Constitutional Churches survived the régime of separation, and these see-sawing policies of the Republican governments.

At times, the refractory clergy seemed to bask in the pious pride of martyrdom. Many of their leaders had taken the path of exile. Forty-one refractory bishops were dead, and only eleven had stayed in France. The *émigré* bishops, living comfortable lives in England, Majorca, or the German courts, were not disposed to compromise with the Republic. Those who remained behind, however, were forced to reach some kind of *modus vivendi* with the government. Amongst these men was Emery, director of St-Sulpice, who had been imprisoned under the Terror, and saved from execution by the 9 thermidor. For men like Emery, Catholic worship had to continue at all costs. The spiritual welfare of the faithful must not be jeopardised for the theological or political scruples of an *émigré* bishop in London or Lubeck.

The *émigré* bishops still tried to maintain contact with their dioceses. They delegated power to '*vicaires ambulants*', or 'the suitcase *curés*', travelling evangelists bound on a campaign of 'reconversion' to the traditional Catholic faith. The Abbé Linsolas, in Lyon, was a particularly successful organiser of this kind of internal missionary activity. In Toulouse, Dubourg organised the clandestine activities of the refractory clergy, reconsecrating churches, remarrying and rebaptising those whose weddings or baptisms had been conducted by Constitutional priests. Louis XVIII hoped to use these missions to spread Royalist propaganda, but the clergy opposed this suggestion.

Nevertheless, the secret Masses held by the refractory clergy were often inspired by anti-Republican harangues. In the Gers, for example, Cablat told his congregation that anyone who attended a Mass celebrated by a Constitutional priest was damned to Hell, and that he himself bet his tongue on this. He counselled against the purchase of the property of the *émigrés*, who, he claimed, were about to return. He denounced the *assignats*, and preached the re-establishment of the tithe to thousands of Catholics, who head him in barns and forest clearings, where they all risked arrest by the National Guardsmen of Toulouse.

The refractory Church was divided. For advocates of the so-called Lyon method, repentant Constitutionals should do strict penance, all Republican oaths should be opposed on principle, and the Church should rely on secret missions, like that of Linsolas in Lyon. Others, like Emery, were proponents of what has been called the Paris method. They believed that there was no intrinsic harm in accepting any *de facto* government, that the Church could be reorganised within the law, and that a policy of reconciliation with the Republic could be in the best interests of Catholicism.

The oath of submission and obedience, demanded of the clergy in the Year 3, exposed these divisions (as was perhaps intended). For Emery, accepting this oath implied an approval of religious freedom, but not necessarily of the divorce laws. No one, after all, was obliged to get divorced. For the moderates, the Church could coexist with any form of government, and since this oath did not affect spiritual matters in the slightest degree, there was no objection to taking it. 'Must religion perish', asked Boisgelin of Aix, 'because the government has changed?' This view was shared by the bishops of Perpignan, Agen, Grenoble, and Luçon, and also by Clermont-Tonnerre, *émigré* bishop of Châlons-sur-Marne. Yet the oath was condemned by other bishops of the emigration, and acceptance was forbidden in the diocese of Lyon. The Bishop of Ax bestowed upon the oath his episcopal curse: 'J'ai dit anathème à la fatale soumission.'

Royalist victories at the elections of the Year 5 encouraged new demands for a return to traditional Catholic worship. *Émigré* priests poured back into France from England, Spain, and the Rhineland. By the *coup* of fructidor, Catholic worship had resumed in 40,000 parishes. In June 1797, Camille Jordan demanded the legalisation of the ringing of church bells, and an end to the deportation of refractories was proposed. In July, a motion to abolish all oaths of allegiance on the part of the clergy was defeated by only six votes. The *coup* of fructidor, however, dashed all hopes of a definitive restoration of Catholicism, sent the *émigrés* scurrying back across the frontiers, and imposed yet another oath.

The new oath was even harsher, for it demanded a declaration of '*haine à la royauté*'. This time even the flexible Emery baulked. Although he declined to make a public statement, he privately admitted that he himself could not accept such a demand. A few bishops, like de la Tour du Pin, took it, but they were by now in a small minority. The Pope, too, condemned the oath. The '*haineux*' comprised about one-third of those who had taken the oath of '*soumission*' in 1795, and only about one-fifth of the refractories of 1791. The proportion of '*haineux*' was perhaps highest in Paris, but in strongly Catholic departments like the Ardèche, for example, there were no '*haineux*'. Plongeron has criticised historians for concentrating too single-mindedly on the oath of 1791. In spite of his warnings, our knowledge of the reception of the subsequent Republican oaths is still defective.

Those who refused to swear hatred to the monarchy risked deportation. Almost ten thousand priests were sentenced to the 'dry guillotine', as the journey to the unhealthy climate of Guiana was known. But not all of these ten thousand were actually arrested, and a few were lucky enough to be rescued by the British Navy before they arrived. In fact only about 230 priests were disembarked in Guiana, of whom over half were to die there. About 750 more, however, were interned on the islands of Ré and Oléron, off La Rochelle. At the same time, the repression after fructidor was taking other forms. Churches were sold, not for profit, but simply to prevent their future use for religious services. Some were destroyed, and others went at derisory prices. The celebrated abbey of Cluny was demolished. Lefebvre found that over four hundred parish churches were sold in this way in the department of the Nord.[1] Once again, a brief period of toleration had been followed by repression. The Directory's claims to religious neutrality looked shallow. In the Year 3, Easter had been celebrated with full ceremony and high Catholic hopes. After the Year 6, however, there were few public bonfires to celebrate the St-Jean or the St-Pierre.

[1] Bibliography no. 29.

The repression was harshest in the conquered territories, where the religious issue was frequently an obstacle to good relations between the French authorities and the rural popula-tion. The full consequences of the post-fructidorian repression were most apparent in Belgium, where popular resentment against French anticlerical legislation ran high. In 1796, the État-Civil was secularised in Belgium, and the inhabitants reacted by recording a predominantly right-wing vote at the elections of the Year 5. Of the ten thousand priests sentenced to deportation, eight thousand were Belgians. In the Year 8, the application of the conscription law to Belgium was to provoke a short-lived peasant rising against the French.

Local authorities, however, were reluctant to arrest refractory priests sentenced to deportation. The religious policy of the Directory failed to overcome the resistance of the local popula-tion and the immobility of its administrators. In the Meurthe, for example, fourteen priests were condemned to deportation in the Years 6 and 7. Only seven of these men were found, however, and only four deported. The priests located were usually the old and the sick, who were too feeble to escape. In the Sarthe, only nineteen refractories were reported to the department, and only eight of them were arrested. The *agents municipaux* would refuse to remove crucifixes from public places, declaring that they 'ne se feraient pas casser le col dans leurs communes pour des croix'.

The Directory was even forced to abandon its attempts to coerce the Pope into a more conciliatory policy. When Bona-parte invaded the Papal States in 1796, there seemed to be a chance of forcing Pius VI to approve the oath of submission, and to reconsider his condemnation of the Civil Constitution of the Clergy. The Pope did agree to recommend 'soumission aux autorités constituées', which appeared to vindicate Emery and the moderates. Even this concession angered the extremist refractories, who suggested that the Papal brief was a forgery. After fructidor, however, nothing more could be extracted from the Pope, who denounced the oath of '*haine à la royauté*'. The Treaty of Tolentino of 1797 subjected the Papal States to a stiff ransom, and the cession of Avignon and the Legations, but there was no longer any question of reaching an agreement over the Church in France. Bonaparte concluded, 'Il faut en finir avec le vieux renard.' After an interlude in Tuscany, the Pope became a French prisoner, but died in the Year 7 in Valence, as 'Jean-Ange

Braschi, exercising the profession of Pontiff'. For some Catholics, however, the death of Pius VI on French soil was equivalent to martyrdom at the hands of the Republic. The possibilities of reconciliation therefore seemed as remote as ever.

Far from reconciling their differences, the Directory and the traditional Catholic Church became, if anything, more intransigent in their relations with one another. As they did so, the Constitutional Church was stranded. Under the régime of separation of Church and State, it was disowned by the government, and struggled on as an embarrassing relic of a failed experiment, a hybrid without issue.

The Constitutional clergy had been decimated by abdications during the Terror, by marriages, deaths, and defections to the ranks of the refractories, encouraged by the moderate policies of Emery. There remained only about twenty-five of the eighty-two bishops of 1792. Leadership was now provided by the Constitutional Bishop of Blois, Grégoire. The government had ceased to finance the Constitutional Church, and it had abandoned the Civil Constitution, but Grégoire set about counting his losses, and reorganising his dioceses.

Grégoire's revivified Gallican Church was to be organised by a committee of 'Évêques Réunis', consisting of Royer, of the Ain, Saurine (Landes), Gratien (Seine-Inférieure), and Desbois de Rochefort (Somme). They issued encyclical letters, purged the Constitutional Church of all married priests, made arrangements for filling vacant cures, and called a National Council in 1797. Grégoire's *Annales de Religion* pleaded for reconciliation, but proposals for the fusion of the two rival Churches were unsuccessful.

Like the refractory Church, however, the Gallican Church was weakened by divisions. A strong current of Presbyterian thought emerged at the Councils of 1797 and 1801. The Church had survived for several years without a strong central organisation. The *curés*, elected by their own congregations, had stronger obligations besides that of submission to their superiors. They had leant to live without episcopal supervision, and were unwilling to submit unprotestingly to Grégoire's new hierarchy. The Évêques Réunis were therefore compelled to compromise with the democratic forces within the Gallican Church, and bishops found it unwise to ignore the views of their own clergy in the sensitive matter of new appointments.

Grégoire had engineered a remarkable recovery, but, in spite of his successes, the future of the Gallican Church was fragile and uncertain. It had been deserted by the Directory. At times, in fact, it acted in direct opposition to government policy. The Directory did not approve of Grégoire's exclusion of married priests from the Gallican clergy, and the Church further condemned the obligatory observance of the *décadi*. Here at least the Gallican Church was closer in touch with popular opinion than the Directory.

The Gallican Church was thus divided, and disowned by the government. It could, however, have survived both these disadvantages, if it had not also been deserted by its congregations. The Constitutional bishops, in their letters to Grégoire, recorded the enormous difficulties they faced. Sermet of Toulouse told Grégoire that in 1791, sixty out of every hundred Catholics had rejected the Constitutional Church, and still continued to do so. Of the rest, twenty-five per cent had apostasised, and the remainder were apathetic and indifferent. 'Seres-vous surpris après cela,' complained Sermet, 'que nous n'ayons encore icy aucune église ouverte et que tout le service se fasse en chambre? Les anticonstitutionnels seuls font foule et chantent à tue-tête.' Laughed at in the street by children, Sermet now found that it was his turn to hold secret Masses behind locked doors, fearing for his own safety. Finally, he brushed the dust of the city off his sandals, and left to face a wilderness, not of temptation, but of indifference.

The state of the Protestant Church was no healthier. According to one Protestant census, there were about 600,000 Protestants in France at the end of the eighteenth century. Outside Paris and Alsace, they were to be found in the Protestant heartland of the Cévennes, and in parts of the Périgord, the Charentais, and Normandy. There were important urban Protestant communities in the southern towns of Nîmes, Montauban, Bordeaux, and Mazamet. The Protestant Church, however, had lost about one-half of its pastors. They had emigrated or died, some had abdicated and did not resume their functions until after the Concordat, while others had found a new career in the Revolution, like Jeanbon St-André, ex-member of the Committee of Public Safety, sent on a diplomatic mission to Algeria, and soon to become prefect of Mainz. Protestant worship was slow to resume after the Terror. In La Rochelle, for instance, worship did not resume until 1798, and regular services were not held in Marseille before 1801, or in Toulouse before 1805. The old synodal organisation was not revived. A synod was organised in the Tarn in 1796, but only four pastors signed its proceedings. The historian Robert feels that the main reason for this stagnation was the lack of enthusiasm amongst rich, middle-class Protestants, whose zeal had cooled after years of political strife.[1] Their defection impoverished the Protestant Church, and deprived it of intellectual leadership.

In spite of itself, however, Calvinism may have indirectly inspired one of the Republic's attempts to create a civic religion in the form of Theophilanthropy. Several attempts had already been made to establish a Republican Church, based on the natural religion of the eighteenth-century philosophers. The cult of patriot saints, and the glorification of the 'Trinity' of Republican martyrs, Marat, Lepelletier, and Chalier, never fully shook off their traditional Catholic framework. Furthermore, they had been to some extent artificially created by the régime. Other suggestions were made for a new religion, based on the ideas of Deism, but influenced by the simplicity of Protestant services, and the symbolism of Freemasonry. Sylvain Maréchal canvassed the idea of a humanist Church, for example, paradoxically named 'Le Culte des Hommes Sans Dieu'. Most Republican intellectuals believed that religion was a social necessity, but they also believed that a truly philosophic religion should be built around a few incontrovertible dogmas, which would not conflict with any other religious creed. The tenets of such a religion would preach reason and toleration. As they would contain the essence of all existing religions, they would embrace them all.

Theophilanthropy itself had several immediate ancestors. Dubermesnil planned a 'Culte des Adorateurs', who would meet in an oval-shaped temple, surrounded by frescoes depicting the seasons of the year and the signs of the zodiac, and would gather around a central altar, on which burned an eternal flame. The quest for a Republican civic religion, which would replace traditional Catholicism, and add some lustre to the clinical ceremonies held in the *mairie*, was thrown open by the Institut. In the Years 5 and 6, a prize was offered for the best essay on the subject which lay at the core of the Republic's religious prob-

---

[1] Bibliography no. 113.

lems: 'Quelles sont les institutions les plus propres à fonder la morale d'un peuple?'

The most constructive answer came from a Norman bookseller, Chemin, whose 'Manuel des Théoanthropophiles' eventually secured government backing. Theophilanthropy claimed to recognise natural laws, and the existence of God as Father of the Universe. It had two simple dogmas: the existence of God, and the immortality of the soul, both deduced from rational principles. Theophilanthropy would also emphasise one's duty to others, and to the *patrie*. Chemin was an ex-Freemason, who had studied Protestantism, and hoped that Protestants would support Theophilanthropy. He argued that both Theophilanthropy and Protestantism were protests against Catholic dogma and ceremony, against pilgrimages and relic-worship, against Mass and the confessional, and against an ecclesiastical hierarchy. La Revellière, who was to become a leading patron of Theophilanthropy, also expressed sympathy for Calvinism. As it turned out, Protestants rejected Theophilanthropy. As Madame de Staël pointed out, Theophilanthropy could not rival the long traditions of the Protestant Church, or the rôle of its pastors. Furthermore, Protestantism was not a political Church, as Theophilanthropy at times seemed to be.

Theophilanthropy was a privately-organised cult until, after fructidor, it received the support of the government, and in particular, of the Director La Revellière, although he never in fact attended a service. The government subsidised the journal *L'Ami des Théophilanthropes*, and the sect was supported by intellectuals like Daunou, politicians like Dupont de Nemours, writers like Chénier and Bernardin de St-Pierre, and Freemasons like Regnault de St-Jean d'Angely. By the winter of 1797–8, the Theophilanthropists were installed in over fifteen Parisian churches, where the congregations heard readings from the Koran, Socrates, Seneca, Confucius, and Pascal, in the eclectic spirit of Theophilanthropic toleration. They would sing patriotic hymns like the 'Chant du Départ', led by an officiator in a tricoloured tunic.

Government patronage of Theophilanthropy, however, did not survive the dismissal of the Jacobin-inclined Minister of Police, Sotin. The Jacobin tendencies of the cult made it unpopular not only with part of the Parisian *bourgeoisie*, but also with the government. The Jacobin *Journal des Hommes Libres* declared its support for Theophilanthropy, and the sect gave up its Sunday services in favour of the *décadi*. The government felt this tendency was too dangerous to encourage, and the sect went into decline. Although it enjoyed a temporary revival after brumaire Year 8, there was no opposition when its services were banned under the Consulate.

Theophilanthropy made little impact outside the capital. It enjoyed some success in the outskirts of Paris, and in the central departments. In the Yonne, for example, where dechristianisation had been particularly destructive, it was very active, and this was the only area where the sect spread into the villages. In the Midi, however, Theophilanthropy left hardly a trace.

Theophilanthropy had always been the religion of a small minority. It was a doctrine of the *bourgeois* élite, and of the Republican intelligentsia. A religion based on such abstract ideas, without colour or emotional inspiration, could not form a basis for popular devotion on a large scale. As Carnot had said, absurdity and unintelligibility were essential ingredients for a successful religion, and on these grounds, nothing could compete with Catholicism. In the Year 6, Catholics physically attacked Theophilanthropic services in St-Merri, in Paris, and similar incidents occurred at St-Etienne du Mont, and St-Eustache.

Something a little less intellectual and a little more spectacular was needed, if the enthusiasm of the masses was ever to be enlisted. The *culte décadaire*, and the series of national festivals which complemented it, were designed to impress the public, and to reduce the Jacobin influences on Theophilanthropy. The closure of shops on the *décadi* was made obligatory. Although this could never be enforced, the civic wedding ceremonies were moderately popular, and the *fêtes nationales* attracted some curious sightseers.

The programme of *fêtes nationales*, devised by François de Neufchâteau, was a masterpiece of propaganda and visual effect. Several of the *fêtes* were political in nature, like the Fête du 9 Thermidor, the Fête du 10 Août, and the anniversary of the Foundation of the Republic. The Fête du 9 Thermidor became a spectacular victory parade for the conquerors of Italy. Rare scientific objects, palm trees, camels, the bronze horses of St Mark, and paintings by Titian and Veronese were carried in triumphant procession to the Champ de Mars. For the Fête du 10

Août, the trees in the Champ de Mars were to be hung with Gobelin tapestries, and the celebrations culminated with a firework display from the terrace of the Chamber of the Cinq Cents. Such exotic spectacles carried clear political messages. At the Fête du 18 Fructidor, a statue of Justice with raised sword was restrained from carrying out an execution by the figure of Mercy, pointing towards the West and Cayenne. The proceedings in celebration of the Foundation of the Republic included the symbolic burning of two statues representing Despotism and Fanaticism, as well as horse-racing, gushing fountains, and the launching of air-balloons.

Once again, however, the *fêtes* aroused little enthusiasm outside Paris. Only in the Yonne did '*Citoyen Décadi*' register a temporary victory over '*Monsieur Dimanche*'. Priests in Sens and Auxerre were forced to celebrate Mass only on the *décadi*. But couples who presented themselves to be married at a civic ceremony on the *décadi* had frequently taken the precaution of marrying before a priest a few days previously. The non-political *fêtes*, in honour of Youth, Old Age, Agriculture, and Marriage, evoked little response. The curiosity aroused by the new cults was soon exhausted. In the Year 7, the government, in an economy drive, limited the budget of the *fêtes nationales*, which were reduced to little more than military parades. These ceremonies now seemed cold and artificial. They could neither convince the sceptic, nor replace the time-honoured rituals of Catholicism. Bonaparte retained only two of the *fêtes nationales:* those of 14 July, and 1 vendémiaire. After 7 thermidor Year 8, the observance of the *décadi* was no longer compulsory.

The Directory's attempts to find a satisfactory form of civic religion, based on the dogmas of Deism, and the social values of Republicanism, had failed. The ideas of a small intellectual élite could not shake the peasant's obstinate loyalty towards *les bons prêtres*. Bonaparte found the Church devastated by death, schism, and apostasy, its buildings in ruins and its leaders in exile. Nevertheless, he found, in the west of France, in Alsace and Lorraine, and in the Massif Central, a population still devoted to traditional Catholicism, ready to welcome the re-establishment of Catholic worship.

Had the Revolution and anticlerical Republicanism then left no trace on French society? The Vovelles, in their study of attitudes to death and purgatory, seen through altar decorations in Provence, described the revolutionary period as a brief hiatus, after which traditional practices resumed, in the Catholic revival of the early nineteenth century.[1] The progress of dechristianisation, of course, had been influenced by sociological changes, which happened quite independently of the French Revolution. The pomp and macabre ceremonies associated with death, for example, with its elaborate processions, and traditional bequests to the poor and the Penitents, were already in decline in busy, urban, mercantile centres like Toulon and Marseille, which Vovelle described as 'la ville de perdition'. The smaller towns of upper Provence, however, rather isolated by the Alps, resisted the impact of dechristianisation. Here, where society did not have to assimilate a mass of uprooted immigrants, in towns which were static and traditional, although not necessarily poorly educated, clerical recruitment continued, and baroque rituals were less easily abandoned. The impact of dechristianisation was therefore received differently in different parts of France, and by different social classes.

Pockets of anticlericalism undoubtedly existed. They existed amongst the purchasers of the *biens nationaux*, they existed among ex-Terrorist circles, and in the Institut itself. In the centre of France, there were areas where the Revolution exposed a surprising degree of dechristianisation. The Directory, however, was mistaken in thinking that these few pockets of anti-Catholicism could form the basis for a radical departure from tradition. 'La République', one might say, 'serait croyante ou elle ne serait pas.'

In spite of the religious revival which followed first the Concordat, and then the Bourbon restoration, the Revolution had imperceptibly weakened the hold of the Catholic Church. Many rural areas had managed for years without priests, without regular baptisms, without First Communions. The legalisation of divorce in 1792 fulfilled an important social need, which Catholic teaching had not recognised. Furthermore, the spread of birth control in the Revolutionary period implies a further undermining of Catholic teaching, if not of faith itself. Historians will never penetrate the secrets of the confessional, but demographers like Dupâquier and LeRoy Ladurie suggest that in the Revolutionary period, techniques of birth control were more generally adopted than in the past.[2] As a result, fertility showed a marked decline,

[1] Bibliography no. 114.
[2] Bibliography nos. 102 and 106.

and families of ten children or more from now on became a rarity. They suggest that although the proportion of childless couples probably did not increase, parents were willing to wait for longer intervals between the births of their children. Southern women tended to be less educated than northern mothers, and the Midi took longer to adopt contraceptive techniques. After the Revolution, however, the birth rate in Languedoc was now below the national average of twenty-nine births per thousand inhabitants per year. It therefore appears that an important change of attitude took place during the Revolutionary period.

In spite of the Directory's failures, then, something perhaps endured. The symbol of the tricolor, and the Fête of 14 July, restored by the Third Republic, have certainly endured. The dream of reconciling the Church to the Revolution lived on in the nineteenth century, and the idea of establishing a humanist Church, based on reason, was to be taken up again by the positivist philosopher Auguste Comte.

8

PHILOSOPHY AND SCIENCE: THE LEGACY OF CONDILLAC

La Révolution est à l'esprit humain ce que le soleil d'Afrique est à la végétation.   –Barère

Both counter-revolutionaries and Republicans have credited intellectuals with a leading rôle in the preparation of the French Revolution. Extremists like the Abbé Barruel, for example, denounced the Revolution as a conspiracy unleashed on France by Freemasons and *philosophes*. At the same time, right-wing commentators have stressed the destructive influence of the Revolution on French intellectual life. The wanton destruction of libraries and the vandalisation of art treasures indicated, for them, a profoundly philistine attitude towards science and learning. Coffinhal is alleged to have declared at Lavoisier's trial: 'La République n'a pas besoin des savants; il faut que la justice suive son cours.' The Revolutionaries thus had to bear the guilt for the execution of the chemist Lavoisier (guillotined as a tax-farmer), and for the suicide of the philosopher Condorcet.

On the one hand, therefore, the Revolution was seen as the work of abstract and atheistical theorists; on the other hand, it was inherently anti-intellectual. This attack on the mainstream of eighteenth-century French thought was echoed during the Directory by La Harpe, notably in his pamphlet of 1797, entitled 'Fanatisme dans la langue révolutionnaire, ou de la persecution suscitée par les Barbares du dix-huitième siècle, contre La Religion Catholique et ses ministres'.

The attitudes of the Republican intelligentsia towards the Revolution were riddled with similar contradictions. The Idéologues of the Directory tried to vindicate the Enlightenment. For them, eighteenth-century philosophy was innocent of the excesses of the Terror. Popular sovereignty had been 'falsely' applied, and the populace, whose ignorance had been prolonged by the Ancien Régime, was not yet ready for democracy. Although the Idéologues denied that the Enlightenment was responsible for the Terror, they nevertheless stressed the links between eighteenth-century philosophy and the Revolution as a whole. Under the Directory, they hoped to renew these links, and to work for the advance of moderate Republicanism. *La Feuille Villageoise* summarised the aims of the Idéologues in brumaire III: 'Éclairons-nous, aimons-nous, rallions-nous.' French thought in this period therefore renewed the traditions of eighteenth-century philosophy. In Moravia's phrase, this was 'the Sunset of the Enlightenment'.[1]

Under the Directory, the prestige of Republican philosophers ran high. Intellectuals released from Terrorist prisons began to assume responsible positions under the new régime, notably in teaching, but also as constitutional advisers. The Revolution and the war effort had already demonstrated how valuable science could be to the Republic. Under the Directory an attempt was made to 'democratise' science, to show that it was not the prerogative of a privileged élite, but that, in the army and the hospitals, it could change the everyday life of French citizens. Under the Consulate, however, the intellectuals fell into disgrace. Bonaparte's own political realism, and the traditional suspicion of the soldier for the intellectual, combined to throw the leading Republican writers and thinkers into opposition. In Bonaparte's vocabulary, '*metaphysicien*' was a dirty word. It was during the Directory, therefore, that the school of philosophers known as the Idéologues was most influential, and that the experiment in the democratisation of science took place. This chapter will discuss the contribution made first to French thought, and then to French science, in this brief period.

The group of philosophers, writers, and scientists known as the Idéologues attempted to apply the inductive scientific method to the moral sciences. Just as Newton had discovered the immutable laws of the physical universe, so they too, by careful observation of the data, planned to enumerate the laws which governed human behaviour and human relations. Volney, for example, in his lectures on history to the École Normale, studied the body politic as a physiologist studies an individual. History for him was 'la science physiologique des gouvernements'. The scientific methods of chemistry and medicine could be adopted for the analysis of society, and of individual psychology. Just as Lavoisier had analysed the composition of air and water, so too,

[1] Bibliography no. 125.

human assumptions and beliefs could be reduced to their basic elements. Thus the title of Cabanis's work *Rapports du physique et du moral de l'homme* implied a whole programme of investigation.

Philosophy, as the Idéologues saw it, was the science of knowledge. That is, they saw their task as that of observing how knowledge is acquired, and how ideas are formed. The word 'Idéologie' itself, coined by Destutt de Tracy in 1796, means literally, the study of ideas. Like Condillac before them, they believed that knowledge was acquired principally through the senses. Our perception of space, time, and distance is derived through the senses of sight, touch, and hearing. Our notion of morality, too, is based on a purely sensual awareness of what gives pleasure, and what gives pain. For the Idéologues, therefore, the study of the acquisition of knowledge could not proceed without a study of how our senses perceive phenomena, and how they react to them. Man as a moral being could not be understood without reference to his physical self.

It would be wrong to give the impression that Condillac was the only precursor of Idéologie, which had a varied philosophical parentage. The Idéologues respected Bacon as a pioneer of the inductive method of analysis based on observation. They looked back, too, to Locke, who had attacked the notion of original sin. Locke had postulated that a child's character was formed not by his inherited faculties, but by his experience of his environment. This idea was central to the thinking of the Idéologues, but it remained a controversial one. Locke's concept of the *tabula rasa* was certainly an appropriate one in the aftermath of a great revolutionary upheaval, for the Directory was itself writing on a slate wiped clean by earlier revolutionary convulsions. In their attacks on Catholicism, and on the idea of inherited guilt, the Idéologues acknowledged the influence of Voltaire, and they owed a considerable debt to Condorcet. When Condorcet's *Esquisse d'un tableau historique des progrès de l'esprit humain* was published in 1795, the Committee of Public Education distributed three thousand copies free of charge. Cabanis, to whom Condorcet bequeathed his last writings, also married his sister-in-law.

Condillac, therefore, was not the only ancestor of Idéologie, which followed the tradition of the eighteenth-century Enlightenment. The Idéologues were indeed to reject many of Condillac's conclusions, but in their central assumptions, they inherited

Condillac's emphasis on the rôle of experience in the formation of knowledge, expressed in his work of 1746, the *Essai sur l'origine des connaissances humaines*. In 1797, the *Décade philosophique* announced the appearance of a new edition of Condillac, in twenty-two volumes.

The Idéologues who met at Madame Helvétius's salon at Auteuil, or in their favourite café in the Rue du Bac, were men of some political experience. Volney, Rœderer, de Tracy, Grégoire, and Dupont de Nemours all began their careers in the Constituent Assembly. Siéyès, Chénier, Lakanal, and Daunou were Conventionnels. Garat had held office as Minister of Justice. For the most part, their sympathies had rested with the Girondins. Volney and Daunou were imprisoned during the Terror, while de Tracy retired to the country. Condorcet had poisoned himself before he could be arrested, but Cabanis survived as a member of the Hospital Commission.

For the historian Picavet, there were three generations of Idéologues: those, like Condorcet, who reached their peak or died before the end of the century; those, like Cabanis, de Tracy, and Daunou, who were most influential under the Directory and the Consulate; and the later Idéologues of the Empire and the Restoration, like Laromiguière and Dégérando.[1] Most of the philosophers with whom this chapter is concerned, however, formed one generation, and were born in a period of fifteen years between the late 1740s and the early 1760s. The work of their leading representatives can be classified as 'Physiological Idéologie', in the writings of Cabanis, and 'Rational Idéologie', in the writings of Destutt de Tracy.

De Tracy had represented the nobility of the Bourbonnais in the Estates-General, but retired to private life and study after 10 August 1792. It was he who was responsible for the label 'Idéologue', and he claimed that his ideas on the science of knowledge were inspired by his reading of Condillac in prison during the Terror. In his work *Éléments d'Idéologie*, de Tracy insisted that an analysis of sense-impressions was basic to an understanding of how ideas are formed. Only by thus dissecting the elements which go to make up human assumptions could their validity be tested. As Rœderer wrote, 'L'analyse ne décompose que pour avoir le secret des bonnes compositions.' For de Tracy, thought was

[1] Bibliography no. 126.

composed of four main elements: sensation, memory, judgement, and will. Sensation was the crucial element in all these faculties.

This had important implications. Was there such a thing as the human personality, or were we simply collections of sensory impressions? Condillac himself had acknowledged the existence of a soul, albeit a very retiring one, '*l'âme oisive*'. De Tracy still insisted that the human being is not just an accumulation of received data, but that a human personality still existed. He refused, however, to refer to it as a 'soul'.

In his *Rapports du physique et du moral de l'homme*, Cabanis studied the links between physiology and psychology. Like Locke, Cabanis was a doctor, and he believed that the methods of continual observation and analysis of apparent symptoms were useful to philosophers. For Cabanis, medicine examined the physical nature of man, on which his moral nature depended. The operations of the mind could be described almost as chemical movements of the brain, and impressions received by the nervous system. Cabanis, however, undertook to correct the theories of Condillac, who had concentrated on the senses of sight and touch, neglecting the influence of 'internal' sense-impressions. As a doctor, Cabanis was well aware of the unconscious action of nausea, hunger, or fatigue on the mental processes.

The philosophy of the Idéologues was more of a methodology than a doctrine. It did not ask why certain phenomena exist, but rather limited itself to an understanding of their mechanism, through patient observation and description. Hypothesising about first causes was less important to them than an objective classification of the available data. Thus Pinel was as devoted to classifying the symptoms of lunacy as he was to discovering its deep-rooted causes.

This obsession with scientific observation and cold analysis was condemned by more romantic temperaments. The Idéologues in the Institut had always to endure the quixotic sallies of Mercier, but within a few years, Madame de Staël was accusing them of sterility, while Rivarol's pamphlet *De la philosophie moderne* declared: 'L'homme qui analyse décompose et tue.' Critics like de Staël found it hard to accept the moral neutrality of the Idéologues. They could not accept that moral decisions, and the sense of good and evil, are predetermined by reflexes to physical pain and pleasure. The Idéologues were materialistic and utilitarian. Their ascendancy significantly coincided with the introduction into France of translations of Bentham's works.

The Idéologues, therefore, had their critics, but the followers of Condillac had a spectacular opportunity to justify themselves in practice, in the celebrated case of the Wild Boy of the Aveyron. An eleven-year-old boy was captured in the forests of the Tarn in 1797. He was incapable of speech, insensitive to pain, covered in scars, and lived on berries and roots. He had apparently been abandoned by his parents at an early age. Experts pronounced him a congenital idiot. One man, however, set out to prove that the boy's idiocy was not inherited. Itard, then consultant at the Institute for Deaf-Mutes in Paris, and a pioneer in the education of backward children, believed that the child was perfectly normal, but suffered only from cultural deprivation. Itard taught him to dress, to eat cooked food, and eventually to perform simple tasks. His success was a triumph for the proponents of education through the senses. The boy Victor was taught to read by following the outlines of letters with his fingertips. His physical senses were forcibly awakened by alternating hot and cold baths, tickling, and slight electric shocks. This treatment induced him to laugh and cry for the first time. Itard's Condillacian theories were unshaken: here was no inherited retardation, but only years of insulation from normal human sense-impressions. Victor's case was an answer to all those who defended the notion of innate ideas, or who saw religion, and not sensation, as the basis of morality.

In spite of this victory, the Idéologues suffered a series of disillusionments. The *coup* of fructidor suggested that the Constitution of the Year 3 had failed to heal the factional conflicts of the Revolution. The Idéologues' dogmatic belief in the inevitability of progress was weakened. Cabanis soon criticised the Constitution, and recognised the need for the strong executive, which Bonaparte was eventually to provide.

The Idéologues had mixed feelings about Bonaparte, in whom they placed their hopes for the future. From the time of the expedition to Egypt, Bonaparte cultivated their support, portraying the expedition as a civilising mission, and winning co-operation in establishing the Institut of Cairo, and the learned periodical, the *Décade Egyptienne*. But Volney, Cabanis, and de Tracy in the new Senate, and the Idéologues in the Tribunat, soon found that they had enthroned not a philosopher, but a military dictator. The Concordat, the amnesty accorded to the *émigrés*, and the end of the Écoles Centrales threw the Idéologues into opposition. The purge of the Tribunat in 1802 signalled their defeat.

Until 1802, the Idéologues had been intimately involved in public affairs. Cabanis and de Tracy expounded their views before the Institut, Daunou was largely responsible for the Constitution of the Year 3, and Garat and Volney taught at the École Normale. In fact, their attempt to turn the École Normale into a seminar for Idéologie was one cause of its failure as a teacher-training institution. From 1794 onwards, the Idéologues had their own journal, the *Décade Philosophique*, which took a moderately Republican line, and defended the *philosophes* against Châteaubriand and de Bonald. The *Décade*, as its name implies, was hostile to Catholicism, and strongly supported the Écoles Centrales. For a brief period, then, in the Institut and the special schools, the representatives of the eighteenth-century Enlightenment had offered their guidance to the Republic. Rejected by the Empire, they nevertheless provided an important link between the eighteenth century and their successors, the Utilitarians and the Positivists.

Just as the Idéologues were rooted in the tradition of the Enlightenment, so French science in this period acquired a distinguished heritage from the Ancien Régime. The century's most notable scientific achievement in France was perhaps Lavoisier's analysis of the composition of air and water, and equally important, his attempts to measure their components quantitatively. The late eighteenth century in France witnessed great popular faith in the power of science. Man's first flight in an air-balloon in 1783 took place amidst a wave of enthusiasm, which Darnton has compared to the reaction to the first moon landings. The Revolution broke out in the middle of a similarly enthusiastic pseudo-scientific vogue for animal magnetism.

The revolutionaries were intent on banishing the charlatanism of hypnotisers and mesmerists, and on making science directly useful to the nation. Science was no longer to be a pastime for aristocratic amateurs, nor was research to be directed in future by parasitical and monopolistic royal academies. The painter David, Romme, and the chemist Fourcroy endorsed a campaign for the suppression of all Ancien Régime learned academies, which included the prestigious Académie des Sciences. The Academies were riddled with factions, they were sectarian, privileged, and the creations of the monarchy. Although Grégoire tried to make an exception of the Académie des Sciences, all the academies were abolished on 8 August 1793.

Historians have stressed the continuity of French science through the Revolutionary period, interpreting the creation of the Institut as the resurrection of the Académie des Sciences. The attempt to 'Republicanise' French science, however, went deeper than this. Science was now to become a citizens' science – that is to say, it was to become less abstract and more directly useful. It should concern the cultivation of the silkworm and the efficiency of waterwheels, as much as speculation about the movement of distant planets. Consider, for example, the strictly practical investigations of Fourcroy during this period, investigations into the control of mineral waters, the analysis of the composition of milk and urine, and the extraction of copper from bell-metal. Science, in a sense, was to be replaced by technology. The limits of scientific knowledge were defined by its usefulness.

How was scientific work to continue after the abolition of the academies? The Académie des Sciences had been entrusted with important tasks, notably, the standardisation of weights and measures. This was an enormous problem: Savary told the Conseil des Cinq Cents that there were 110 different measures of grain in the Maine-et-Loire alone. Work continued in a special commission, and then under the auspices of the Institut. By 1799, the standard metre and kilogram had been perfected, although their adoption was not made obligatory until 1837. Here was one important way in which science could be seen to serve the Republic.

Above all, Republican science served the needs of war. The greatest achievements of French technology in this period had a military purpose. Chappe's telegraph was installed between Lille and Paris in the spring of 1794, and the news of the victory at Valenciennes was relayed to the last stage on the roof of the Louvre. Air-balloons were adopted for military reconnaissance, although they also had an important psychological effect on superstitious Austrian soldiers. Only two balloons had operated at the battle of Fleurus, but by the Year 7, France had twenty-three, at the Aerostatic school at Meudon. The balloons, however, did not last. Hydrogen was difficult to obtain. Sulphuric acid, from which it was usually extracted, was too valuable for the production of sulphur for gunpowder. The alternative method, of decomposing water over red-hot iron, involved cumbersome and dangerous furnaces. Chemists like Monge, Hassenfratz, and Chaptal were employed in the extraction of saltpetre and the manufacture of cannon. Monge was to write a treatise on the manufacture of cannon, which summarised progress to date in metallurgy. Even the creation of the Bureau des Longitudes, in 1795, for the perfection and popularisation of navigational instruments, was advertised as a way of helping the Navy to defeat English sea power.

The old learned scientific community had been dispersed. Science, however, had been enlisted by the State. With the expedition to Egypt, military conquest seemed fully confused with both France's scientific mission and with tourism. Bonaparte took Monge and Berthollet with him to Egypt, where the soldiers knew them as a two-headed monster called 'Mongéberthollet', and compared them unfavourably with their Egyptian donkeys. They set up the Institut of Cairo, and became the unwitting instruments of French colonisation. They visited the Pyramids, fought the Mamelukes, and pondered the possibilities of clarifying the waters of the Nile and planting vines on its banks. Here, in the deserts of Egypt, they glimpsed the mirage of what *La Clef des Cabinets des Souverains* called 'l'alliance imposante de la philosophie et des bayonnettes'.

The creation of the École Polytechnique was to contribute to the great achievements of French scientists in the first half of the nineteenth century. Its chief aim was to train military engineers, and its popularity can perhaps be gauged from the success of scientific courses at the Écoles Centrales (see Chapter 6). In fact, teaching at the specialist schools like the École Polytechnique, the École Normale, and the Muséum d'Histoire Naturelle became a vital medium for the dissemination of scientific ideas. Rivalries between competing engineering schools had meant that Monge's descriptive geometry had for years been a jealously guarded secret at Mezières. It was only the need to lecture on the subject which forced him to publish his ideas for the first time. Similarly, Lamarck first presented his ideas on evolution in his lectures at the Muséum. Fourcroy, the most brilliant lecturer of his day, spread the ideas of Lavoisier, and helped discredit the phlogiston theory, according to which all inflammable substances contained the 'essence of fire', an elusive and mysterious substance which could not be isolated. At the École Normale, Daubenton, in his eighties, lectured, Republican-style, on Buffon and his assertion that 'le lion est le roi des animaux'. 'Le lion n'est pas roi', countered Daubenton, 'puisque tous le fuient et qu'aucun ne le flatte; il n'y a point de roi dans la nature.'

The most characteristic advances of this period were in the field of medicine and hygiene. We have seen that Cabanis and the philosophers attached great importance to the methods of medical science. The emphasis on observation and experiment gave a new status to the hospitals. They became the workshops of a new type of medicine, the place where symptoms could be examined, and clinical instruction given. Doctors were not associated in this period with a teaching post, or with a research laboratory (as in the era of Pasteur); they were principally the directors of hospitals.

War was a powerful stimulus for medicine and hygiene. Bonaparte's expeditions gave French medicine a totally new experience. Military doctors had to deal with conjunctivitis in epidemic proportions in Egypt, to say nothing of leprosy and elephantiasis, with bubonic plague in Syria, and later, with yellow fever in the West Indies. If the Revolution had not fully rehabilitated surgery, then the battlefields of Europe certainly did so. Larrey, whose mobile ambulances had first been used in the Rhineland in 1792, was now surgeon-in-chief to the armies, expounding the virtue of quick amputation as the best method of treating gunshot wounds. At the new Écoles de Santé, medicine and surgery were linked in what was known as '*La médecine pratique*'.

The end of the eighteenth century saw the beginnings of 'social medicine', for instance in the popularisation of improved methods of hygiene. Jenner's smallpox vaccine was adopted in France, and local vaccination committees were opened to overcome popular prejudices. The vaccine was known at first as 'English poison', but opposition was overcome, and by 1808, over a quarter of a million vaccinations were being performed a year.

Hygiene, as taught at the Écoles Centrales, consisted mainly of midwifery. The contemporary expert Baudelocque was always ready to explain his techniques. Baudelocque had delivered the offspring of celebrities like Madame Fouquier-Tinville, and

Theresia Cabarrus, and he was later promised ten thousand francs on delivery of every new baby in the Imperial family. He was reputed to be adept in delivering babies feet-first, and he would perform a Caesarian operation if necessary, although at this time deliveries by this method were successful in only about one case in three.

It is impossible to tell how far medicine did become socialised, and how often the poorest sections of the population had recourse to medical help. Revolutionary plans to provide free medical assistance were only imperfectly realised. The Comité de Mendicité's plea for medical aid to the indigent in their own homes was based on an assessment of domestic hygiene that was still probably over-optimistic. Typhoid, for instance, was endemic in France until the 1860s. The Committee of Public Safety's plan to provide three medical practitioners for every district was not fully implemented. How easy was it to consult a doctor in the late eighteenth century? In the Year 8, in Paris, Jussieu charged only two francs for a consultation. In rural areas a visit might cost as little as fifty centimes, although charges would be higher if the doctor was called out at night. Vaccination against smallpox might cost as much as two francs, while a bleeding would rarely cost over one franc. However, the availability of doctors in the rural areas of France remains something of an open question, as does the extent to which the suspicious peasantry still rejected medical advice and innovatory techniques of treatment. Nevertheless, Balzac's portrayal of the fictional Benassis, the well-meaning philanthropist, and respectable country doctor, suggests the new regard in which the medical fraternity was beginning to be held.

The Republic thus exploited the intellectual and scientific heritage of the eighteenth century. Both philosophy and science emphasised the utilitarian aims of knowledge, and advocated learning by clinical observation and direct experience. It was no coincidence that advances were made in that most practical of the sciences, medicine. Progress was made not so much into the causes of diseases, but in the study of their symptoms and treatment, on the battlefields of Europe, and at the bedsides of Pinel's Salpetrière.

9
TASTE UNDER THE DIRECTORY

On 13 January 1793, the French representative in Rome, Bassville, was killed by a rioting crowd. The subsequent flight of the French colony in Rome marked the end of an era. The multitude of foreign artists, students, and aristocratic patrons who gathered around the ruins of classical antiquity had formed, until 1793, a truly cosmopolitan community. For them, classical art was the proper concern of every educated and cultivated man of the Enlightenment. After 1793, however, the sophisticated study of Europe's artistic heritage was interrupted by the rude blasts of nationalism. The invading armies of the Directory were to plunder the art treasures of Italy, and parade them in triumph on the Champ de Mars.

Nevertheless, art in this period continued to draw its inspiration from antiquity, and from the movement known to art historians as 'Neo-classicism'. Neo-classicism helped to provide the form and subject-matter for official attempts to define and promote a specifically Republican style in the visual arts, the theatre, and even costume. This survey of art and literature in the late 1790s must therefore begin with some explanation for this respect for the civilisations of Greece and Rome.

The roots of Neo-classicism went back much further than the eighteenth century – to the painting of Poussin, for example, to the poetry of Milton, to the architecture of Palladio. In the late eighteenth century, however, respect for the classics was transformed into a veritable obsession. The excavations of Herculaneum, after 1738, and of Pompeii, after 1748, brought to light a series of wall paintings, for example, which were to be particularly exploited by interior decorators under the Directory. The art criticism of Winkelmann, and its ecstatic descriptions of the smooth serenity of Greek sculpture, also helped to awaken enthusiasm for classical art. Winckelmann's rapturous, and perhaps homosexual, admiration for the naked male form in no way mitigated the impact of his aesthetic ideal of noble simplicity and tranquil grandeur. The literature of ancient Rome, taught in the *collèges* of the Ancien Régime, was part of the general culture of the educated eighteenth-century Frenchman. Virgil's *Aeneid*, Horace's *Ars Poetica*, Ovid's *Metamorphoses*, the first three books of Livy, and Cicero's *Orationes*, as well as Plutarch's *Lives*, were to provide rhetorical window-dressing, and a fund of constructive examples, for the orators of the revolutionary generation.

Above all, French Neo-classicism was a reaction against the frivolity and purely decorative indulgence of the Rococo. Admirers of the stern morality and stoic values of antiquity were appalled by art which seemed destined purely for the titillation and superficial amusement of a corrupt court. Perhaps the development of middle-class patronage also helped to encourage a taste for works of art and literature which had some moral content. This particular aspect of Neo-classicism was emphasised by the Revolutionaries. The leading critic, Quatremère de Quincy, championed a more didactic form of art before the Committee of Public Education in 1791. For the Republicans, art should not primarily delight the eye, but ennoble the sentiments; it should serve not only to amuse, but also to teach moral precepts distilled from the examples of Rome, Athens, and Sparta.

Neo-classicism, however, was not so much a homogeneous style as a recognisable vocabulary, which provided a medium for very different forms of expression. In the paintings of Greuze, for example, championed by Diderot, the ideals of modesty and family loyalty were compounded with a strong dose of sentimentality, which modern audiences might excusably find nauseating. With David, however, to whom we must return, Neo-classicism was theatrical, statuesque, and heroic. In the architectural projects of Ledoux, it became starkly functional and even futuristic. The classics could provide examples to justify the Republican form of government; they were just as often plundered by conservative commentators, for warnings against the dangers of an excessively democratic political system. Important nuances distinguished the preference of a man like Desmoulins for Athens, from that of Montagnards like Lepelletier for Sparta.

Although the vogue for Neo-classicism continued under the Directory, tastes were changing. There was a world of difference between the proud, virile patriotism of David's *Oath of the Horatii* (1785), and Gérard's portrait of Madame Récamier, painted in Greek costume before a set of pillars, but in a languid and negligent pose. It is significant, too, that the proportion of paintings on classical themes shown at the Salons of 1798 and 1799 dropped to less than ten per cent of all the exhibits. By the end of the Directory, the relevance and utility of classical models were no longer generally appreciated, except as the source of motifs which decorated the drawing-rooms of the rich. The moral element was discarded; the decorative element triumphed.

The end of court life, and the aristocratic emigration, forced artists to seek new patrons. Painters could obtain a precarious income from commissions from the government and local authorities, if they were prepared to commemorate the Republic's military victories, and the great *journées* of the Revolution, and to contribute to the *fêtes nationales*. If art was to teach Republican virtue, it must cease to be the monopoly of a privileged élite, and become public art, available to the masses. The period of the Directory saw a sudden democratisation of the arts, with the breakdown of the monopolies of the Comédie Française, the relaxation of the control of the Académie des Beaux-Arts over the Paris Salon, and the new freedom given to the periodical press. This chapter must consider not only the official attempt to find a Republican form of art and drama, but also the tastes of a middle-class, and even more general, public, which now attended public concerts, visited the Paris salons, flocked to the theatre, and bought cheap novels and engravings. For the historian, the way in which the *nouveaux riches* decorated their town houses, and the popularity of boulevard theatre, are as much a part of the history of taste as official propaganda art. The scope of this book and the present state of historical knowledge have confined the following discussion of the visual arts, theatre, literature, dress, and décor to Paris. It was in the capital that new developments in the arts and fashion first saw the light of day, and where foreign influences first penetrated.

The world of French painting was dominated by David, who had become a national figure when he led the revolt against the restrictive practices of the Académie des Beaux-Arts. The Academy was a closed circle of about sixty members, under royal patronage, who monopolised the biennial Salon of the Ancien Régime, and supervised the allocation of government commissions. David's breakaway Commune of the Arts supported a more democratic organisation of the profession. In 1791, it succeeded in opening the Salon to all artists, whether members of the Academy or not, and in 1793, the Academy was abolished outright. From now on, the Salons became annual events.

The immediate result of this democratisation was to swamp the Salon of 1791 with over eight hundred items, many of them mediocre. It was clear that some selection of the exhibits was still necessary, but not until 1798 was a jury constituted, nominated by the government. Criticisms of government interference, however, succeeded in temporarily abolishing the jury in 1799.

After David's release from prison, his studio acquired international fame. In the *Intervention of the Sabine Women*, David abandoned the harsh tone of the *Oath of the Horatii*, and attempted something softer and more refined, in what was known as 'the Greek style'. For modern audiences, however, the contrived theatricality of this composition does not have the impact of his more realistic paintings, like the *Marat*, or the *Lepelletier*, or of the portraits he continued to paint. The painting of his wife's sister and her husband, Monsieur and Madame Sériziat, for example, was completed in 1795. In 1799, David began work on his *Léonidas at Thermopylae*, but this was not a timely moment to produce a painting on the theme of a military hero facing defeat. Appropriately enough, the *Léonidas* was not finally completed until 1814.

David's own paintings were not his sole contribution to the art of this period. He also had an important rôle to play as a teacher of other painters. His pupils Gérard, Girodet, Gros, and Ingres, however, who all passed through his studio, were to lead French Neo-classicism along new and different paths. Gérard's rather mannered *Cupid and Psyche*, shown at the Salon of 1798, had none of the strident character of his teacher's work. In 1793, Girodet allowed shafts of romantic moonlight to illuminate the sleep of *Endymion*. Gros's *Bonaparte on the Bridge at Arcole*, also shown at the Salon of 1798, certainly had a heroic quality reminiscent of David, but in his subsequent works for Napoleon, he developed a more personal style. The glorious colour of his *Battle of Aboukir* was in marked contrast to David's deliberately subdued tones and biscuit-coloured nudes. Ingres, the greatest of David's pupils, made an emphatic departure from Davidian precepts. Inspired by Raphael, Ingres described the sensuousness of the female body in a way which the spartan David would never have contemplated.

The revolutionary governments tried to harness this artistic talent for propaganda purposes. David, who had eulogised Republican self-sacrifice in his *Brutus*, and his *Assassination of Marat*, as well as designing the *fêtes nationales*, offered a model for Republican artists. The régimes of the Terror and the Directory, however, had little success in fostering a specifically Republican style of art and architecture. The Committee of Public Safety planned a competition for the design of public monuments to the victims of the Revolution of 10 August 1792, and to the victory of the people over fanaticism and despotism. The prizes were not awarded until 1795, to Gérard for his sketch of 10 August, and to Vincent, for another sketch celebrating Republican heroism in the Vendée. These sketches, however, were never completed.

Why were such attempts to encourage Republican art unsuccessful? Firstly, the political climate remained uncertain. A commission carried out for the Terrorist régime, for example, might prove fatally compromising if and when that régime was overthrown. Thus, in 1791, Lebarbier was commissioned to paint Desilles, the captain who had died trying to prevent a mutiny at Nancy. By the time the painting was completed, Desilles was already considered a reactionary figure.

Artists continued to paint political pictures in allegorical form. David's *Intervention of the Sabine Women* (1799), was seen as a plea for reconciliation, after the factional conflict which had divided France since 1793. Political allusions were also perceived in Guérin's *Return of Marcus Sextus*, shown at the Salon of 1799, in which the exile returns to find his wife dead, and his daughter prostrate with grief. Analogies were readily drawn with the returning French *émigrés*. These controversial interpretations were attributed to paintings which were intrinsically very equivocal.

For in general, artists were afraid of unambiguous and openly committed political art. Fragonard discarded his plan for a painting about the recapture of the rebel city of Toulon, in favour of a painting of a slave auction. In 1798, François de Neufchâteau revived the idea of a government-sponsored competition, intending to reward painters of Republican themes, which carried a contemporary moral lesson. The jury, however, was compelled to award the prizes to politically neutral, traditional paintings, like Girodet's *Sleep of Endymion*, and Lethiers's *Philoctetes on the Isle of Lemnos.*

There were other reasons why the Directory failed to mobilise the arts behind the Republic. It could not afford to sponsor an expensive programme of public monuments, like the one envisaged by the Committee of Public Safety. In the Year 6, the government had only 350,000 livres earmarked for cultural patronage, and half of this was still owed to the prize-winners of 1795.

Furthermore, the public itself had other ideas about the paintings it wanted to buy. Just as the number of artists exhibiting at the Paris Salon had swollen, so too the painting-buying public had grown. Contemporaries remarked on the wide social origins of the visitors to the Directorial Salons. At the Salon of 1798, 12,800 catalogues were sold, compared with only 5,000 in 1755.

The exhibits themselves reflected the taste of private, middle-class patrons. In the Salon of 1799, only five per cent of the paintings exhibited referred to contemporary political events, or portrayed classical scenes celebrating heroism or civic virtue. On the other hand, portraits were immensely popular, accounting for almost forty per cent of exhibits. Another third were landscapes, interiors, and genre paintings. David continued to design Republican costumes, to encourage his brilliant pupils, and to receive official approval for his most ideologically sound paintings. The Directory, however, could not afford to continue a lavish programme of Republican festivals, and the richer *bourgeois* public preferred to immortalise itself by commissioning portraits.

The two art forms with potentially the largest and most popular audience at this time were public architecture and the theatre. The Directory was forced to abandon schemes for great public works, but, like its predecessors, it intended to use the theatre to educate France in Republican morality and patriotism.

At first, the French Revolution had a liberating effect on the Paris stage. Until 1791, the Comédie Française held a monopoly of the works of dead authors. Outside the Comédie Française, the Comédie Italienne, and the Opéra, there were severe restrictions on the use of spoken dialogue on the stage. The smaller theatres infringed these rules, but they relied for the bulk of their repertoire on mimed tableaus, dance, acrobats, and jugglers. After 1791, however, these restrictions were abolished, and royal censorship was replaced by supervision by the municipal authorities.

As a result, a host of small theatres opened up all over the capital. Within one year of the lifting of the ban on spoken dialogue, twenty-three café theatres opened in Paris, which then had a total theatre seating capacity of 60,000. By the time of the Terror, the capital had over forty theatres, as well as perhaps two hundred amateur houses. A new freedom and opportunity were suddenly offered to the struggling publicists and pamphleteers who formed the literary proletariat of Paris. In 1793 alone, over two hundred new plays appeared, by about 140 different authors.

Nevertheless, the theatre remained a precarious industry. Collot d'Herbois was paid only thirty livres per act by the Théâtre de Monsieur, for the first ten performances of his plays, supplemented by sixty complementary tickets, which he and other authors sold, to add to their income. The government's attempt to revive the Comédie Française as the Republican Odéon failed, and the Directory did not assist theatre managers by levying a ten per cent tax on all receipts, destined for poor-relief. Smaller houses had to compete with the pleasure gardens, and rival attractions like balloon ascents and firework displays. By the end of 1797, there were only about twenty professional theatres left in Paris. The entrepreneur Sageret, who rented the Feydeau, the République, and the Odéon, grew rich as others failed, but even he could not produce continuous successes at all his theatres, and he went bankrupt in 1799. The Opéra, too, was bankrupt by this time. There were, of course, other hazards. In 1798, Lazzari's Variétés Amusantes was burnt down, after a performance of Don Juan, which ended as the hero was engulfed in a blazing hell – blazing, with the aid of fireworks, all too realistically. Lazzari, facing complete ruin, committed suicide.

In spite of such difficulties, the revolutionary theatre enjoyed amazing vitality. The theatre of this period was generally oval-shaped, with an orchestra, a *parterre* of plain benches, and, behind these, tiered boxes. The spectators mixed freely with the actors, and both cast and audience might retire for refreshment to one of the cafés which were frequently attached to the theatres. The seating arrangement thus emphasised social differences, until the

Terrorist régime tried to abolish the distinction between the *parterre* and the *loges*. In the experiment at the Odéon, spectators were accommodated along a single raked gallery, without boxes. The thermidorean régime, however, considering that this was carrying Republicanism to an intolerable extreme, replaced the private boxes, erased the tricoloured decorations, and installed the traditional central chandelier.

The Directory nevertheless fully intended that the theatre should be a platform for the education of the public in the tenets of Republican patriotism. What did the Revolutionaries mean by this? They intended, for example, that Republican plays should no longer take as their subjects the love affairs, intrigues, or even tragedies of aristocrats and monarchs. The *Journal des Spectacles* denounced the Opéra in these terms: 'How can it be tolerated that in a Republican theatre, the execrable doings of the House of Atreus are still celebrated; that the names of Agamemnon and Achilles are offered for public acclamation?' All mention of nobility and monarchy was to be deleted from scripts, which should now have a didactic, if not entirely a popular content. The entire *œuvre* of Racine was banned. Chénier's most successful play, *Charles IX*, was held up as an ideologically correct play, and was repeated many times after its first performance in 1789. It was an attack on absolute monarchy, which was blamed for the Massacre of St Bartholomew's Day. Chénier appreciated the didactic nature of Republican theatre when he subtitled this play *L'École des Rois*, and his *Jean Calas* was similarly subtitled *L'École des Juges*. The future Minister of the Interior, François de Neufchâteau, however, broke this rule in his play *Pamela*, which had an aristocratic heroine. *Pamela* earned François two days in prison, and led to the arrest of the actors of the old Comédie Française in 1793.

In official terms, the most popular type of Republican theatre was that based on classical themes. These, for instance, accounted for twenty out of seventy performances subsidised by the Paris Commune in the summer of 1793. Amongst them were Voltaire's *Brutus* and his *La Mort de César*, as well as plays about Scaevola, Spartacus, Regulus, and Caius Gracchus. Classical authenticity, however, did not go very deep on the stage. It was quite common to see actors in togas, sporting eighteenth-century wigs, and rubbing shoulders with characters in harlequin costume. The actor Talma asked David to design authentic classical costume, but this was exceptional, and not particularly appreciated by audiences.

Anti-religious plays were also acceptable throughout this period, especially those which dealt with the evils of convent life. A number of plays appeared with plots built around lecherous monks, and lovers separated by monastery walls, with titles like *Les Rigueurs du Cloître,* and Monvel's *Les Victimes Cloîtrées.*

Pièces de circonstance, on contemporary events, were favoured by the authorities. Many were simply commemorations of military victories, or general eulogies of the patriotism of the Republican soldier, like *Le Départ des Volontaires,* and *Les Ennemis aux Frontières.* Others had a very specific propaganda aim, like *Les Véritables Honnêtes Gens,* a justification of the *coup* of fructidor, and the series of plays on peace, which followed the Treaty of Campoformio.

These, then, were the commonest types of Republican plays, but they had a mixed reception during the Directory. During this period, the theatre became a political battleground, where Jacobins and the thermidorean and Royalist *jeunesse dorée* confronted each other. Fights broke out in the *parterre,* actors would be shouted down or acclaimed, according to their political sympathies, forced to make their *autocritique* on stage, and to sing either the thermidorean *Réveil du Peuple,* or the Jacobin *Marseillaise* or *Ça Ira.* The Directory banned singing of the *Réveil du Peuple,* but this did not prevent the right-wing following of the Théâtre Feydeau, for example, from noisily interrupting the *Marseillaise.* Bonaparte, entrusted for a time with the surveillance of Paris theatres, singled out the Feydeau for its lack of sympathy for the Republic, and Merlin de Douai was forced to close it.

Thermidorean and moderate theatre audiences had their own gallery of anti-Republican heroes, and a dramatic taste which often proved embarrassing for the government. They applauded Cange, commissioner of St-Lazare prison, who helped suffering prisoners during the Terror. He was immortalised in *Cange ou le Commissionnaire Bienfaisant,* and was hailed as a hero when he appeared in person at the Théâtre de la Cité. Perhaps the most successful anti-Jacobin play, however, was Ducancel's *L'Intérieur des Comités Révolutionnaires.* The Terrorists were here portrayed as ignorant, illiterate, black marketeers, embezzlers, and false denunciators. The play enjoyed a national success, and at Bordeaux, for instance, it sparked off the drawing up of anti-Terrorist blacklists, and the brutal assassination of Groussac, Jacobin ex-mayor of Toulouse, in 1796. Once more, White Terrorist plays drew on classical models, but their main characters were now the tyrant Nero rather than Brutus, the Decemvirs rather than the Horatii.

Popular dramatic taste had a completely different mythology, ambience, and geography. A festive atmosphere reigned in the Boulevard du Temple, known as the '*boulevard du crime*', with its hawkers and peddlars, jugglers and pickpockets, acrobatic and equestrian displays, and tiny theatres offering pantomime, farce, song, and dance, in a multitude of ephemeral productions, full of spectacle. The only truly popular theatre to survive the revolutionary period was the Vaudeville which, far from following political orthodoxy, or Neo-classical imitations, parodied them both. It satirised Chénier on the one hand, and the muscadin dandies on the other, but it remained the only new boulevard theatre to survive when, in 1807, Napoleon reduced the number of Paris houses to eight.

Popular audiences greatly appreciated satires on the *nouveaux riches*, especially those in the *poissarde* tradition. The *poissarde*, or Parisian fishwife, was, like the Père Duchesne, a stock character, portrayed in her natural Parisian setting, usually Les Halles, speaking her own unique argot. Eve caused a sensation when he created the character of Madame Angot in 1796, in *Madame Angot ou la Poissarde Parvenue*. Here, the fishwife, intent on marrying her daughter above her station, aped the manners of her social superiors, and fell into grotesque social blunders which betrayed her popular origins. Madame Angot, together with the simpleton Janot, and the naive valet Jocrisse, remained a figure of Parisian folk culture until well into the nineteenth century, beginning under the Directory with Aude's *Madame Angot dans son Ballon*, and *Madame Angot au Sérail de Constantinople*.

The popular drama had always shunned Diderot's ideal of the sentimental *bourgeois* comedy, and classical adaptations, in favour of spectacle, exotic settings, and banal tales of oppressed innocence. Some critics see the birth of French melodrama in this period, emerging from the pantomime tradition, with its complicated apparatus of caves, prisons, desert islands, battle and storm scenes. Popular taste forced the adaptation of several 'stage classics' along melodramatic lines. Ducis, for example, the contemporary adaptor of Shakespeare, added a happy ending to his *Othello*, and a happy ending was also added to *Robert, Chef des Brigands*, a play loosely based on Schiller.

We can therefore conclude this brief summary of the theatre under the Directory by suggesting that official attempts to sponsor a Republican form of drama had a mixed success. If the convent plays were relatively popular, the authorities always ran the gauntlet of vociferous Royalist heckling, and could not undermine the fertile and resilient tradition of the most popular forms of French drama.

The literary critics of the Directory deplored the vulgarity of popular taste as much as they deplored the comedies and novels about lecherous aristocrats, who composed elegant epigrams while entangled in improbable love intrigues. For Duval, in the *Décade Philosophique*, 'on avait transformé le théâtre en boudoir'. Duval had a healthy suspicion of authors who dashed off patriotic plays merely in order to advertise their own Republican zeal, and he was not afraid to suggest that much Revolutionary literature was completely devoid of talent.

The critics' conception of Republican theatre and literature was still inspired by the classical aesthetics of the *Ars Poetica*. For Duval, Republican comedy should have an element of serious social satire, and La Chabeaussière reiterated that comedy should be a weapon of ridicule, to expose vice and praise virtue. The society of the Directory, it is true, offered a wide range of subjects for the satirist. The pretensions of public officials and of the *nouveaux riches* had great comic potential. The Directory, however, never found its Aristophanes to exploit it to the full.

For Madame de Staël, there were two main requirements for the ideal novel: '*le naturel*', and '*la moralité*'. The novels of Fielding and Richardson, she felt, were admirable, and La Harpe, too, regarded *Tom Jones* as the best novel ever written. This novel was thought to combine a refreshing natural realism (*candeur*) with a clear demonstration of the triumph of virtue.

Arguing again from the basis that art should be moral and, at the same time, close to nature, de Staël and her contemporaries felt, quite rightly, that 'high comedy' had never equalled the achievement of Molière. Without detracting from Racine's poetic genius, many critics at this time felt that Voltaire, if not a superior tragedian, was at least Racine's equal. They based this surprising judgement on the belief that Voltaire's characters were less conventional and more realistic than Racine's. The continuing prevalence of Neo-classical literary aesthetics was demonstrated under the Directory by the appearance of new complete editions of Racine, Lafontaine, Bacon, and the *Essays* of Montaigne.

The converse of these preferences was the ambiguous attitude of contemporaries towards Shakespeare. Although his tragic genius was recognised by Madame de Staël in her *Essai sur les fictions*, his mixture of tragic and comic elements was considered in bad taste. He was guilty of incoherence, a penchant for the grotesque (as in Caliban and Richard III), and vulgarity. Ducis's adaptations of *Macbeth*, *Othello*, and *King John* tried to disguise these 'aberrations', and attempted the impossible task of assimilating Shakespeare into the conventions of classical tragedy. Molière and Racine thus remained the models for the comedy and tragedy of the future.

The *Décade Philosophique* did not find that the popular novel lived up to the high standards it set for Republican literature. It is difficult to describe the extent or nature of the reading public to which cheap popular novels were addressed, but it was clearly restricted at least by illiteracy. In estimating the literacy rate in eighteenth-century France, however, important regional differences must be taken into account. North-east of a line running roughly from the bay of St-Michel to Geneva, literacy was relatively high: never less than twenty-five per cent, and in some areas, over fifty per cent. In the rest of France, however, the rate of literacy on the eve of the Revolution was notoriously low. It was particularly low in the Breton departments, the Centre, and the South-west. Women's literacy was universally worse than that of men. These differences corresponded to the geographical distribution of primary schools during the Ancien Régime, to linguistic differences, and to the general level of prosperity in any area. Taking France as a whole, about forty-seven per cent of men could read and write, and about twenty-seven per cent of women. These figures, however, are based on the ability to sign one's name on a marriage contract, and probably overestimate the proportion of the population capable of reading a novel or a newspaper.

Nevertheless, there was at least a Parisian market large enough to support the publication of almost a novel per day by the end of the Directory. Although many of them ran to three or four volumes, each volume rarely cost more than 1fr.50. A German visitor to Paris remarked on the voracious literary appetite of Parisians in 1786: 'Tout le monde lit à Paris. Chacun, surtout les femmes, a un livre dans sa poche. On lit en voiture, à la promenade, au théâtre, dans les entr'actes, au café, au bain. Dans les boutiques, femmes, enfants, ouvriers, apprentis lisent; le dimanche, les gens qui s'assoient à la porte de leurs maisons lisent; les laquais lisent derrière les voitures; les cochers lisent sur leurs sièges, les soldats lisent au poste, et les commissionaires à leurs stations.'

The Alsatian bibliophile Fleischer compiled, for the benefit of the book trade, a complete catalogue of all books published in Paris during the Year 9, which gives some indication of the material available to the Parisian reading public during this period.[1] The list confirms the suggestion of Ehrard and Roger that the eighteenth century saw a declining demand for theological books, and a soaring demand for books falling into the category of belles-lettres.[2] If engravings, musical scores, maps, and newspapers are subtracted from Fleischer's list, then just under two thousand items were published in the Year 9, of which only about two per cent are classified as theological and religious books. Many of these, it should be noted, were on the subject of Theophilanthropy. On the other hand, about seven hundred or over one-third of all publications, were in the field of literature and belles-lettres, and, of these, a majority were novels, editions of poetry, or *contes*. Book production seems to have declined at the beginning of the Empire, but in 1799, the annual output of novels reached its peak for the century. At the end of the Directory, one book in every eight published was a novel. Their titles suggest a staple diet of love stories, often with an exotic location destined to satisfy the most predictable sexual fantasies of the reader, like *Les Dangers de la mauvaise compagnie, ou les nouvelles liaisons dangéreuses, Ma Tante Geneviève ou je l'ai échappée belle*, and *Les Jolis Péchés d'une marchande des modes*.

Alongside this ephemeral literature appeared several Gothic novels, or *romans noirs*, usually English in origin, which perhaps presaged an important change in literary taste. By 1797, the Paris stage was already gripped by dramatisations of Ann Radcliffe's *Mysteries of Udolpho*, which had many imitators, and Lewis's *The*

[1] Bibliography no. 135.   [2] Bibliography no. 134.

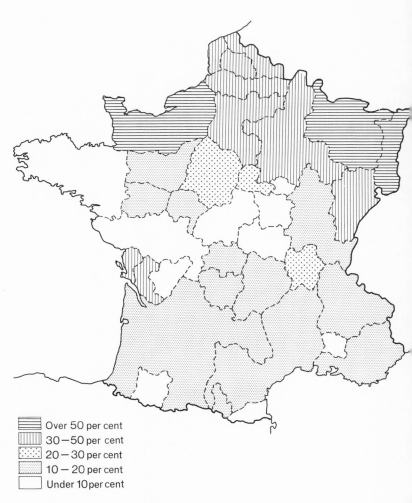

Over 50 per cent
30 — 50 per cent
20 — 30 per cent
10 — 20 per cent
Under 10 per cent

Map 2. Proportion of brides able to sign their names, 1786–90

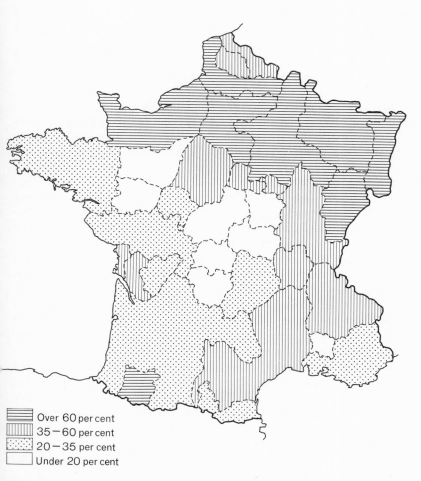

Over 60 per cent
35 – 60 per cent
20 – 35 per cent
Under 20 per cent

Map 3. Proportion of bridegrooms able to sign their names, 1786–90

Monk. The vogue for these novels and others like them satisfied a growing taste for the supernatural, and were roundly condemned by the critics of the *Décade Philosophique.* Less violent, and more melancholic romantic tastes could be accommodated in this period by translations of Goethe's *Werther,* the poems of Ossian, and Châteaubriand's *Atala.* Madame de Staël's increasing respect for the more sombre and primitive aspects of northern European literature was clearly a sign of the times.

Just as the democratisation of the Paris Salon and the liberalisation of the stage opened up new careers for struggling painters and dramatists, so, too, the flourishing revolutionary newspaper press gave thousands of would-be journalists a platform and a voice. In 1788, there were only sixty newspapers in France; after the freedom granted to the press in the Constitution of the Year 3, there were approaching two hundred in Paris alone. One did not have to be rich to buy a single wooden printing press, and to print a single folded sheet on coarse paper every two or three days. This is how most journals appeared. There was, as yet, no mass newspaper readership. Papers were sold by the subscription method, and an annual *abonnement* might cost anything from eighteen to thirty-six livres.

Only a handful of Parisian papers had a circulation which ran into four figures. Among them were the *Moniteur,* and the official *Rédacteur.* Most privately-run newspapers had only a few hundred subscribers. Babeuf's *Tribun du Peuple,* for example, had 590 subscribers all over France, fewer than the most successful fashion paper of the Directory, the *Journal des Dames et des Modes.* Like many provincial newspapers in France even today, papers were often the mouthpiece of one political figure. This was true, for instance, of Babeuf's paper, of Lebois's *Ami du Peuple,* and of Fréron's *Orateur du Peuple.* The contents of these papers accordingly tended to be polemical in tone, although they generally carried a summary of debates in the Legislature, and had a rudimentary foreign news coverage. The lack of a sophisticated libel law encouraged their polemical nature.

Until the end of the Year 7, the French press perhaps enjoyed more liberty than at any other time during the Revolution, and certainly more than under the Empire. The liberalism of the Directorial régime was however threatened by the strength of a flourishing Royalist press. The Directory made several half-hearted attempts to check this unlimited freedom. In messidor IV, the postal rate for newspapers sent into the departments was raised, and the successive *coups d'état* were followed by the suppression of newspapers. After fructidor, for example, the editors of thirty-two Parisian journals were arrested, including the editors of the *Courrier Républicain*, the *Messager du Soir*, and *La Quotidienne*. Similarly, after floréal VI, some Jacobin journals were suppressed, including the *Journal des Hommes Libres*, the leading Jacobin paper under the Directory, which survived by changing its name. In nivôse VI, the Directory issued a directive to editors, encouraging them to defend the Constitution of 1795, condemn the Ancien Régime, point out the dangers of 'anarchy' if the government fell, and encourage the prompt payment of taxes. These warnings were not enough to create a loyally Republican press. Security could only be assured by violating the principle of press freedom. In thermidor VII, for example, deportation orders were issued for over sixty journalists, including editors of the *Anti-Terroriste* of Toulouse, the *Courrier* of Lyon, and the *Actes des Apôtres*.

Nothing reflects more vividly the rising influence of the *bourgeoisie* on French taste in this period than fashions in dress and interior decoration.

Styles of dress expressed the new social freedom of the post-Terrorist period, as well as the popularisation of Neo-classical designs. The dandies of the Directory, the 'Incroyables', wore large felt hats, and colossal cravats, which were commonly an object of ridicule. Their partners, the 'Merveilleuses', adopted rather more enduring fashions. Madame Tallien, for example, who was largely responsible for dictating the taste of society women, wore a light, high-waisted, Greek costume, known as a '*robe à l'athénienne*', made of muslin or gauze, which was white and practically transparent. Greek-style sandals, and rings on the toes were fashionable accessories for such an outfit. Although light, simple, and elegant, the Greek tunic was also cold, and discriminated against women who did not have delicate hands and feet, or who were reluctant to bare their arms and legs.

The Directory saw the return of Ancien Régime habits of dress, in the revival of the wig. Blonde wigs were particularly fashionable in the thermidorean period, and Madame Tallien was said to own thirty of them, each one a different shade. At the same time, the lightness and transparency of the Greek tunic offended puritan sensibilities. On one afternoon, Madame Hamelin, wife of the government contractor, could be observed strolling through the streets of Paris in a topless costume. This was not repeated, but curious readers of the period could refer to a book which suggested exactly how far the reaction against Jacobin austerity had progressed. It was entitled *Éloge du sein des femmes; ouvrage curieux, dans lequel on examine s'il doit être découvert: s'il est permis de le toucher, quelles sont ses vertus, sa forme, son langage, son éloquence, le pays où il est le plus beau, et les moyens les plus surs de le conserver.* By the end of the Directory, however, Parisians had turned to a rather more practical style of dress. Gripped by the anglophilism of the late 1790s, they donned shawls and straw hats, while the men sported high hats and Spencer jackets.

Taste in interior decoration was equally dominated by a preference for simple, elegant lines, and classical motifs. Antiquity had dominated taste long before the Directory, and the *style grecque* was nothing new to the aristocrats of the reign of Louis XVI. It was only during the Directory, however, that archaeology influenced furniture and décor on a wide scale. The mahogany furniture of designers like Jacob retained the elegance of the Louis-Seize style, without the lugubrious monumentality of the Empire. From the wall paintings of Pompeii, the Directory style borrowed dark hues of brown, violet, and black. Beds were surrounded by columns, and decorated with paintings of Greek gods and goddesses. Consoles were supported by caryatids, and a small tripod table, known as '*l'athénienne*', made its appearance. Interior decoration incorporated a series of mythological figures, winged genii, and nymphs.

More exotic motifs might accompany these Greek and Pompeian styles of decoration. The expedition to Egypt aroused interest in Egyptian civilisation, and a new series of designs entered the decorators' repertoire. '*Lits à l'égyptienne*' had Isis at their head, and were supported by lions' feet. Swans adorned the bed Berthault created for Madame Récamier in 1798. Sphinxes and griffons sprouted on chair-arms, serpents lurked around candelabra. Obelisks and pyramids appeared on walls and furniture. It was not long before the simple, intimate style of the Directory was superseded by the cold, heavy, gilt ornamentation of Imperial pomp.

Artists and writers no longer worked for the court or the aristocracy, and luxury craftsmen had lost their pre-Revolutionary clientèle. Instead they chose to satisfy official pressure for Republican art, patriotic theatre, or the decoration of public buildings. Alternatively, they worked for a relatively new, and recently enriched *bourgeois* market, which imposed its own distinctive tastes – for portrait-painting, for the sentimental and Gothic novel, and for the mahogany *secrétaires* and Pompeian décor which embellished the new drawing-rooms of the Chaussée d'Antin.

Popular tastes, however, were barely influenced either by official Neo-classicism, or by the anglophile fashions of a snobbish middle class. The average Frenchman still preferred pantomime to Voltaire, and Madame Angot to Mutius Scaevola. He still bought the brochures and almanacs sold by peddlars or *colporteurs*, relating, in simplified and pictorial form, historical legends and stories from the Bible, giving instruction to the practical housewife, and describing age-old popular superstitions.

10

THE NATION IN ARMS

Il faudrait que dans chaque condition, le citoyen ait deux habits, l'habit de son état et l'habit militaire.

–Diderot

Since the Revolution, the rôle of the army in French society has always been a sensitive issue. While those on the right have, in the past, argued for the military effectiveness of a professional army, an *armée de métier*, others have seen the danger of entrusting military power entirely to a specialised body, cut off from the nation as a whole. It may seem particularly baffling to English audiences that France has retained national military service in a nuclear age, when advances in military technology demand highly-specialised skills. The answer lies partly in the endurance of the Jacobin ideal of the national army, in which every citizen has a duty to serve, and whose composition is an accurate reflection of French society itself. The deputy Charrier described the idea of the nation in arms when he asked, 'Qu'est-ce que l'armée? C'est la France entière. On a voulu mettre de la distinction entre les troupes de ligne et les gardes nationaux et c'est un piége qu'on a tendu. Tous les citoyens français sont l'armée. Pourquoi recruter l'armée? Le tocsin sonnant tous les patriotes seront sous les armes.' For the Revolutionaries, the virtues of the national army, and of the *levée en masse*, had been demonstrated at Valmy, Jemappes, and Fleurus. The modern heirs of Jacobinism, from Jaurès onwards, are still convinced of these virtues, and this explains why even the Communist Party resists left-wing protests against conscription.

After briefly examining how the armies of the Republic had been formed, this chapter considers the main characteristics of the Republican national army. These were, for example, the extent to which the composition of the army reflected French society as a whole, the rôle of the army in fostering fraternity and national unity, and the way promotion within the army reflected the new social opportunities created by the Revolution. Finally,

146

since Republican soldiers were ideally motivated by patriotism, and were citizens with political rights and duties, the growing political consciousness of the Republican armies must be taken into account.

Until J.-P. Bertaud has completed his research on the army under the Directory, we must rely quite heavily on illustrations from the earlier revolutionary armies. But this chapter goes on to suggest that the army of the Directory was becoming more of a 'praetorian' army, following its generals rather than the nation as a whole, and developing a professional *esprit de corps* of its own.

The art of war was traditionally the *métier* of the aristocrat, and the army of the Ancien Régime was distinguished by its social exclusiveness, and dependence on aristocratic leadership. In the eighteenth century, about ninety per cent of regular officers were of strictly aristocratic origin. Nobility, of course, could be acquired by reaching the rank of general, but only five per cent of marshals and generals before the 1780s had acquired aristocratic status by this method. Noble status was also conferred on families whose members had served in the army for three generations, and on those who were awarded the Croix de St-Louis, after thirty years' army service. Only a very small number of commoners benefited from these stipulations. According to the Loi Ségur of 1781, all army officers had to prove four quarters of nobility on their paternal side. This was not so much a new measure of discrimination against the promotion of commoners, since they had always been virtually barred from becoming officers; it was rather an attempt by the *noblesse d'épée* to check the promotion of men recently ennobled by the purchase of venal offices. The Navy, too, was noted as a stronghold of aristocratic exclusiveness and arrogance.

The hierarchy of military rank reflected the Ancien Régime social hierarchy of orders, which the Revolution overthrew. The colonelcies and higher ranks were shared by the court nobility, while the lesser nobility occupied the ranks of officers below the colonels. The *bourgeoisie* could aspire to the posts of junior, or *bas officiers*, as they were known until the Republic gave them the less condescending name of *sous-officiers*. Thus commoners could hope only for a lieutenancy, and lesser nobles for a lieutenant-colonelcy at the most, but years of service were needed to achieve even this much. The '*cascade de mépris*', which characterised the attitudes of social classes during the Ancien Régime, certainly applied in the armed forces of France.

The Bourbon army was recruited by its captains, who often used local contacts with neighbours, or the peasants on their fathers' seigneuries to enlist men. They might delegate recruiting work to their sergeants, who employed all the pressures and cunning deceptions associated with the press-gang. Hoche, for example, was tricked into enlisting in the Gardes Françaises, in the belief that he was joining a colonial regiment. In war-time, the ranks would be supplemented by the *miliciens*, selected by lot in the towns and villages of France. In theory, the *milice* might have become the basis for a system of national military service, and its fusion with regular units during the Seven Years' War has been seen as an earlier form of the revolutionary *amalgame*. In practice, however, liberally-accorded exemptions, and the practice of 'buying' a replacement conscript meant that *milice* duty fell chiefly on the popular classes, who were neither influential enough to secure exemption, nor wealthy enough to afford a substitute. The *milice* rarely provided more than 14,000 recruits per year, but the resentment it aroused showed that in the Ancien Régime, military service was regarded not as a duty, nor as a profession, but as a burden involving loss of personal liberty, and the severing of local and family ties.

Projects for reform had been mooted. Servan, future Rolandist Minister of War, envisaged a system of recruitment which would create a more national army, replacing the odious press-gang, and selection by lot for the *milice*. He even considered the election of officers and the abolition of humiliating corporal punishments.

The disciplinary code of the Bourbon army punished fighting, duelling, and drunkenness with dishonourable discharge, and the theft of goods from civilians for resale might be punished with a term in the prison hulks. A soldier who threatened or assaulted a sergeant also risked a life sentence in the convict ships, or even death. After the Seven Years' War, discipline became even tighter, as the high command attempted to reform the French army along Prussian lines.

The Republic was to take up some of Servan's ideas later. For a revolutionary army of citizen-soldiers would not require the brutal discipline needed to motivate the soldiers of the Ancien Régime army. Bohan described the eighteenth-century infantry as one 'composée aux deux tiers de vagabonds, déserteurs et coquins, [which] doit nécessairement être conduite comme des forçats'. Under the Republic, the army would no longer resemble a vast penal settlement, nor would it suppress leaders of merit in order to preserve the aristocratic monopoly of higher ranks. The enemies of France, however, took some time to realise the powerful resources unleashed by the Revolution. The Prussian aide-de-camp Bischoffswerder rashly prophesied in 1792 that 'les fumées de l'ivresse de la liberté se dissipent à Paris. L'armée des avocats va être convenablement rossée dans les Pays-Bas; en automne nous serons chez nous.' The misplaced confidence of the coalition's leaders in their own armies, composed by their own admission of the 'scum of the earth', helped revolutionary France to record the victory of Valmy.

In place of the so-called 'mercenaries' of the Ancien Régime, the Revolution gave birth to the National Guardsmen, and the volunteers of 1791, who came mainly from the ranks of the National Guard. The latter, formed during the breakdown of public order in 1789, were not fully 'national', since membership was restricted to active citizens – that is, those wealthy enough to qualify for political rights. In many towns, however, this qualification was not enforced. The National Guard and the volunteer regiments elected their own officers, but the volunteers only engaged for one campaign, and disbanded in 1792.

Although the volunteers numbered 170,000 by the summer of 1792, they alone could not provide the army the Republic needed to defeat the First Coalition. In February 1793, bachelors and widowers between the ages of eighteen and forty were liable to be called up, and in August, the *levée en masse* was ordered. The conscription of able-bodied males between eighteen and twenty-five was to produce an army of three-quarters of a million men. For the first time, the principle of universal obligation to military service was established. On 19 fructidor Year 6, the Loi Jourdan called up conscripts in the twenty to twenty-five age-group, for a five-year term of service. What is more, military service was now obligatory in peacetime.

The new revolutionary army had to be trained and equipped, and in some way assimilated into the units of regular soldiers of the line. *Représentants en mission* were sent out from Paris to speed up conscription, and to organise the mobilisation and elementary training of the new recruits. The experience of the regulars,

and the raw revolutionary enthusiasm of volunteers and conscripts were to be combined in the *amalgame*. According to the
proposals of Dubois-Crancé, one battalion of regulars would fuse
with two battalions of new recruits, to form a new *demi-brigade*.
The first *amalgame* of 1794 was never complete, since many units
succeeded in escaping fusion with other battalions. A new *amalgame* was ordered by the Directory, to bring units up to full
strength, and to reduce the element of segregation between
regulars and conscripts. The new *amalgame* operated at the
company and battalion level, and not, as previously, at the level of
the *demi-brigade*.

Too much has perhaps been made of the differences and
suspicion which divided the regular soldiers, *les blancs*, named
after their white coats, and the new volunteers and recruits, *les
bleus*. At first it was true that conditions of service varied considerably in the army of the line, and in the volunteer units. The
volunteers received a higher rate of pay: fifteen *sous* per day,
compared with eight *deniers* for the regular soldier (1 *sou* = 12
deniers). The volunteers enrolled for only one campaign, and they
elected their own officers. On the other hand, *les bleus* and *les
blancs* had much in common. Many regular soldiers joined the
volunteers, attracted by better rates of pay and chances of
promotion. Many volunteers enrolled as regular soldiers at the
end of their first campaign, like the Parisian diarist and carpet-
weaver Bricard, who went on to become a lieutenant in the Year
10.[1] Discrepancies in the terms of service were gradually reduced, in the interests of administrative convenience. Soldiers in
the army of the line soon engaged to serve for only three years,
instead of eight, as previously. The army of the line did not wither
away: in 1791 and 1792, it enjoyed a recruitment boom, especially in the infantry. Bonuses were paid on enrolment, and the
emigration of officers opened up new opportunities for promotion. By 1793, two-thirds of the army of the line had enlisted since
the beginning of the Revolution. The French army could not
tolerate units with different recruiting systems, different rates of
pay, different codes of discipline and methods of promotion. One
standard training scheme was needed, and the fusion of separate units reduced the excessive numbers of officers and their
staff. The *amalgame* was thus dictated by the needs of adminis-

[1] Bibliography no. 148.

trative rationalisation. The similarities between the infantryman of the line and the volunteer made the *amalgame* possible.

These were the foundations on which the Republic built the war machine that was to defeat the First and Second Coalitions. By 1794, the great European powers faced a Republican citizen army which had revolutionised the concept of warfare. It had its own Republican system of discipline, which punished looting ruthlessly, but was otherwise more lenient and humane than before. It had its own tactics, for in Italy, where the army lived off the land, Bonaparte's army had the enormous advantage of superior mobility. It had its own weapon – the pike, the very symbol of the popular revolution in arms, originally adopted because of the shortage of rifles. Its officers now required not a pedigree of noble birth, but a *certificat de civisme*, and an oath of loyalty to the nation. Victories were no longer celebrated by a Te Deum, but by a Republican fête. In the Navy, Jeanbon St-André replaced almoners by Republican *instituteurs*, and a Phrygian bonnet flew from every mast.

These were the outward signs of the changes that had occurred. How was the composition of the army specifically Republican? In theory, if the army was not to become an exclusive élite, its composition should reflect that of French society as a whole. In fact the Republican army, like its predecessors, continued to draw its soldiers mainly from the traditional areas of recruitment in the North and East. One-third of the infantry regulars of 1793, and over one-half of the cavalry and artillerymen came from the six provinces of Flanders, Artois, Picardy, Champagne, Lorraine, and Franche-Comté. Here, local economic crises, the good physique of the inhabitants, and the presence of many garrisons made recruitment easier. Perhaps, too, the attitudes of the frontier population made enlistment relatively popular. The Midi, where there were fewer garrisons and men were smaller, always provided fewer recruits than the North-east in proportion to its population. There were of course exceptions, like the old Comté de Foix, where enlistment had always been a possible alternative to the poverty of Pyrenéan peasant life. After the minimum height of new recruits was reduced in 1792 from five feet two inches to five feet, more southerners did enlist. Military service, by contrast, was always unpopular in the West, where conscription had sparked off the revolt in the Vendée in the spring of 1793. Brittany and Poitou provided less than four per cent of the army of the line in 1793. Garrisons were fewer and farther between in the West, and in the coastal regions of Brittany at least, recruits joined the Navy, not the Army.

The urban centres of France were over-represented in the Republican army. Two-thirds of the army of the line were of rural origin, but one in every two infantry officers was born in a town with a population of over 2,000. Many of them came from large urban centres, for twenty-five per cent of infantry officers lived in towns with populations of over 25,000 and one in ten lived in Paris. The volunteers of 1791, drawn principally from the urban National Guard, were of course predominantly urban in origin, but two-thirds of the volunteers of 1792 came from the countryside.

The aristocratic monopoly of the officer corps was broken. The popular classes still found it difficult to accede to the rank of colonel, but if all the officers are considered, one in five was from the liberal professions, another one in five was an artisan, and one in eight was now a *laboureur*.

At the same time, the army reflected the youth of the French nation. Sixty-three per cent of the regulars were under twenty-six, and seventy-nine per cent of the volunteers were under twenty-five.

The army became an important medium in the unification of the French nation. Young conscripts, whose horizons were normally limited to the world of their own village or neighbourhood, were thrown together with fellow-recruits from all over France. Conscription thus helped to break down linguistic barriers and the spirit of localism, which the Republic 'Une et Indivisible' tried to replace with a sense of national loyalty. This process, however, was not a smooth one, and many recruits found the regiment a poor substitute for the bonds of family and community from which they had been uprooted. Military doctors treated homesickness, known as '*nostalgie*' or '*mal du pays*', as a serious disease, which caused fever, apathy, and even prostration. Volunteers were recruited on a local basis, and so were not immediately severed from the consoling company of their compatriots, but units with a marked regional identity were prone to epidemics of *dépaysement*. Such epidemics of homesickness were recorded, naturally enough, in Egypt, and in the Army of the Alps in the Year 8. The only treatment offered was a period of leave. The *amalgame*, which threw together soldiers of very different local backgrounds, aggravated local tensions within army units. In the Year 2, for example, a group of officers in the Army of the Eastern Pyrenees demanded a transfer from a unit composed of men from the Moselle to one composed chiefly of southerners, arguing that 'l'intérêt de la République n'en sera servi qu'avec plus de zèle par des citoyens qui combattent à côté de leurs amis et de leurs parents'. The Republic hoped that, in time, they would come to regard all Frenchmen as their compatriots.

With the abolition of aristocratic privilege, officer ranks were thrown open to merit. Merit was generally interpreted as seniority of service, but promotion also incorporated the democratic principle of the election of officers. After 1790, captains were to be co-opted from a short list drawn up by corporals, and three out of four *sous-lieutenants* were appointed after a competitive examination, every fourth post being reserved for the most senior *sous-officier*. A similar system was introduced for the Navy, where recruits qualified by examination for the special rank of *enseigne entretenu*. After a period of training, they would go on to become lieutenants and captains. This was designed to facilitate the recruitment of merchant seamen into the Navy. The volunteers and the National Guard elected their own officers.

The mass emigration of army officers led to an extension of the elective principle. It is estimated that 2,000 out of 9,500 serving officers refused the oath of loyalty to the 1791 Constitution. The defection of the naval base at Toulon to the English and the mutiny in the Brest squadron in 1793 provoked the exclusion of many aristocrats and Royalist sympathisers from the Navy. As a result, naval officers were to be elected to the vacancies, although half of the captaincies were reserved for experienced merchant captains and senior lieutenants.

The Republican principle of the election of officers was compromised in the interests of military discipline and the desire to ensure that the armed forces were led by technically capable men. The higher posts, for instance, were filled by the Committee of Public Safety, through its *Représentants en mission*. Negligence or lack of patriotism could lead to a denunciation to the local Jacobin club, dismissal, imprisonment, and even execution. During the Terror, the highest army posts were hardly secure positions. When Schérer arrived to take up his post in Perpignan in prairial Year 3, he was the fourteenth commander-in-chief of the Army of the Eastern Pyrenees in two years. Four generals of this army had been guillotined, one died in prison, another blew his brains out, Dugommier was killed in action, and many more were suspended. Soldiers became inured to constant changes of leadership.

The Convention took precautions to ensure that the best-qualified candidates were appointed to command its armies. After 1793, all corporals and higher ranks had to be able to read and write. One-third of officers' posts were now to be filled by the government, with the help of *conseils d'administration* within each unit. Although all officers had to possess a *certificat de civisme*, it was realised that patriotism alone was not sufficient qualification for promotion. As Jeanbon St-André, the architect of the Republican Navy, told the revolutionary committee at Lorient, 'le patriotisme va devant tout, c'est une maxime incontestable, mais à la mer il doit nécessairement être accompagné d'une habilité et d'une expérience suffisante'. Guided by such level-headed principles, he was not afraid to promote the ex-aristocrat Villaret-Joyeuse to the rank of rear-admiral.

After the Year 2, however, the principle of election of officers was gradually diluted, and, eventually, virtually abandoned. The army, increasingly conscious of its own power and its own needs, succeeded in thwarting government policy in the promotion of officers. In the Year 3, the election of officers by their troops was replaced by a system of co-optation by the officers themselves. By the Year 4, the generals abrogated patronage rights at the expense of the civilian authorities. The officers on the *conseils d'administration*, for example, might oppose the appointment of an officer from another *demi-brigade*, and even falsify the qualifications of their own internal candidate, in order to circumvent the orders of the government. In the Army of Italy, promotion lay almost entirely in the hands of Bonaparte himself, and by the end of the Directory, the fastest way to achieve promotion was to join the clientèle of an influential general. The army was thus originally a genuinely Republican institution, which rewarded seniority, talent, and patriotism. But it acquired a professional exclusiveness of its own, becoming an organisation in which favouritism and private patronage played an increasingly large part.

If all citizens were expected to be soldiers, then the converse was also true. The Republic expected all soldiers to be loyal and committed Republicans. The armies of revolutionary France were never politically neutral. The strength of their political will was apparent in the series of mutinies of 1790, often provoked by the counter-revolutionary attitudes of the officers of the royal army. Republican soldiers were not the blindly obedient automatons of the Ancien Régime army: they were proud of their political consciousness and civic spirit. They refused to allow the King to escape at Varennes; they refused to answer Dumouriez's call to march on Paris after the battle of Neerwinden. In the Year 2, the government maintained a barrage of propaganda to keep the troops abreast of political developments, and to alert them to their patriotic duty. Military journals encouraged discipline, reported news from Paris, and expounded Republican principles. Bouchotte, at the War Ministry, sent out free copies of newspapers like the *Père Duchesne* and *La Montagne* to the men at the front. The official military journal, *La Soirée du Camp*, had a daily printing of 10,000 copies. After thermidor, when the government preferred an army of docile Republicans to an armed force of fervent Montagnards, these journals disappeared. The Directory was to discover, however, that the army had not abdicated its political rôle.

The armies of the Directory were becoming professional armies. The inexperienced, patriotic volunteers of 1791 were now hardened soldiers, with bitter experience of several revolutionary campaigns. They grew increasingly indifferent to domestic political squabbles, and increasingly aware of the special skills and interests of the soldier's trade. Bricard, who volunteered in 1792, became disgusted with politics after 9 thermidor, and began to count himself among the '*vrais militaires*', as opposed to the '*scélérats*', whose looting dishonoured the army.

His colleagues seemed increasingly motivated by financial and careerist interests rather than by Republican patriotism. This was partly because their material lot was often appalling. In the Year 3, they froze to death, and in hostile country their *assignats* would buy them nothing. They had to endure food shortages and lack of elementary equipment like boots, which they blamed on fraud by the *fournisseurs*. Bricard tells of men seasoning their soup with gunpowder, because there was no salt, and of soldiers cutting grass and killing cats in order to stay alive.

In 1792, they may have accepted such hardships more easily. Dumouriez had exhorted them: 'Soldats, vous n'êtes pas si à plaindre que les allemands qui restent parfois quatre jours sans pain et mangent leurs chevaux morts. Vous avez du lard, du riz, de la farine, faites les galettes, la liberté les assaisonnera!' By the Year 4, however, they would answer such exhortations by desertion or indiscriminate looting, in which their officers often joined.

Material hardships were not new to the French army. Insufficient pay had played its part in the grievances of the Toulon arsenal workers who had let in the English. Short rations and arrears of pay lay behind the mutinies in Metz in the Year 5, and in Rome in the Year 6, and provided fuel for Royalist propaganda in the Army of the Rhin-et-Moselle. Even when Bonaparte crossed into Italy, however, where the plains of Lombardy stretched before the French like a land flowing with milk and honey, and even when his soldiers were paid in cash, the looting did not stop. In Italy, French soldiers took all possible advantages of their situation. For Stendhal, 'L'amour des plaisirs s'était empiré des officiers et même des simples soldats, bien accueillis par les belles italiennes; ils vivaient dans les plaisirs et dans l'abondance.' Bonaparte's aide-de-camp Sulkowski commented ruefully on this new cynicism. 'Si l'on admet', he wrote, 'que la soif de l'or suffit pour éteindre toute vertu civique, il est constant que l'amour du pillage a attiédi dans nos guerriers celui de la Patrie et de la Gloire.' Bonaparte tried to keep the army in check by instituting a system of financial bonuses, and a series of fines to discourage the private sale of vital equipment. The troops entering Verona were paid twenty-four livres each *not* to loot the city.

The army was growing more distant from the nation. As the terms of service lengthened, so an *esprit de corps* developed within each unit, and each army. The Army of Italy was known as a Jacobin army, while the Army of the Rhin-et-Moselle was renowned for its Royalist sympathies. In Italy, Bernadotte's division, where the form of address was the counter-revolutionary 'Monsieur' rather than the Republican 'Citoyen', clashed with the Republican division of Masséna. Soldiers developed a strong sense of loyalty to their own particular general, especially Bonaparte, who, by paying his troops in cash, had transformed the army of Italy into virtually his own private army. Soldiers began to regard their generals almost like feudal barons, paternal figures who distributed gifts and patronage to their faithful followers, just like the Ancien Régime *seigneurs* who had recruited their own peasants to their regiments. For Bricard, 'chaque soldat voyait dans son général [e.g. Kléber] un père, un ami, aussi capable que vertueux', and in the Year 8, many were willing to sacrifice five days' pay for a monument to Désaix and Kléber.

The army still had a political rôle to play, but in fructidor Year 5 and brumaire Year 8, it acted against the expressed wishes of the electorate. It had forgotten the phrase in the Constitution of the Year 3 which stipulated that 'la force publique est essentiellement obéissante', to become the tool first of the Directorials, and then of one ambitious general. It had ceased to be a national army. In the referendum on the Constitution of the Year 3, the army had voted in favour by a margin of over 73,000 to less than 2,000, and it remained faithful to the thermidorean majority in the Year 3, and in vendémiaire Year 4. Under the Directory, troops on active service did not vote. In theory perhaps, the army was still the nation in arms, composed of thinking Republicans, but in practice it was becoming a passive tool in the hands of its leaders. Under Napoleon, it became 'un corps établi, docile, honorifique, et ouvre carrière à l'ascension sociale' (Reinhard).[1] General Stanislas de Girardin addressed his troops thus in the Year 10: 'Camarades, il est question de nommer Bonaparte consul à vie. Les opinions sont libres, entièrement libres. Cependant, je dois vous prévenir que le premier d'entre vous qui ne votera pas pour le Consulat à vie, je le ferai fusiller devant le front de son régiment. Vive la liberté!'

The Republic had lost control of its armies. It had attempted to maintain liaison through its *commissaires,* who were given the same functions as the *Représentants en mission,* but, unlike them, could not issue decrees on their own initiative. They failed to stop looting and indiscipline, or financial waste by generals and officers, with whom they frequently came into conflict. The government, which needed the support of its generals, was not prepared to back the *commissaires* up to the hilt against them. After floréal Year 5, the *commissaires* were abolished, and only temporarily re-established in frimaire Year 7. Then their attempt to curtail the authority of the generals threw the military leaders into the camp of the brumairiens.

By the end of the Directory, the army was no longer the natural extension of the Republican nation which its creators had

[1] Bibliography no. 156.

intended it to be. The election of officers had been abandoned, and its 'patriotism' had become a pliable instrument in the overthrow of the representatives of the political nation. The army was becoming a praetorian army, with its own professional interests. In Imperial society, its leaders enjoyed elevated status, wealth, and respect. Military service was no longer regarded as the patriotic duty of every citizen, but as a specialised career. Perhaps this growing professionalism was inevitable. Many were to think so, like General du Barail at the beginning of the Third Republic, when he argued that 'Rien que par sa devise, La République est la négation de l'armée, car Liberté, Egalité, et Fraternité veulent dire indiscipline, oubli de l'obéissance et négation des principes hiérarchiques.' The ideal of the nation in arms, however, remains a basic principle for some socialist societies, and for anyone who wants to minimise the distinctions between the soldier and the civilian. The armies of the First French Republic will keep their place in political mythology, by virtue of their victories, at Fleurus, in Egypt, and, above all, in Italy.

ADMINISTRATION AND THE 'CONSPIRACY OF INDIFFERENCE'

C'était la conspiration de l'insouciance, insouciance perfide qui laisse le
champ libre au royalisme et à l'anarchie.
                              —*Tableau analytique de la Seine*, germinal Year 7

Under the Terror, political indifference was a crime. Failure to
denounce one's neighbours' indiscretions, or to put in a regular
appearance at sectional meetings made one suspect in the eyes of
the Jacobin authorities. Under the Robespierrist dictatorship, the
government aimed at correcting vice and rewarding virtue in the
merest details of private life. The messengers of the Terror
propagated a Republican code of morality, which even regulated marital relations, forms of dress and of conversation. At
every turn, politics impinged on individual privacy. The private
individual needed to think before he spoke in public: a careless
phrase might be reported to an over-eager informer. His mail
might be intercepted, the company he kept was noted, and it was
dangerous for him to visit a brothel or a gambling-house. He was
told that even his children belonged to the *patrie*. His private life
was a public concern.

Under the more liberal régime of the Directory, the central
government was weaker and less intrusive. It was easier to retire
from the exhausting pressures of five years of Revolution, and to
devote oneself, undisturbed by the rhetorical sermonising of
prying officialdom, to peaceful pursuits like raising a family or
running an estate. A cloud of political apathy settled over France.
It was this lack of any passionate enthusiasm for or against the
régime which followed it to continue for four years: longer than
any of the previous revolutionary régimes. It was the same lack of
enthusiasm which allowed Bonaparte to end it, with hardly a
ripple of resistance.

The Directory made the minimum of demands on the private
citizen. The public administration of France touched his private
life at three main points: at election time, in demands for the
payment of taxes, and for military service. This chapter is chiefly

concerned with these three topics, and the passive resistance encountered by the administration in all of them.

Private obscurity was a comfortable alternative to an insecure and poorly paid public post. The Directory never succeeded in breaching the impenetrable wall of indifference with which the régime came to be regarded, both by individuals and local communities. Both individual apathy and the surviving spirit of local independence prevented the régime from taking a firm grip on the administration of the provinces. In previous chapters I have already pointed out the most spectacular consequences of the central government's ineffectiveness, such as the White Terror in the Rhone valley, and outbreaks of banditry in many other areas. The sullen resistance of local populations, often aided by the complicity of government officials themselves, thwarted the prompt execution of the Directory's decrees. Local authorities would connive at the illegal activities of refractory priests, and at the protection of returning *émigrés*. In order to preserve the continuity and tranquil equilibrium of social and political life in the small towns and villages of rural France, the eye of vigilance winked at such misdemeanours.

The Royalist insurrection of the Year 7 in the South-west, to be discussed more fully in Chapter 15, is a typical illustration of the impotence of the central government. The presence of large bands of deserters in the Pyrenéan departments escaped the vigilance of the local authorities, trees of liberty were felled with impunity, and refractory priests were not effectively pursued. The rebellion was signalled long in advance. Not only was the government unable to prevent its outbreak, but it played little part in extinguishing the rebellion. The crushing of the revolt was a purely local responsibility, the burden falling chiefly on the shoulders of the Jacobin municipality of Toulouse.

In spite of popular apathy, however, the Directory's administrative record was not entirely a negative one. The régime created the beginnings of a permanent government bureaucracy, and it established a system of taxation, which provided the basis of the French fiscal system for decades to come. If posterity has reason to respect the Directory's achievement, this raised no spark of enthusiasm amongst contemporaries.

This chapter, therefore, must also consider the positive aspects of Directorial administration. First, however, a brief outline of local and central administration under the Directory is necessary.

The thermidoreans considerably modified the centralised administrative system outlined in the Terrorist law of 14 frimaire II. The Constitution of the Year 3 abolished municipal councils in communes which had less than 5,000 inhabitants. Instead, small communes were to elect an *agent municipal*, and his *adjoint*, who attended the newly-created cantonal administrations. The canton thus replaced the unit of the district, which had played an important rôle under the Terror. The communes were left with the tasks of keeping tax-rolls, and the État-Civil; in other spheres of administration, the canton was to combine the powers of the old communes and the districts, and to provide a link between the commune and the department. This scheme was reminiscent of the Girondin plan to create *grandes communes*, to submerge the Jacobin influence of the urban areas in larger and more rural administrative units. Only in larger cities, like Toulouse and Dijon, did ex-Jacobins continue to exert a dominant influence over municipal administration.

Directly above the canton in the local administrative hierarchy was the department, which now enjoyed wide powers. The department was responsible for police, justice, education, public works, the collection of taxes, and the sale of the *biens nationaux*. The *agents municipaux* were accountable to it. The departmental council was composed of five men, one of whom was to be renewed annually. It was generally composed of town-dwellers and sat in the *chef-lieu du département*.

At every level of local administration – commune, canton, and department – the authorities were supervised by an agent of the central government, the *commissaire du Directoire*. The *commissaire central du département*, for example, was to be present at every meeting, and although he did not officially have a vote, no decision was to be taken until he had given his opinion. He was responsible for supervising the execution of the laws, corresponded directly with the Minister of the Interior, and could postpone the execution of decrees and recommend the suspension of administrators. His rôle resembled that of the Napoleonic prefects.

The *commissaires* were powerful men. Many had served as *procureurs-généraux* of the districts and departments in the Year 2, or as mayors. Many ex-deputies resumed their political careers as *commissaires du Directoire*, like Garnier in the Meuse, and Laloy in the Haute-Marne. Robert Lindet was appointed *commissaire central* in the Eure. Ex-Conventionnels who were appointed frequently clashed with the more moderate departmental authorities. In spite of the purges which followed fructidor and floréal, they were a relatively stable body of administrators. Twelve departmental *commissaires* remained in office throughout the Directory.

Unlike the *Représentants en mission* of the Year 2, and the prefects of the Empire, the *commissaires* were mainly local men. Their departments often rewarded their services by electing them as deputies. The career of Veyrieu of Toulouse is typical in this respect. In 1790, he was a judge in the district tribunal. In 1791, he represented the Haute-Garonne in the Legislative Assembly. He did not hold office during the Terror, but in the Year 4 he was chosen as *commissaire central* in the Haute-Garonne. Within a year he was sitting as a deputy in the Conseil des Cinq Cents. Other *commissaires* attained even greater heights. François de Neufchâteau, like Veyrieu, represented his department of the Vosges in the Legislative Assembly. After the Terror, he was to become the Directory's *commissaire* in the Vosges, then Minister of the Interior, and Director.

The local deputies, too, had a powerful influence over local affairs. They usually formed a coherent group, united by their local origins, often sharing accommodation in Paris. The Conseil des Cinq Cents often seemed as if it was formed out of a collection of local lobbies. The local *députation* was consulted by the government on local appointments, and thus had wide patronage within its own department. The *députation* of the Haute-Garonne, coming from an important administrative centre like Toulouse, might even have a voice in appointments in other neighbouring departments. The *députation* was the medium through which local interests were sympathetically presented to the ministries.

There was no such *esprit de corps* amongst the ministers of the Directory, whose rôle was that of subordinate clerks. They did not discuss their affairs in common, they were excluded from the legislative chambers, and the Directors received them one at a time. At first six ministries were established, but in pluviôse IV, a seventh was added, when the Ministry of the Interior spawned a separate Ministry of Police. Ministers were replaced frequently, and the Ministry of Police, politically an extremely sensitive post, was a particular casualty, changing hands eight times under the Directory (see Appendix to this chapter). Nevertheless, a few individuals held their ministries long enough to make a lasting impression on the conduct of policy. Ramel, for example, the longest-standing minister, held the Ministry of Finance for over three years. The Ministry of Foreign Affairs was held by Charles Delacroix for twenty months, and by his successor, Talleyrand, for two years. Of the thirty-two men who held ministerial positions under the Directory, nine were ex-Conventionnels, and of these, several had been Montagnards: Cochon, Merlin de Douai, Génissieux, and Delacroix in the Year 4, and later Fouché, Dubois-Crancé, and Robert Lindet, who held office briefly at the end of the Year 7. More typical of the Directory's ministers were moderate men like Truguet (Navy), Merlin de Douai (Police), and committeemen like Cambacérès (Justice), and Ramel. Perhaps most typical was Charles Cochon (Police), a faceless and uninspiring bureaucrat, tailor-made for the prefectures of the Empire. An undistinguished provincial lawyer from the *bourgeoisie* of Fontenay-le-Comte, in the Vendée *bleue*, Cochon only became a deputy by accident in 1789, when he took the place of a dead colleague. He was a man of little imagination or originality, but had a clear head, and could present a sound brief. He was an energetic Conventionnel. He owed his appointment as Minister of Police to the influence of Carnot, and when in office, he reacted to the inevitable puns on his surname with humourless inscrutability. He became an efficient and merciless administrator in the suppression of the Babeuf conspiracy, and the attack on the military camp of Grenelle.

The diplomatic corps, from which several ministers were recruited, amalgamated Ancien Régime expertise with revolutionary vigour. Barthélémy, for example, had been trained in the tradition of Vergennes, while Delacroix served his apprenticeship as secretary to Turgot in the intendancy of Limoges. Faipoult, on the other hand, the Directory's *commissaire* in Rome, had been *chef de bureau* in the Committee of Public Safety. Reinhard, French minister to the Hanseatic ports, and then in Florence, was by origin a Wurtemburger. At first a professor of German in Bordeaux, he had been promoted by the Girondins. Service as a diplomatic representative of the Directory often preceded appointment to a ministry in Paris. Sotin, for example, served in Genoa, and Lecarlier arrived at the Police Ministry via his post as *commissaire* to the Helvetic Army. Bernadotte, too, spent a brief but tumultuous term of office in the embassy in Vienna before becoming War Minister. Except for the disastrous appointment of Bernadotte, the Directory did attempt to be tactful in its appointment of diplomatic representatives to the European courts. As a general rule, no regicide was given a diplomatic post. The Madrid embassy, a very sensitive post, was the only one entrusted to an ex-noble (Pérignon).

Alongside the ministries, the Directors employed their own private secretaries, and built up a series of specialised bureaus, which, with the staffs of the ministries, formed the nucleus of a permanent civil service. Church, in his study of over five thousand men employed in the ministries, found that Directorial civil servants were comparatively young, and predominantly from the north-east of France, a traditional area of immigration into the capital, and also the best-educated part of France.[1] The Directory succeeded in the civil service, where it failed in politics and in education, in reconciling the extremes of French opinion. For the civil service amalgamated Ancien Régime *fonctionnaires* with new revolutionary personnel. Two-thirds of the corps had entered the civil service since thermidor II, and one-third had been employed before 1788. The personnel were becoming increasingly permanent, and dynasties of civil servants were developing: Arnould, chief of the *bureau de commerce*, was succeeded in 1798 by his son. Both the Arnoulds had served under the Ancien Régime. There was little political animosity within the ranks of the civil service. When, after the rising of vendémiaire IV, a special commission was set up to purge the civil service of royalist infiltrators, very few were found. Only about nine per cent of the 11,000-strong Parisian bureaucracy was accused of Royalism, and the ministries ignored over one-third of the commission's recommendations for dismissal. The mixture of Ancien Régime experience and new revolutionary practice was able to survive the political fluctuations of the Directory, and ninety per cent of civil service personnel held their jobs under Napoleon. This was one of the many ways in which the Consulate built on the work of the Directory.

[1] Bibliography no. 161.

The Directors themselves are discussed elsewhere (see Chapter 1). Here only their recruitment must be noted. New Directors had either distinguished themselves as ambassadors abroad, like Barthélémy, or had risen from the ranks of the ministries, like François de Neufchâteau, and Merlin de Douai. Siéyès had a unique political reputation which makes him an exceptional case, and he brought with him an important political clientèle, in the form of Roger-Ducos, and Quinette, the Directory's last Minister of the Interior.

The list of men who failed to become Directors is equally instructive. The former ministers Cochon and Delacroix were turned down by the Conseil des Anciens. Cochon was perhaps too Royalist, and Delacroix too Jacobin. Moderate nonentities like Gohier and General Moulin were more successful. With the exception of Moulin, the Conseil des Anciens repeatedly rejected the candidatures of military leaders. Augereau, for example, the executioner of fructidor, was twice rejected in favour of Merlin and François de Neufchâteau; Masséna, four times a candidate, was four times passed over. Barras, too, claimed to have dissuaded Bonaparte from standing as a candidate for a Directorship. This was a significant riposte to those who accused the Directory of being the pawn of its generals.

The administration of the Directory was thus apparently very diffuse. It was divided at the centre between five men, who had private links with their ministers, who were, in their turn, with some notable exceptions, victims of abrupt political changes. At a lower level, administration depended too heavily on the cumbersome and rather artificial unit of the canton. Between the localities and Paris, the informal pressures exerted by local deputies were often decisive. Amidst this dispersal of authority, two centralising and stabilising influences can be discerned: the *commissaires du Directoire auprès des départements*, and the growing government bureaucracy. In the last resort, however, authority lies with those who hold the power of appointment. In these terms, the balance of power seemed to lie with individual Directors like Carnot, Barras, and Siéyès, who could command personal followings, and with the departmental lobbies in the legislature.

The successful working of this administrative system was vitiated from the start by the almost universal reluctance of officials to take up their posts. The resignations of the *agents municipaux*, in particular, amounted to what has been called an 'administrative strike'. In the Year 4, for example, in the recently-assimilated Mont-Terrible, the presidents of five cantons, together with forty-one *agents municipaux*, and twenty-four of their *adjoints*, refused to serve. Those who did not resign were far from assiduous in their attendance at meetings. Many *agents* used the meetings of the cantonal administration simply as excuses for social gatherings, leaving the work and the decisions to the *commissaire du Directoire*.

Some resignations were forced by the exclusions of the relatives of *émigrés* from public office, but the majority were offered with lame excuses which showed how little confidence the régime inspired. Some pleaded illiteracy, old age, or illness, like the administrator at Gemeaux (Côte d'Or), who, in case he should be asked to serve again, made it clear that 'il ne guérirait probablement jamais'. For others, the journey from their commune to the *chef-lieu du canton* deterred them from taking office. Others had to attend to their personal affairs, neglected since the beginning of the Revolution. Some agreed under pressure to serve 'provisionally'. The anonymity of private life was everywhere preferable to taking up a poorly-paid post with unpleasant duties. The *commissaires* of the cantons, for instance, were paid only three hundred francs per year, which they often supplemented by taking employment as schoolteachers, or as secretaries to the municipalities. Later, especially in the Year 7, local administrators were asked to perform tasks which made them very unpopular in their local community. Rather than incur the hostility of their neighbours by executing requisitioning orders, or by collecting the forced loan, they preferred to resign. Discretion got the better of patriotic duty for those who, in the words of the *Journal de la Côte d'Or*, retired 'paisiblement dans leur famille méditer à leur aise sur les vicissitudes de la fortune'. This lack of confidence in the régime was apparent even at the highest echelons. Pléville le Peley resigned as Minister for the Navy, pleading old age and infirmity (he did have a wooden leg). Gaudin refused the Police Ministry, and Siéyès the Ministry of Foreign Affairs.

The Directory attempted to bring local communities to heel by threatening to appoint *agents municipaux* itself, if none could be found, but this was not calculated to encourage the growth of civic spirit. Recalcitrant villages were forced to request the services of the *agents* of neighbouring communes, at their own expense. The purges which followed the *coup* of fructidor V, '*le valse des agents*', threatened to eliminate the majority of those who were eligible and willing to serve, and made recruitment even more difficult. In the Sarthe, for example, the elections of 807 *agents municipaux* and their *adjoints* were at first annulled, but one-third of them were reinstated. In the areas of the West affected by the *chouannerie*, posts were filled by nominations from the central government.

This *grève des administrateurs* was accompanied by a *grève des administrés*. Electoral results are a vivid illustration of popular apathy, and of the extent to which successive *coups d'état* had devalued the electoral process. Judging from the local studies available, the primary electoral assemblies of the Year 5 attracted barely one voter in three: 28 per cent voted in the Sarthe, 28 per cent in Colmar, and 29 per cent in Toulouse. In some cities, however, a much heavier poll was recorded. Le Mans, where 82 per cent of the electorate voted, was one of these exceptions, and in Dijon, about 50 per cent went to the polls. Abstentions had multiplied, however, by the Year 7, when the proportion of voters was perhaps nearer one-tenth of the electorate. Only 8 per cent voted in the Meurthe in the Year 7, less than 10 per cent in the Sarthe, and 12½ per cent in Colmar. The stagnant calm of this year expressed the population's total lack of concern for politics.

Popular antipathy towards revolutionary and Republican taxation also undermined the administrative reforms of the Directory. This, however, was not the only obstacle to the Directory's fiscal policies. Revenue from taxes was limited by the administrative inadequacies of all eighteenth-century régimes, and by the inflation of the *assignats*. It is therefore to the Directory's credit that some degree of organisation was imposed on the fiscal system by the Year 8.

The Constituent Assembly had accepted the principle of fiscal equality, but the collection of a truly universal direct tax would have put an intolerable strain on any government of the period. Accurate land surveys, for example, equitable assessments, and the task of keeping these up to date demanded a sophisticated administrative apparatus, which no government of this period yet possessed. Hence the collection of taxes itself was inordinately expensive, and the monarchy had entrusted it to tax farmers.

What methods of taxation lay open to the Directory? The Revolutionaries considered any form of poll-tax a tyrannical practice, more appropriate to countries under the yoke of 'Oriental despotism', than to free citizens. Taxes on consumption were roundly condemned by the Physiocratic school, which argued that they were hard to collect, discriminated against the poor, and encouraged contraband. The Constituent Assembly had abolished indirect taxation, but on the insistence of Ramel, they were tentatively reintroduced under the Directory. The most satisfactory, direct, and universal form of taxation at this time was a tax on land. This was entirely appropriate to a predominantly agricultural country, whose main source of wealth, as the Physiocrats never ceased to emphasise, was its territory. The Constituent Assembly supervised the compilation of tax-rolls based on the value of land in 1791, the *matrices foncières*. The information provided to assess liability during the Revolution was largely supplied by the taxpayers themselves. A more sophisticated organisation would have taken years to establish. The Directory, always short of money, and in need of quick returns, relied on the assessments made by its predecessors.

The Directory inherited considerable tax arrears. In the Year 4, the taxes of 1793 and the Year 2, and in some cases those of earlier years, had not been fully collected. The administration was thus burdened with the collection of arrears throughout the Directory, and it is thus hardly surprising if some areas continually paid the land tax a year in arrears throughout this period. The abolition of the district administrations did not make the task of collection any easier. In brumaire VI, an attempt was made to accelerate tax collection by the establishment of departmental collecting agencies, the *Agences des Contributions Directes*, but as long as assessment was still left to the municipalities, it remained arbitrary, and was still based on out-of-date surveys.

The decline in the value of the *assignat* reduced the real value of the taxes which were collected. Half of the land tax of the Year 3 could be paid in *assignats*, and taxpayers took the opportunity to fulfil their patriotic duty at little personal expense, by unloading worthless *assignats* on the government. The Treasury was flooded with valueless paper currency, and receipts for requisitions. As Barras remarked, 'Le contribuable qui paie s'enrichit véritablement à l'instant qu'il s'acquitte.' It seemed as if the only purpose in collecting such taxes was to take an enormous amount of paper currency out of circulation.

The nation's tax-paying capacity, however, increased with the good harvests of the Years 6 and 7, and the stabilisation of the currency helped to increase government revenue from taxation. Until this happened, the Directory, pressed by the needs of war, was forced to supplement its revenue from the principal direct taxes by a series of expedients. The forced loan, and new indirect taxes increased the régime's unpopularity.

The Directory inherited the land tax and the *patente* from the Constituent Assembly. The land tax provided the bulk of the government's revenue from taxation. In the Year 5, its yield was forecast at 240 million francs. At first, however, its collection was complicated by the order to pay one-half in *assignats* and one-half in grain. Although taxpayers were ready to rid themselves of the *assignats*, only armed force could compel them to part with grain, especially in the famine year of 1795.

The *patente* was a direct tax on trade licences. It was estimated at one-tenth of the rent paid on commercial premises. The *patente* was an unpopular tax, falling sometimes on peasants who were engaged in a trade on a part-time basis, and including the poorest artisans who were technically engaged in commercial activity. By the Year 6 and the Year 7, however, revenue from the *patente* continued to increase.

The *impôt mobilière, personnelle et somptuaire*, repeatedly clarified under the Directory, was, together with the land tax and the *patente*, the third of the four main taxes on which the Directory relied. The *impôt somptuaire* was a tax on luxuries like chimneys, domestic servants, and carriages. This was naturally very rarely levied in the countryside, unlike the tax on movable property (*mobilière*), which tended to hit the peasantry hardest. After nivôse VII, this tax was calculated from the tenant's rent. The *impôt personnelle*, which resembled a poll-tax, was levied at the equivalent of three days' wages. Only the indigent were exempt.

The fourth tax of the quartet, levied on doors and windows, survived until 1925. Introduced in the Year 7, this tax had the virtue of clarity, requiring a payment of twenty centimes on every window, and one franc on every door. Within a few months, the tax was doubled.

Ramel, at the Ministry of Finance, was largely responsible for this rationalisation and reconstruction of the fiscal system. In spite of reluctance to pay the *patente*, and the massive arrears, these reforms formed the basis of financial recovery under Napoleon. Nevertheless, the land tax, the *patente*, and the taxes on movable property, doors, and windows, were never enough to meet the government's expenditure. In the Year 6, the deficit was estimated at 250 million francs. The government was forced to seek extra income from the conquered territories and from the sale of *biens nationaux*.

The forced loan of the Year 4 was a desperate measure, hastily improvised to meet the deficit. The tax was to be levied on France's wealthiest citizens, and it was optimistically expected to provide 600 million francs. Recent purchasers of *biens nationaux* immediately took fright. The tax was assessed in the most arbitrary way by the municipalities. In Toulouse, for example, the Jacobin municipality discriminated against its political opponents. Men described as '*agioteurs*' in the tax-rolls were assessed for large sums, and Brouilhet, editor of the thermidorean newspaper *L'Anti-Terroriste*, was asked for an astronomical 300,000 livres. Objections were raised, and this delayed collection. Some communes flatly refused to draw up a list of their wealthiest citizens. The government recovered only a fraction of the sum intended.

The government was thus induced to supplement its revenue by reverting to Ancien Régime practices of indirect taxation. There was no return, however, to possibly the most lucrative source of indirect taxation: salt. The Conseil des Anciens, well aware of the sinister connotations of the *gabelle*, vetoed a proposal for a salt tax, which the lower chamber had taken twelve sessions to approve. The other indirect taxes which were introduced in the Year 7 were the least popular aspects of the Directory's fiscal policies.

The most productive of these indirect taxes were those on the registration of legal documents, and the stamp tax on newspapers. The most controversial was the resurrection of a form of *octroi*, or municipal toll. The hated *barrières* were rebuilt on the outskirts of towns to collect this tax, which proved an expensive one to administer. Municipalities had to find the money to build the toll-gates, and to pay guards to man them. Money sometimes could not be found to pay guards to work at night, and travellers and salesmen were able to evade the toll under cover of darkness. Furthermore, the tax-collectors themselves might always be susceptible to bribery. The toll levied was never more than one franc, and the revenue barely covered the cost of its collection. The main consequence was to raise the price of goods on the urban market. The *barrières* were the scenes of several popular riots, like those at Le Mans and Toul. Elsewhere, they were destroyed by arson. So unprofitable was this *droit de passe* that it was first leased out to farmers and then abolished in 1806, when Napoleon decided to replace it by a salt tax.

In 1795, France was in the throes of famine, while large areas of the West had not yet recovered from the ravages of civil war. These were not propitious conditions for the organisation of an efficient system of taxation. In spite of the troubled state of France at the beginning of the Directory, in spite of tax arrears, and in spite of the ill-will of taxpayers, Ramel succeeded in laying the foundations of an enduring fiscal structure. Direct taxation was still relatively arbitrary in its distribution, however, and never succeeded in meeting the Directory's expenses. The various expedients employed to eliminate the deficit incurred popular hostility, even if they may have helped the Directory to keep direct taxes low.

Meanwhile an attempt was made to establish the assessment of France's taxes on a sounder basis. In his second term at the Ministry of the Interior, François de Neufchâteau began an ambitious scheme to catalogue France's resources. He aimed at collecting statistical information on the population, topography, agriculture, and industrial resources of every French department. The departmental authorities were slow to react to his requests for information. By germinal VIII, only seven departments had submitted answers to the government's extensive questionnaires. Nevertheless, the work of compiling statistical information about every aspect of French life was carried forward by his successors, Lucien Bonaparte and Chaptal. This programme, inaugurated by François de Neufchâteau, was an important step in acquiring the information which would enable future governments to arrive at a more equitable geographic distribution of taxation.

The most spectacular index of apathy towards the régime was the reaction to a different form of imposition, the 'blood tax'. The events leading up to the reintroduction of conscription in messidor VII will be described in Chapter 15. Here it is enough to suggest that desertion, or more frequently, refusal to obey the call-up, was eloquent testimony to popular contempt for the Directory.

Desertion had begun to take on alarming proportions in the Years 3 and 4, when the foreign invading armies seemed to have been defeated, and near-famine conditions prevailed at the front. Desertion then became not just an isolated phenomenon, but a mass movement, as bands of deserters roamed the countryside. In the Pyrenees, for example, official calculations estimated the number of deserters in the district of St-Gaudens at 3,000 in the winter of the Year 4. Here the mountainous terrain offered safe hiding-places for deserters and '*insoumis*'. They enjoyed the protection of local communities; in Faget (Haute-Garonne), the mayor himself had deserted from the 22nd regiment of dragoons. These wandering bands of deserters were to become the rank and file of the Royalist insurrection of the Year 7.

In response to the call-up of the Year 7, desertion again continued on an alarming scale, particularly in the Nord, the Pyrenees, the Massif Central, and the Mediterranean coast. Deserters were likely to see their family's property confiscated, or soldiers billeted in their parents' homes, and yet in France as a whole, the *levée* was only about sixty per cent effective. In the Meurthe, where the desertion rate was relatively low, the *gendarmerie* arrested 1,200 deserters in the Year 7. The Charente, another comparatively docile department, produced little over forty per cent of its allotted contingent for the first two *levées* of the Year 7. In the Mont-Terrible, over one-half of those called up did not appear. After desertion, and elimination of the physically unfit, only nineteen per cent of this department's contingent actually stayed to fight. Amongst those turned away were men who had deliberately severed their right thumbs with an axe, or removed their canine teeth, so repugnant to them was the idea of serving the armies of the Directory. Without their thumbs, they could not handle a gun, and without their teeth, they could not tear a cartridge. Others feigned deafness or short-sightedness, and demonstrated their claims of epilepsy or incontinence of the bladder. If France was reluctant to go to the polls, then its armies certainly voted with their feet in the Year 7. Cobb has seen the massive desertion of this period as a kind of walking referendum in condemnation of the régime.[1]

[1] Bibliography no. 15.

Once again, the central government proved incapable of enforcing its own decrees. It could not persuade local administrators to accept office. It could not persuade electors to vote. It could not force recalcitrant authorities to levy the forced loan, pursue refractory priests, or answer government questionnaires. It could not prevent them from condoning massive desertion.

These glaring failures, however, should not disguise the important reforms initiated during the period of the Directory. The *commissaires du Directoire*, at municipal, cantonal, and departmental level, formed part of a logical administrative hierarchy. A government bureaucracy was developing, which combined Ancien Régime experience with revolutionary talent, and survived the repeated political shifts of the régime. The basis was laid for a rational and enduring fiscal structure, and the government began to collect much-needed information on the activities and resources of its subjects. The administrative reforms of the Directory were an important part of its work of reconstruction; but it was left to future generations to reap the benefit.

Appendix. *The ministers of the Directory*

Date of appoint- ment	War	Navy	Justice	Interior	Finance	Foreign Affairs	Police
Brum. IV	Aubert du Bayet	Truguet	Merlin de Douai	Bénézech	Faipoult	Delacroix	
Niv. IV			Génissieux				
Pluv. IV	Petiet				Ramel-Nogaret		Merlin de Douai
Germ. IV			Merlin de Douai				Cochon de Lapparent
Mess. V		Pléville-le Peley		François de Neufchâteau		Talleyrand	Lenoir-Laroche
Therm. V	Schérer						Sotin
Fruct. V				Letourneux			
Vend. VI			Lambrechts				
Pluv. VI							Dondeau
Flor. VI		Bruix					Lecarlier
Prair. VI				François de Neufchâteau			
Brum. VII							Duval
Vent. VII	Milet de Mureau						
Mess. VII	Bernadotte	Bourdon de Vatry		Quinette			Bourguignon
Therm. VII			Cambacérès		R. Lindet	Reinhard	Fouché
Fruct. VII	Dubois-Crancé						

12

ECONOMIC LIFE

The Revolution removed many of the legal obstacles which had hitherto hindered the development of modern capitalism in France. The abolition of the seigneurial system ended restrictions on private property. The abolition of internal tolls created a single, unified domestic market. The restrictive practices of the guilds were swept away, and the Directory continued to harass the *compagnonnages*. When the *compagnons du Devoir* met at Tours in the Year 7, some of them were arrested as anti-Republicans, on the pretext that they had assembled illegally on Sundays and religious holidays. In the Year 4, after a series of strikes in Paris, workers in paper manufactures had to give their employers forty days' notice before leaving their jobs. The introduction of a *livret* system was to strengthen employers still further against workers' associations.

In spite of these changes, however, the French economy failed to seize the opportunities offered for the rapid advance of capitalist enterprise. During the nineteenth century, France fell further behind her European competitors, losing the strong economic position she had held in the Ancien Régime. France's failure to achieve an English-style industrial revolution has been variously attributed to the lack of cheaply available natural resources like coal, to political instability in the nineteenth century, and to psychological or cultural factors, like the timidity of the French entrepreneur. In this chapter, however, the discussion is restricted to the state of the French economy immediately after the revolutionary years. It examines why the forces released by the Revolution did not immediately lead to rapid economic growth. The Revolution had a significant impact on patterns of population growth, but the distribution of population remained stable. The land settlement of the Revolution reinforced the conservatism of French agriculture. The Directory's short-term problems of inflation and deflation disrupted economic life, and delayed the elaboration of a sophisticated system of credit. Finally, the impact of war on the economy will be assessed. The Directory had enormous problems to solve, but after the confusion of its early years, it began to stabilise its finances. While war inevitably and brutally interrupted the traditional progress of trade and industry, it also redirected economic activity towards new goals. Although France could never compete with the new industrial might of Britain, the Directory's work of reconstruction helped lay the basis for economic resurgence in the future, and for the continuous, if relatively slow, economic progress of the nineteenth century.

France's chief economic resource at the end of the eighteenth century lay in her reserves of manpower. The increase in her population during the Ancien Régime varied from region to region, but in Upper Languedoc, for instance, it had amounted to forty-five per cent since 1730. By 1801, France's total population was about 27·5 million. In Dupâquier's phrase, France was the China of Europe. This demographic strength was an essential condition of French expansion during the Revolutionary and Napoleonic wars. France could quickly replace the one million men lost in the wars of the Empire, and Napoleon could boast that he had an annual income of 100,000 men.

There were signs, however, that a new pattern of demographic change was emerging. In place of the high mortality and high birth rate of the Ancien Régime, the revolutionary period saw a decline in the birth and death rates, which were tending towards the relatively low levels familiar to modern industrial societies. The birth rate, measured in terms of the number of births for every one thousand inhabitants, declined from about thirty-five per year in the early 1780s to under thirty-two by the end of the Empire. The wider use of contraceptive methods, always difficult to assess, perhaps played a part in this. The death rate, too, fell from about thirty-two to about twenty-seven in the same period. The absence of plague epidemics and the diminishing risk of famine made this possible, while improved midwifery and the gradual popularisation of vaccination reduced the appalling infant mortality of the Ancien Régime.

The depression of the birth rate during the Directory was especially remarkable, since the period immediately following the Revolution was characterised by an astonishing increase in the marriage rate. The relaxation of the legal restrictions on divorce and the conscription of bachelors led to a stampede to the *mairie*. Although the number of illegitimate births rose in this period, especially in urban areas like Paris, the Nord, the Gironde, and the Bouches-du-Rhône, the fertility of married couples was in decline. Between the middle of the eighteenth century and 1815, the average number of children per family fell from about six to only four.

In some aspects, therefore, population growth was assuming a more 'modern' character. In others, traditional 'backwardness' prevailed. For instance, there was little progress towards increased urbanisation during the Directory. The definition of a town is not a question on which historians and sociologists can readily agree. Agulhon, for example, saw the most vital changes occurring in the life of Provençal communities when their population exceeded a threshold of only eight hundred inhabitants. For administrative purposes, French towns were arbitrarily defined as communities with over two thousand inhabitants. According to this over-rigid classification, only one Frenchman in five lived in a town by the time of the Empire. The emigration and economic crisis tended to reduce the population of many large towns. Nancy lost one-twelfth of its inhabitants between 1789 and the Consulate, but the population of Reims fell by one-third, and in Lyon, a centre of civil war and severe economic hardship, near the Swiss border, the population fell by almost one-quarter. Paris, with a population of over half a million, was five times as large as either Lyon or Marseille, its nearest rivals in size.

Eighteenth-century France therefore had a predominantly agricultural economy. The insistence of the Physiocratic school that France's main wealth lay in the land was entirely appropriate to such a pre-industrial society. Neither their efforts, nor the changes brought about by the Revolution succeeded in introducing any far-reaching alterations in French agriculture. The attachment of the peasants to tradition and routine was unshaken. They were, for the most part, content to till the soil in a three-year, or even a two-year cycle, leaving large stretches of arable land lying fallow for long periods. The most common form of fertiliser was still the limited supply of horse manure. Although the Revolutionaries tried to popularise the potato, and Napoleon temporarily raised the production of sugar-beet, the

forces of rural inertia generally stifled such attempts to introduce new forms of cultivation.

The development of manufactures in France was inevitably
retarded by industry's long dependence on the very low level of
peasant consumption. They still used implements of wood, rather
than of metal, and while most of their needs were satisfied by the
local craftsman, there was little domestic incentive for the mass
production of manufactured articles, with the possible exception
of textiles. A bad harvest, by reducing peasant purchasing power,
regularly had disastrous effects on industry. In the novels of
Eugène Leroy, the *métayers* of the Périgord, as late as the
mid-nineteenth century, worked only for their own subsistence,
and acquired money only for the purpose of paying their taxes.

Changes in agriculture could therefore prove fundamental for
the whole economy. A rapidly-expanding industrial economy
needs to recruit labour from the countryside, while greater
agricultural productivity is necessary to feed growing urban
populations. In agriculture, however, the Revolution did not
succeed in breaking the hold of the accumulated ignorance of the
centuries, or in releasing the forces of commercialism and
individual initiative. The criticisms made by Arthur Young in the
late eighteenth century remained valid. French agriculture was
retarded, in his view, by the proliferation of small-holdings, and
the snail-like pace of enclosures. The property transfers of the
revolutionary period multiplied small-holdings, which barely
supported their owners' families, and gave little possibility for
investment of profits, or agricultural improvement. In the Nord,
for example, three-quarters of the peasantry possessed no more
than one hectare (two and a half acres) per family, and relied on
collective grazing rights for their survival. Alsace was another
classic area of *morcellement*. In a sense, therefore, the sale of the
biens nationaux delayed the commercialisation of agriculture.
There were still large numbers of landless peasants in many
areas, but by increasing the number of small peasant proprietors, the Revolution did not hasten the growth of a mobile labour
force, which is an important ingredient in any industrial revolution. The economic promise of the Revolution was slow to
materialise. In spite of François de Neufchâteau's *sociétés agricoles*, innovations rarely attracted more than a few pioneers, and
the increase in the number of small-holdings perhaps prolonged
agricultural inefficiency. Political uncertainty and price fluctua-

tions dissuaded proprietors from granting leases longer than nine years.

The Revolution and the Directory hastened the disintegration of the peasant community itself. The proprietor of Picardy or the Flanders plain, who produced for the market, the *métayer*, or share-cropper in the South-west, and the landless labourer had very different economic interests. The wealthy farmer was perhaps in a position to profit from the sale of the *biens nationaux*, the abolition of the tithe, and the grain shortage. But the landless peasants of Normandy, or the Versaillais hardly shared his satisfaction. They were threatened, too, by the partition of common land, authorised by the Convention in June 1793, if this was demanded by one-third of the inhabitants of any commune. This legislation might have satisfied Arthur Young, but it threatened poorer peasants with extinction. Their cherished grazing rights would be lost, the members of their family might draw by lot completely dispersed plots of land, and would be forced to sell out to the wealthier farmers.

During the Directory, however, the defence of ancient communal rights against capitalist acquisition by larger landowners won some success. Since 1793, only a few communes had actually carried out the partition of their common land. Elsewhere difficulties were insuperable. Parts of the common had perhaps been usurped by individuals, and litigation was necessary to dislodge them. The expense involved in paying surveyors, and organising partition, frightened many communes. In some cases, the demand for the partition of valuable and fertile land was embarrassing. How could the commune of Grenade (Haute-Garonne), for example, share eighty acres of common land between 4,500 inhabitants? The peasants themselves were divided. Even the prefect of the Bas-Rhin opposed the scheme in 1802, arguing that a minority of one-third should not be allowed to impose its will on the majority, and voicing another complaint rather more typical of an Imperial administrator, namely that partition was likely to cause rowdy public meetings. In prairial IV, the Directory abandoned the campaign to partition common land. The preservation of collective rights had triumphed over the commercial interests of the larger proprietors.

In industry, too, the opportunities open to ambitious entrepreneurs were not immediately seized. Industry had a predominantly rural character. In Normandy, for instance, the textile industry was organised on a domestic basis by the merchants of Rouen or Elbeuf, through their peripatetic agents, the *fabriquants de campagne*. Carding wool or spinning cotton gave the peasantry a profitable occupation on long winter evenings, and provided an essential supplement to their incomes. In the Ariège, too, to take another example, metal was produced by the independent masters of small charcoal forges in the Pyrenéan forests. Large concentrations of industry were rare. Apart from a few well-known exceptions, like the ironworks at Le Creusot, or Chaptal's chemical works at Montpellier, the most developed sectors of French industry were those geared to luxury production, like the manufacture of porcelain, tapestries, or silk. French industry was predominantly artisanal in scale. In revolutionary Paris, only seventeen enterprises employed over two hundred workers. Thus, except for the booming Atlantic trade, capitalism was only in its embryonic stage on the eve of the Revolution.

No progress could be made until the Directory had restored financial stability. The Revolution interrupted the growth of trade and industry for as long as the inflation of the paper currency postponed a resumption of normal business activity. At the beginning of the Year 4, the *assignat* had fallen to less than one per cent of its face value. To some extent this decline betrayed a lack of confidence in the Republic, and the military successes of the Year 3 could no longer redeem the situation. The fall of the *assignat* was encouraged by the dismantling of the economic controls of the Terror, and the end of the demonetisation of gold and silver. Depreciation was further exacerbated by the over-issue of the *assignats:* in pluviôse IV, Ramel estimated that there were 39,000 millions of *assignats* in circulation. Above all, the food shortage and the soaring price of bread made the *assignat* worthless.

Merchants advertised their goods for sale at two prices: one in coin and the other in paper. They generally preferred to sell to regular customers, whose cash resources were well known. Manufacturers faced gigantic rises in the cost of labour and raw materials. The Directory itself granted wage increases to its employees, amounting to 3,000 per cent of wage levels in 1790. In the Dauphiné, the price of charcoal rose by 500 per cent between 1790 and the Year 3, while the price of steel increased by 1,500 per cent. By the end of the Year 6, an estimated 60,000 were unemployed in Paris.

The government found it difficult to find a way of replacing the *assignat*, without descrediting still further the currency already in circulation. Cambon planned its extinction, while his public speeches tried to bolster its value. The thermidorean government found only short-term remedies for the problem. The forced loan, for example, was intended to take *assignats* out of circulation, but perhaps encouraged merchants to raise prices still further, by passing the cost of the loan on to the consumer. The new *mandats territoriaux*, introduced to replace the *assignat* in ventôse IV, and again guaranteed by the unsold *biens nationaux*, were a failure. The Directory made the mistake of tying the value of the *mandat* to the discredited *assignat*, for thirty *assignats* could be exchanged for one *mandat*. By 1 floréal, the *mandats* had lost ninety per cent of their value, and in pluviôse V, they too were demonetised.

Faipoult and bankers like Lecouteulx canvassed the idea of a semi-independent bank, which would be allocated a proportion of the tax revenue, in return for a fixed monthly issue of banknotes. Jacobins, however, were unwilling to 'lock up the Constitution of 1795 in the bankers' vault'. The left wing still hoped to salvage the *assignat*, and instinctively distrusted the secret manoeuvrings of Parisian high finance. This project was defeated.

The Directory found, however, that the inevitable return to metallic currency created almost as many problems as it solved. Before the Year 5, there was far too much currency in circulation: after the Year 5, there was a desperate shortage of cash. A period of spiralling price rises was suddenly followed by a marked fall in prices. Commercial dealings and private contracts were temporarily thrown into a state of confusion. During the period of inflation, debtors hastened to acquit their debts in valueless paper currency, and in ventôse V, the government had reintroduced imprisonment for debt. In the subsequent period of deflation, however, borrowers of *assignats* found repayment in coin impossible, and demanded protection from the government.

Hoarding of cash during the political turmoil of the Revolution, and the flight of capital in the periods of the emigration created a shortage of money. Credit was expensive as interest rates soared. Short-term loans cost up to five per cent per month in the Corrèze, for example. Thus deflation brought in its wake a new kind of economic stagnation. There was even a partial return to a natural economy. Deputies' salaries were calculated in grain, employees demanded payment in bread or grain, and in Languedoc, in the Year 5, the eighteenth-century practice of paying leases in grain and other agricultural produce was current.

Production flagged in many areas. In Grenoble, for example, the glove industry worked at only half its capacity on the eve of the Revolution, and in Cholet, in the West, half of the looms lay idle by 1798. Elsewhere, however, the return to hard currency brought a revival of industrial activity. The mines of the Gard, which produced over 5,700 tons of coal in 1792, reduced their output by eighty-five per cent by the Year 4, but they produced 9,000 tons in the Year 6. Similarly, production in the mines of Anzin reached over eighty per cent of their pre-revolutionary level by the end of the Directory.

The peasantry had survived inflation better than urban consumers, but falling prices and good harvests were to reverse this situation. In Vienne, the price of wheat fell by twenty-eight per cent in three years, and in Thiers (Puy-de-Dôme), the lowest prices of the revolutionary period were recorded in the Year 7. The peasant found it increasingly difficult to sell his produce profitably, and he could no longer pay his taxes in depreciated paper currency.

It took rather longer for wages to follow this decline in prices, and as a result, their real value rose at the end of the Directory. According to Chabert, the average wages of an urban labourer rose by two-thirds between 1789 and 1806, but the counter-revolutionary economist d'Ivernois considered that the rise in agricultural wages was even higher.[1] In the Puy-de-Dôme at least, a man earning twelve sous for a day's labour in 1791 might be paid as much as one franc in the Year 7. Thus the rise in the value of wages experienced during the Empire had begun in the period of deflation at the end of the Directory.

Economic reconstruction could not be achieved overnight. Manufacturers found it difficult to resume normal business when raw materials, and especially fuel, were so costly, and when they were besieged with demands for higher wages. The monetary famine made credit scarce and expensive, and conscription complicated labour problems. The Revolution had created a

[1] Bibliography no. 171.

unified market. The abolition of internal tolls could not bear fruit, however, until more money was available to improve France's deteriorating roads and canals, and until the main communications routes were no longer infested with robbers.

France still lacked a sophisticated credit system. The Caisse des Comptes Courants, established in the Year 4, and the Caisse d'Escompte et de Commerce (Year 6), failed to reduce the lending rate below three or four per cent per month. They were, however, to provide the basis for the Banque de France. In the provinces, banks hardly existed, and borrowers were frequently dependent on private money-lenders, or the local municipal pawn-shops (Monts-de-Piété).

At a time when money was expensive, when prices fluctuated wildly, and profits were elusive, land seemed a gilt-edged investment. The Revolution encouraged the conservatism of the French *bourgeoisie*, by encouraging it to immobilise large amounts of capital in land, instead of in more productive commercial and manufacturing enterprises. Francis d'Ivernois asked, 'What Frenchman is mad enough to risk his fortune in a business enterprise, or in competition with foreign manufacturers? He would have to be satisfied with a profit of 10, or at the most 12 per cent, while the state offers him the possibility of realising a return of 30, 40, or even 50 per cent, if he places his money in one of the confiscated estates.' Inflation, the effects of war, and the shortage of credit made bankruptcy a commonplace in the police reports of the Directory. Large profits were not to be made from business in this period, except by speculators who were prepared to run enormous risks, or by those prepared to cultivate influential connections in order to secure government contracts.

The flight of capital into land, however, was not always a symptom of economic retardation. Landed property was frequently the indispensable accompaniment to a successful business career. In 1803, the list of the twelve largest contributors to the land tax in the department of the Ardennes included five manufacturers, and in the Nord, too, there were five businessmen on the list. Land was an important source of credit, and a guarantee against bankruptcy. It is perhaps significant that in this period the Directory developed the *code hypothécaire*, to help the peasantry to obtain mortgages on their property.

Amidst the confusion of the revolutionary period, the Directory laid the basis for progress in the future. In vendémiaire Year

6, in the '*liquidation Ramel*', the government 'consolidated' its debts. In other words, it declared its own bankruptcy. Two-thirds of the government's debts were to be repaid in bonds, which were valid for the purchase of *biens nationaux*. The government found itself in a strong position after the coup of fructidor, and wanted to seize the opportunity to renounce the whole debt, but Republican misgivings forced it to abandon such a drastic solution. In the Conseil des Anciens, the liquidation of the debt was denounced as an attack on property as immoral as highway robbery, and as callous as the frauds perpetrated by the government's own *fournisseurs*. The deputy Rousseau criticised the government's haste in carrying out the liquidation. He was amazed 'qu'on ait mis si peu de refléxion dans un projet qui tend à ruiner deux cent mille familles, et qui serait tout au plus digne de figurer dans le code d'un Gengis-Kan ou d'un Schah-Nadir'. The plight of the *rentiers* was indeed a pitiful one, and the police reports of the Directory are full of their miseries.[1] The government argued that it was better to guarantee one-third of their investments, than to leave them in continual uncertainty about interest payments. Critics replied that if the government could unilaterally refuse to honour its previous engagements, it could hardly expect *rentiers* to be confident about the security even of the remaining 'consolidated third'.

Enormous risks were involved. Public credit would be shattered, and the government might find it difficult in future to borrow money at home, or attract investment from abroad. Furthermore, the issue of yet another new paper bond played into the hands of currency speculators. On the other hand, the 'consolidation' reduced the government's annual expenditure by 160 million livres, and it removed the odious necessity of raising the level of taxation. This desperate and humiliating measure at least made possible a regular and balanced budget, although the renewed outbreak of war was to send government expenditure soaring again. Together with the new taxes described in chapter 11, the 'consolidation of the two-thirds' helped the Directory to stabilise the finances of France.

The régime also prepared the way for the introduction of decimal currency, after silver five-franc pieces were put into circulation in the Year 4. The Directory can further be credited

[1] Bibliography no. 1.

with putting the trade balance in surplus in 1799, for the last time for twelve years. The return to metallic currency was eventually to lead to an economic revival.

It was above all the war which first interrupted, and then redirected the economic development of eighteenth-century France. The war destroyed the leading sector of the Ancien Régime economy – foreign trade. The revolt in San Domingo and the loss of French colonies had already hit the West Indian trade, but the English blockade was to strike a decisive blow at prosperous Atlantic seaports, like Bordeaux, a wine-exporting centre, and an international entrepôt for colonial produce, and Nantes, which specialised in the slave trade. Not only did the economic life of these cities suffer, but so too did the ancillary industries which built and supplied their merchant fleets. The rope-makers of Tonneins, the sugar refineries and the tobacco manufactures of the Bordelais were all affected by the collapse of the Atlantic trade. Some colonial trade was still possible with the help of neutral vessels, and wine exports to the United States remained an important asset. Even these outlets, however, were closed by the bad wine harvest of 1797, the rupture with America, and later, by legislation which discriminated against neutral shipping.

Although Mediterranean trade managed to improve during the Directory, the war cut valuable overland trading routes. The loss of the Spanish market, for instance, deprived the textile industries of Languedoc of an important outlet, and affected the industry as far afield as the Dauphiné. The dispersal of the court and the emigration reduced demand for luxury silk articles produced in Lyon, and now Piedmont became an enemy power. In 1789, the city supported 8,000 workshops; in 1800, only 3,500 were still active. Foreigners no longer visited the international fair at Beaucaire. On the eve of the Revolution, foreign trade, expressed as a proportion of France's gross physical product, amounted to twenty-five per cent, but in 1796, according to Marczewski, it stood at only nine per cent.[1]

Certain industries benefited from the war, if they provided cloth for military uniforms, metal for weaponry, or munitions. The coal mines of Littry, in Normandy, studied by Lefebvre,

[1] Bibliography no. 183.

survived the Terror on government orders, and inaugurated a phase of mechanisation before the end of the Directory.[1] French conquest encouraged the metallurgical industries of the Saar and Luxembourg, while the annexation of Belgium improved France's coal resources. The annexations of Mulhouse and Geneva were intended to assist Lyon, as was Moreau's destruction of machinery in the rival town of Constance. The conquest of Italy could provide Lyon with raw silk, and a captive market, and the south of Italy could provide extra grain supplies for the Midi. While cities engaged in maritime trade hoped for peace, the war gave other towns a new and profitable commercial rôle. Bordeaux was to welcome the Bourbons back ecstatically, but during the period of French expansion, Strasbourg grew rich on the continental transit trade, as an entrepôt for Levant cotton. Strasbourg was to prove a centre of Bonapartist support.

The cotton industry was in fact the main beneficiary of the war. The exclusion of British goods removed competition from France's chief rival in the textile industry, and gave a new, although artificial, boost to the production of cheaper types of manufactured cloth. In 1786, the Bourbon monarchy had breached the mercantilist traditions of the Ancien Régime, by concluding a Free Trade Treaty with England. While supporting free trade within France, the Directory renewed the policy of protectionism abroad. Foreign conquest, and alliances with satellite Republics were aimed at the exclusion of British textiles from continental markets, where French goods could now supplant them. At the same time, borrowings and imitations of British mechanical inventions continued during the Directory. The first spinning-jenny was set up in Strasbourg in the Year 8. By 1810, prefects estimated that cotton production in Alsace had quadrupled since the 1780s. The cotton industry could easily adapt to machine production, and required little initial capital. In the period of Directory and the Empire, the industry expanded rapidly in Mulhouse, Lille, and Roubaix, and in Paris itself. Between the 1780s and the middle of the Empire, cotton became the leading sector of French industry, attaining an annual growth rate estimated by Marczewski at five per cent.[2]

War therefore had mixed effects, but it sent reverberations through all sectors of the French economy. Brief consideration of

[1] Bibliography no. 179. [2] Bibliography no. 183.

the chequered career of one manufacturer illustrates its influence better than global and impersonal statistics. Boyer-Fonfrède, the younger brother of the Girondist Conventionnel, came from a Bordeaux family which owned large West Indian plantations, and was involved in the naval armaments industry. In 1791, he set up a small textile factory in two convents in Toulouse, where he had little competition. He recruited skilled workers in Manchester, and by the Year 6, he owned forty-eight looms, under the direction of Isaac Gouldbroof of Leeds. The Terror temporarily interrupted production. The convents became military hospitals, his English employees were interned as enemy aliens, and war with Spain deprived him of his chief export market. Peace with Spain enabled Boyer-Fonfrède to resume production. He now concentrated the activities of carding, weaving, spinning, bleaching, and dyeing under one roof in his mill on the Garonne. He defeated the manpower problem by recruiting orphans and indigent children, under the guise of philanthropy. In the Year 9, he introduced Crompton's 'mule', and he was one of the first men in France to use Kay's 'flying shuttle'. His enterprise prospered until war once again forced its closure in 1809. The Revolution clearly placed difficulties in the path of such an entrepreneur. The Wage Maximum, the Terror, conscription, and the loss of export markets all had to be overcome. Nevertheless, Boyer-Fonfrède could find cheap premises available amongst the *biens nationaux*, and enjoy a period of production without substantial competition. Perhaps the most positive and constructive aspect of his career in this period was the increasing pace of mechanisation, and the absorption of imported English techniques.

The Revolutionary period thus only temporarily interrupted a process of continuous growth, which had its roots in the eighteenth century. For a time, war and inflation placed a barrier in the path of economic expansion. The period of the Directory, however, had important positive aspects. François de Neufchâteau attempted to improve agriculture through the *sociétés agricoles*, and in the Year 6, he optimistically opened the first Exposition Nationale. Mechanisation continued, and cotton advanced. The economy of the Ancien Régime left important traces, in lingering peasant atavisms, the protectionist policy of the Directory, and in the timidity of the French entrepreneur, who sought security in land and government tariffs. Although the gap which separated Britain from her continental rivals was allowed to widen, industrial production at the end of the Directory reached two-thirds of its pre-revolutionary level. The basis was being laid for economic development in the future.

The maritime trade of France had collapsed. As Professor Crouzet puts it, the axis of the European economy was shifting from the Atlantic to the Rhine.[1] The decline of the western seaboard, and the growth of textiles and metallurgy in the North and East, were to transform the economic geography of France. The decline in small-scale industry in Aquitaine and the Garonne valley made the South-west an increasingly backward area, until, in the twentieth century, the chemical and aeronautical industries went some way towards restoring the balance. This process, originating in the revolutionary period, perhaps corresponded to cultural differences. Under the Bourbon Restoration, Stendhal described the North as 'La France moderne et civilisée, la France des machines à vapeur', in the process of 's'angliser'. But the Midi, he wrote, 'n'a pas le caractère âpre qu'il faut maintenant pour gagner et conserver de l'argent...son brio naturel, sa vivacité, l'empêchent de s'angliser, comme le Nord de la France. Un homme du Midi fait ce qui lui fait plaisir au moment même, et non pas ce qui est prudent.' After the Revolution and the Empire, the French economy looked to new horizons.

[1] Bibliography no. 174.

13

FOREIGN POLICY: THE
MEDITERRANEAN DIMENSION

The Directory inherited a continental war which was to convulse Europe for two decades between 1792 and 1815. War had been promoted by both Republicans and the Counter-Revolution. Through Marie Antoinette's correspondence with the Austrian Emperor, the French Court had urged an armed conflict as a means of restoring the full powers of the monarchy. Lafayette, on the other hand, had perhaps envisaged victory as a stepping-stone to the establishment of his own military dictatorship in France. For the Brissotins, foreign war would divert attention from internal problems, and would necessitate more extreme policies and a more democratic form of government, from which they themselves would benefit. 'We cannot be calm', urged Brissot, 'until Europe, all Europe, is in flames.' But in launching a war which assumed the characteristics of an ideological crusade against Ancien Régime Europe, Brissot plunged France into a military adventure for which she was ill prepared, and whose consequences were to be far-reaching. Only Robespierre added a note of sanity, when he emphasised that the Revolution's real enemies were to be found not in Koblentz, or in the courts of Europe, but within the *patrie* itself, and when he prophetically warned that 'La liberté ne se porte pas à la pointe des baionnettes.'

The defections of generals like Dumouriez and Lafayette weakened the army, and the loyalty of others like Custine was suspect. The emigration of army officers undermined morale, just as massive desertions were later to reduce its fighting strength. New recruits had to be equipped and trained, and the suspicion in which they were held by the regular army, *les bleus*, had to be dispelled. In the summer of 1793, the Girondin war policy seemed to have ended in disaster. France was invaded, the Vendée was in open revolt, Toulon and Corsica were in the hands of the English, while Lyon, Bordeaux, Marseille, and parts of Normandy were in rebellion against Paris. Furthermore, the Girondin majority offered no effective solution to these problems.

Collapse was averted by the Terror, which imposed the total mobilisation of France's resources for the war effort, and by Carnot's successful amalgamation of regular professional units with the inexperienced conscripts of France's citizen army. It was averted by the adoption of revolutionary methods of warfare. The armies of the Ancien Régime, accustomed to the sedate progress of siege warfare, were opposed by the massed bayonet charges which fully exploited France's military advantages: numerical superiority and the enthusiasm of the nation in arms. 'Point de manoeuvres, point d'art', ran Hoche's formula, 'du fer, du feu, et du patriotisme.'

The initial successes of Jemappes and Fleurus, which opened up Belgium to the French, owed as much to allied divisions as they did to the Republic's own achievements. The diplomatic rivalries and disputes of the Ancien Régime had not been settled, and until they were resolved, they provided an essential condition of French military success under the Directory and the Empire.

Until 1792, the eastern powers were at war against Turkey, while the fate of Poland still occupied the thoughts of European diplomats. Neither Prussia, Austria, nor Russia would allow any of the others, jointly or severally, to seize the advantage in Poland, and both Austria and Prussia feared that, by committing themselves on the Rhine, they would leave Russia free to take the lion's share behind their backs. Until Poland was partitioned, the war against France was regarded merely as a sideshow. Austria resented the lack of Russian support for Joseph II's scheme to exchange the Austrian Netherlands for Bavaria, and Austro-Prussian rivalry in Germany made cooperation against France difficult. As recently as 1790, Prussia had encouraged the Belgian revolt against the Austrian Emperor. At Pillnitz in August 1791, the Emperor Leopold and Frederick William had avoided genuine commitment to a war against France, by making their intervention conditional on British participation, which was only forthcoming after the French occupation of Belgium and the execution of Louis XVI.

On the French side too, unity of purpose was sorely lacking. The Directory's foreign policy was the resultant of many conflicting forces. At times, the individual Directors, the generals, ambassadors, and ministers seemed to be pursuing contradictory aims, and divisions within the Directory itself prevented it from imposing any single policy, to the exclusion of 'le secret de

Bonaparte', or 'le secret de Talleyrand'. Directorial foreign policy oscillated between the defence of France's natural frontiers, on the one hand, and the creation of semi-independent sister republics on the other, between the defence of the Rhine, and expansion in Italy. At the same time, the diplomatic barometer responded to the chances of military victory, and to the successive *coups d'état* of fructidor, floréal, and prairial. Within the Directory, Reubell favoured expansion to France's natural frontiers, while La Revellière was sympathetic to the idea of Republicanising Europe – two policies which were not always incompatible. Barras and Carnot lacked any consistent policy. Hoche in the Rhineland, Bonaparte in Lombardy, and later Championnet in Naples set up independent republics for their personal ends. The Directory was frequently embarrassed by ambassadors like the volatile and provocative Bernadotte in Vienna, and the more able, but more moderate Barthélémy in Berne. In Italy, Saliceti and General Brune pursued policies sympathetic to Italian Jacobins, which were not officially approved, and only rarely did the government's *commissaires* work in harmonious co-operation with the generals in the field. The conduct of foreign policy was further complicated by more venal considerations: Barras was offered substantial payment to protect the interests of the Venetian Republic, while Talleyrand at the Foreign Ministry solicited bribes from English and American negotiators. The Prussian ambassador Sandoz reported in January 1798 that 'Everything can be bought here in the field of foreign affairs, not from the Directory, but from the ministers subordinate to it.' It was Sandoz who summarised for Frederick William the confusion at the centre which consistently blurred the Directory's strategic aims: 'I hear politics is managed now as finance', he wrote in June 1797, 'from day to day, and from event to event...When I wanted to know the state of the present negotiations with Austria...I could verify that no member of the Executive Directory knew exactly of what they consisted.'

Yet across the jumbled mosaic of Directorial foreign policy, a few recurring *leitmotivs* can be discerned. The government's financial difficulties influenced French policy throughout the years of the Directory. Shortage of funds forced France to support its armies out of the resources of foreign territories. Thus profit and propaganda went hand in hand. Europe might be Republicanised, but it was to pay a heavy price for its liberation in requisitions, war contributions, and art treasures. Propaganda was often the prelude to the conquests which were necessary to support the army and satisfy the avarice of its generals, and the demands of government contractors and army suppliers.

A second permanent factor was perhaps the French public's desire for peace, which was instrumental in forcing the Directory to accept Bonaparte's negotiations with Austria, and at the same time, its anglophobia, nurtured on years of propaganda, which had erroneously attributed the Revolution's difficulties to English espionage and 'Pitt's gold'. In the government, only perhaps Talleyrand did not share this hatred of England.

Reubell's firm support for the annexation of the left bank of the Rhine was also a stabilising influence within the Directory. This is not to say that the defence of France's natural frontiers was a generally accepted policy, even before the Treaty of Campoformio committed an unwilling Directory to gains in Italy. On 23 ventôse III, Rühl's motion to make recognition of France's Rhine frontier the *sine qua non* of peace was not even seconded in the Convention. Carnot, too, thought that the Meuse was far more easily defensible. In thermidor III, however, when Rœderer's *Journal de Paris* offered a prize for the best essay on the desirability of pushing France's frontier to the Rhine, most of the entrants concluded in favour of annexation, not only for reasons of military security, but also for economic motives. The mineral deposits of the left bank would be an economic advantage for France, and ecclesiastical land in conquered territory could be used to redeem the *assignats*.

Reubell could not dictate French foreign policy. The election of Barthélémy to the Directory and the replacement of Delacroix by Talleyrand at the Ministry of Foreign Affairs undermined his authority. His knowledge of German and English, however, his stubbornness, and his ability gave him an important influence. He brought to discussions on the security of the eastern frontier a keen perception of the interests of his native Alsace, which he had already defended against the German princes, against the *émigrés*, and against the Jews. He vowed to go unshaven until Mainz was once more a French city.

In order to consolidate the French occupation of the left bank of the Rhine, Prussian co-operation was necessary. An alliance with Prussia to this end, together with alliances with Spain and

Holland against British sea-power, became the primary aims of French policy after thermidor.

Progress was made towards the first of these aims in the Treaty of Basle, concluded between Barthélémy and Hardenburg in germinal III, which established Prussian neutrality. Prussia was now free to concentrate on her Ostpolitik, while the creation of a neutral zone in northern Germany made the French conquest of Holland secure. Only Austria, which still held the fortress town of Mainz, could now oppose French occupation of the Rhineland.

Although the future of the Rhineland was still in doubt, France was officially to annex Belgium in vendémiaire IV, and she was already master of the United Provinces. The cold winter of 1795 and the ice on the rivers deprived the Dutch of their traditional means of defence – the flooding of the dykes. In pluviôse III, the French entered Amsterdam. The flight of King William, and the abolition of the stadtholderate opened the way for the creation of a Batavian Republic. The French desire to 'liberate' the Dutch, however, was, as always, tempered by more mercenary and strategic motives. At the Hague, Reubell and Siéyès negotiated an offensive and defensive alliance with the Dutch, which condemned them to pay an indemnity of one hundred million florins. The policy outlined by Chabot in the Jacobin club in 1793 was fulfilled. 'Où trouverons-nous de l'or pour faire la guerre?' he had asked, 'À Amsterdam et à Madrid...Portez la liberté en Hollande, elle vous tend encore les bras, elle vous offre son or et ses vaisseaux.' Holland was further asked to support a French army of 25,000 men, and yield all her territory south of the Meuse. Dutch naval strength was now at the disposal of Britain's enemies.

Dugommier's advance into Catalonia brought about the Spanish withdrawal from the war. By the Treaty of San Ildefonso, in thermidor IV, France guaranteed Spanish possession of her colonies, although the fate of Louisiana was still undecided, since Godoy insisted on exchanging it for Gibraltar. The French alliance with Spain gave her naval control of the western Mediterranean.

In fact, any hopes placed in these reinforcements of French naval power were to prove illusory. The Spanish fleet, never eager to fight, was blockaded in Cadiz after the battle of Cape St Vincent, while the Dutch fleet was destroyed at Camperdown. Neither the Spanish nor the Dutch fleet gave the French any naval assistance in the Irish expedition of the Year 5. Not only was Britain mistress of the Channel, but she could also deprive France of her West Indian colonies, and the French western ports of their colonial imports, as well as seize the vital Dutch possessions of Ceylon and the Cape of Good Hope.

Prussia had withdrawn from the coalition, and alliances were concluded with Spain and Holland. The war, however, continued, until a settlement could be reached in Germany which satisfied both Paris and Vienna. France was sympathetic to the Austrian plan to exchange Belgium for Bavaria, but this scheme was unacceptable to Prussia. On the other hand, Prussia could be compensated for French acquisitions on the Rhine out of secularised German territory, but Austria would not accept the violation of the Holy Roman Empire. The French war effort was now concentrated against Austria. Carnot's plan was to hold the Alpine frontier, while the armies of the Sambre-et-Meuse and the Rhin-et-Moselle launched a two-pronged attack across the Rhine, meeting at Ratisbon. Bonaparte, meanwhile, was to force Austria into peace by penetrating into northern Italy. The Directory appreciated the value of Italian conquests as bargaining counters for the security of the left bank of the Rhine. Military failure in Germany, however, and Bonaparte's spectacular success in Italy were to impose a new set of priorities on the Directory.

Advances over the Rhine were slow and hazardous. Pichegru's Royalist sympathies, and later, Moreau's hesitancy prevented a decisive thrust. Desertion and Royalist propaganda in the Army of the Rhin-et-Moselle undermined morale, and discipline was lax, as indiscriminate pillage and the headlong retreat of the Year 5 were to reveal. Jourdan advanced down the Main, while Moreau pressed forward as far as Munich, demanding a contribution of four million francs from Frankfurt, concluding profitable armistices with Baden, Wurtemburg, and the Swabian circle, and threatening Austria with insurrections in southern Germany. The two armies never co-ordinated their advance. The Archduke Charles was to defeat Jourdan's isolated Army of the Sambre-et-Meuse, and Moreau, afraid that he too would be cut off, beat a discreet retreat to the safety of the Rhine bridgeheads.

In Italy, however, glittering horizons beckoned. While the French armies in Germany were weakened by desertion, Bonaparte was strengthened by reinforcements from the Pyrenéan

Map 4. Central Europe during the Directory

fronts. While Moreau crossed the barren Palatinate, Bonaparte promised his troops rich pickings in the fertile plain of Lombardy. The financial rewards of the German campaign were insignificant in comparison to the forty million francs extorted from Italy in 1796. Bonaparte could afford to send some of this plunder back to his grateful government, finance an expedition to Corsica, and pay his troops half in cash. This privilege, denied to Moreau, threatened to turn the army of Italy into Bonaparte's private mercenaries.

In 1796, Italy was a patchwork of tiny states, divided by long-standing municipal rivalries, and vulnerable to foreign invasion. The Kingdom of Sardinia, which ruled over Piedmont, Nice, and Savoy (annexed by France in 1792), guarded the Alpine passes. The Milanais was a dominion of the Austrian Habsburgs, and merchant oligarchies governed the declining republics of Genoa and Venice, which included the Trentino, Istria, Dalmatia, and the Ionian Isles. Here the Austrian defence of northern Italy could fall back on the 'Quadrilateral' formed by the fortresses of Mantua, Verona, Peschiera, and Legnago. Austrian influence was strong south of the Po, in the miniature duchies of Parma, Piacenza, and Modena, and in Tuscany. The Papal States straddled the peninsula, from Rome in the west, to the port of Ancona in the east, and including the Papal Legations of Bologna, Ferrara, Ravenna, and Forlì, also coveted by Austria. In the south, the Neapolitan Bourbons gave the British fleet access to the harbours of the Kingdom of the Two Sicilies.

In spite of reinforcements from Spain, and from the Vendée, the Army of Italy still numbered less than 50,000 men, and it was essential that Bonaparte should prevent the junction of the Austrian and Piedmontese forces, if his campaign was to be successful. His surprising mobility achieved this aim, and he defeated first the Piedmontese at Mondovi, and then the Austrians at Lodi, on the Po. His policy was now to conclude an armistice with Piedmont, weaken Austria by Republicanising Lombardy, to intimidate the neutral duchies into providing loans and indemnities, and then to threaten Vienna through the Tyrol.

An armistice was signed with Piedmont at Cherasco, and Bonaparte entered Milan, where, in response to appeals from the Italian Jacobins, he set up a Jacobin municipality. The smaller Italian states now withdrew from the coalition, although this cost Parma an indemnity of 2 million lire, and Modena 7·5 million lire.

Map 5. Italy on the eve of the Revolutionary Wars

France soon disposed of this 'antipasto' before going on to devour Italy's richest prize. The Papal Legations, and then Rome, were occupied. The Directory's negotiations with Rome, discussed in Chapter 7, had foundered on the Pope's refusal to revoke his condemnations of Republican oaths. In the Treaty of Tolentino of ventôse V, Bonaparte discarded these demands, forced the Pope to abandon his claims to Avignon, the Legations, and the port of Ancona and to exclude British shipping from his harbours, and condemned him to an enormous indemnity of 21 million lire.

Neither the richness of these fruits, nor their gargantuan quantity, could satisfy the ravenous appetite of the French. Even Tuscany, nominally a neutral state, was not immune from armed French intervention. The Directory wished to force Tuscany to expel the *émigrés* who had taken refuge on her territory, and to eject the British from their naval base at Livorno. This was a project which particularly appealed to Bonaparte and his fellow-Corsican Saliceti, the Directory's *commissaire* to the Army of Italy. For the capture of Livorno would open up Corsica again to the French. The British, however, evacuated their supplies to Elba before the French forces arrived, and although they abandoned Corsica, this was the only tangible benefit accruing to the French from the raid on Tuscany. This time the cupboard was bare.

Although Bonaparte, by paying his troops in cash, had established his personal control over the Army of Italy, the conduct of the Italian campaign so far described was entirely consistent with the Directory's war aims. But the creation of an independent Cispadane Republic, comprising Modena and the Legations, in vendémiaire V, served as a warning to the Directory. The government in general, and Carnot and Reubell in particular, interpreted France's Italian conquests as temporary assets which could be traded for territorial gains on the Rhine. The establishment of sister republics, although welcomed by Italian Jacobins and by La Revellière, suggested that Bonaparte had personal objectives of his own, and his aspirations to European statesmanship included the creation of client republics dependent on his own authority. For Reubell, French obligations to such a republic would prove embarrassing and expensive. 'Ces Republiques-là', he sneered, 'Brissot les appelait des petits patés; mais c'est avec la graisse de la viande que se fait le petit paté; et c'est aux dépens de la grande République que les petites Républiques environnantes s'engraisseraient.' Austria could never tolerate the existence of a French satellite in northern Italy. The Cispadane Republic, which was to become, with the inclusion of Lombardy, the Cisalpine Republic, was to dash the hopes of all those who wished for a lasting peace with Austria.

The Austrians had retreated to the Quadrilateral, but French victories at Arcole and Rivoli in the winter of 1796–7 forced them to evacuate the vital fortress of Mantua. Bonaparte invaded the Tyrol, and forced the Austrians to sign an armistice at Leoben, only eighty miles from Vienna itself, on 29 germinal V. His army was too weak to press further towards the Austrian capital, and he had an anti-French revolt in the Tyrol on his hands. Furthermore, the rapid conclusion of a cease-fire would minimise Directorial interference in Bonaparte's own diplomatic projects. In the Preliminaries of Leoben, Bonaparte gave French foreign policy a new dimension. Austria surrendered Belgium, but Bonaparte also insisted on acceptance of his northern Italian Republic. The problem of the left bank of the Rhine, which had hitherto been the government's chief objective, was now shelved. Bonaparte forced the Directory's hand by committing France to permanent gains in Italy. Austria was to be compensated not in Bavaria, which might antagonise Prussia, but by the partition of Venice. French *agents provocateurs* instigated the rising which provided the excuse for the French invasion of the Venetian Republic. In vendémiaire VI, the Treaty of Campoformio confirmed the provisions of the Leoben armistice. The future of the Rhineland was referred to a congress of the Imperial Diet to be held at Rastadt, while possession of Corfu gave France the enticing possibility of further gains in the eastern Mediterranean.

Bonaparte had presented the Directory with a *fait accompli*, which it did not accept without considerable misgivings. Many interpreted the French failure to insist on the left bank of the Rhine as a feeble surrender to Austria. For Reubell, indeed, only '*chouans*' could support the settlement. Nevertheless, Thugut presented the Treaty of Campoformio to the Court of Vienna as an almost unmitigated disaster. Austria had lost Lombardy, and without Mantua or the Papal Legations, she felt powerless to resist the growth of Republicanism in Italy. In fact, the Treaty of Campoformio made Austria a potential sea-power, and she was still in a good position to give support from Venice to the Pope and the Neapolitan Bourbons. Because Austria could never accept the permanent existence of the Cisalpine Republic, however, the peace could only be temporary, and this reorientation of French policy condemned her to a continuation of the war.

Jacobins saw the cession of Venice as a cynical betrayal of French revolutionary ideals, and of the Constitution of 1793, which had promised the liberation of oppressed peoples from the tyranny of the Ancien Régime monarchies. The Jacobins of Lombardy, who had hoped to absorb Venetia into the Cisalpine Republic, regretted that the defensive position of the Cisalpine had not been reinforced by the settlement. The presence of the bronze horses of St Mark on the future Place de la Concorde was an indictment of the Directory's preference for financial profit and strategic security over the Republican ideals of 1793.

Nevertheless, the Treaty of Campoformio was accepted. Although Reubell continued to oppose it, La Revellière acquiesced, Carnot did not desire to alienate Bonaparte, and Barras feared he would be compromised, if it emerged that he had been offered large bribes to protect Venetian interests. The Directory could not overrule the only general who could guarantee victory, and without either peace with England or an alliance with Prussia, there seemed little alternative. Above all, the Directory bowed to the popular demand for peace. Yet it was a precarious peace, which constituted a victory for France's Mediterranean interests over expansion on the Rhine, a victory for Bonaparte over Reubell, and a victory for the generals over the government. The First Coalition was destroyed.

France was not yet at peace with Europe, One enemy remained: England, whose money had been the most powerful unifying force in the history of the Coalition. Irish patriots like Wolfe Tone had repeatedly tried to persuade the French that an expedition to Ireland would unleash a rebellion and bring London to its knees. The Directory was soon to regret its faith in their optimistic promises. The force which left Brest in the winter of 1796 was dispersed by bad weather and worse navigation, and a French landing was not achieved. Encouraged by mutinies in the British navy, which sent the value of stock on the Paris Bourse soaring, and by the renewed prospect of a rising in Ireland, the French made another attempt at an invasion in the summer of 1798. A force of about 1,000 men disembarked from three frigates on the remote west coast of Mayo. Ireland was perhaps the weakest link in Britain's armour, but her people were surprisingly unreceptive to this foreign brand of Republicanism. The French general Humbert found the Irish reluctant to leave their fields at harvest-time, even to support the invincible armies of the Grande Nation, and those who did join the French were a liability rather than a military asset. Unfavourable winds and lack of financial support prevented French reinforcements from arriving before the English had destroyed the ephemeral provisional government of Connaught.

A diplomatic settlement with Britain was not ruled out. Negotiations between Delacroix and Lord Malmesbury in 1796 had come to grief over the British refusal to recognise the French annexation of Belgium, or to make a separate peace without Austria. By the time negotiations had resumed, however, in messidor V, prospects for an Anglo-French rapprochement seemed brighter. The armistice of Leoben had been signed, and England now consented to make a separate peace. The death of Catherine II of Russia and the determined neutrality of Prusia seemed to leave England diplomatically isolated, while mutinies at Spithead and the Nore, and the Bank of England's difficulties induced her to make further concessions in the discussions at Lille. England now seemed prepared even to recognise the Batavian Republic. For Pitt, Britain's minimum terms included British retention of Ceylon and the Cape, together possibly with Trinidad. France, however, had guaranteed the colonial possessions of her Dutch and Spanish allies. Even if Talleyrand, who had replaced Delacroix at the Foreign Ministry, was prepared to abandon the Dutch if the price was right, Reubell could not agree to abandon France's allies. Once again, therefore, the Anglo-French negotiations proved abortive. This time they crumbled over the problem of the restitution of colonial conquests, and over impossible French demands for the cession of the Channel Islands. The British perhaps hoped that the new Royalist majority in the Conseil des Cinq Cents would give their offers a more sympathetic hearing, and this consideration certainly made the rupture with Britain popular in France, reinforcing the probably false impression that Malmesbury was not a sincere negotiator.

The offensive against England seemed about to resume when the Directory assembled the Army of England, in preparation for a landing on the south coast. A patriotic loan was raised to support this expedition in the winter of the Year 6, to be repaid from the receipts of taxes to be levied in conquered English territory. The response to this loan suggests that the popular pressure for peace stopped at the English Channel.

By ventôse, the *armée d'Angleterre* had been allotted a new strategic rôle. The plan to invade England had been rejected in favour of an expedition to Egypt. French foreign policy was thus redirected once again towards the Mediterranean, and Reubell suffered another defeat at the hands of Bonaparte. How did this *volte-face* come about? The French fleet was no match for the British naval forces which commanded the Channel, and after Camperdown, France could expect no aid from the Dutch. Reubell still maintained that England was France's main enemy, but Bonaparte and Talleyrand persuaded the government that by diverting the Army of England to the Near East, it would strike a blow at British trade, by cutting the route to India. Egypt, as a provider of cotton, rice, and coffee, could perhaps compensate France for the loss of her Caribbean empire, while for men like La Revellière, the expedition provided an opportunity to carry the benefits of French civilisation to the confines of the despotic Orient.

Talleyrand's argument rested on the assumption that in overthrowing the Mamelukes, the Albanian and Circassian military élite which effectively ruled Egypt, France could draw the Ottoman Sultan himself into an alliance. The Battle of the Nile, in thermidor VI, made this only a very remote possibility, and was to pave the way for the Second Coalition. The story of Nelson's pursuit of the French across the eastern Mediterranean, his premature arrival on the coast of Egypt, and ultimately his skilful destruction of the French fleet as it lay at anchor in Aboukir Bay, is now part of the heritage of every English schoolboy. In fact, a great opportunity had been missed. If Nelson had succeeded in making contact with the poorly-protected French transport vessels before they disembarked Bonaparte's army, the consequences might have been enormous. Not only would he have destroyed the French Adriatic squadron, but he might also have immobilised an entire French army and the cream of French generalship.

In his memoirs, La Revellière insists that the Directory did not send Bonaparte to Egypt in order to be rid of him.[1] He claims that

---

[1] Bibliography no. 7.

the conception and execution of the whole enterprise were Bonaparte's. There may have been advantages in keeping an embarrassingly ambitious conqueror at a distance. They did not, however, outweigh the risk involved in committing an experienced army so far afield. It is far more likely that Bonaparte wanted to be rid of the Directory. In Egypt, he was immune from interference from the government's *commissaires*, and could freely indulge his ambitions to statesmanship on a world scale.

In his absence, from prairial VI until vendémiaire VIII, the Directory was able to pursue a more independent foreign policy. In Bonaparte's absence, François de Neufchâteau was to represent France at the Rastadt conference, where the Directory hoped to mitigate the effects of Campoformio. After the *coup* of floréal in particular, the Directory installed more conservative régimes in the sister republics.

The Directory had failed to extricate France from the European conflict. Britain was still at war. The uneasy peace did not satisfy Austria, which still hoped for further compensation for French gains, preferably in Bavaria or the Legations. The uncertainties of the Directory made it a prey to circumstance. It wavered between annexation and the creation of sister republics. It had preserved the *status quo* in Piedmont, but subverted it in Milan. It had liberated the United Provinces and the Cisalpine Republic, but in agreeing to the cession of Venice, it had acted within the traditions of Ancien Régime diplomacy, cynically disregarding the wishes of its inhabitants. Meanwhile, the Directory had been reluctantly committed to a permanent war footing in Italy, and Bonaparte's spectacular victories unveiled new horizons in the Mediterranean.

14

FOREIGN POLICY: PROFIT
AND PROPAGANDA

The victory of the Directorial Left in the *coup* of fructidor V inaugurated a new period of French expansion, during which Switzerland, Liguria, Rome, and then Naples were occupied. The Directory saw no contradiction in levying forced loans and maintaining armies of occupation in liberated territories. The army was paid and supplied out of its own conquests, or, as the Directory preferred to put it, it was 'nourished with the fruit of its courage'. The spread of Republicanism progressed at the same pace as the enrichment of the generals, and of the companies who supplied them. Such a policy could not fail to provoke first the hostility of Austria, and ultimately the renewal of the Coalition against France. In Zaghi's phrase, France devoured the surrounding states like a man peeling the leaves of an artichoke.[1] The Directory professed peaceful intentions, but it accepted expansion because of financial need, and because it relied on the support of the Republican generals, to whom it had already turned in fructidor. Time and again, the Directory's hand was forced by acts of aggression committed by agents it could not control.

It is now time to consider some of the causes and consequences of French intervention in the sister republics.

Negotiations between Reubell and the Swiss patriot Ochs long preceded the French invasion of the Swiss cantons in the winter of the Year 6. The French, however, did not act simply to oblige the Swiss democrats. They had other financial and strategic motives at heart. Seizure of the Berne Treasury might help to finance the Egypt expedition, while the expulsion of *émigrés* and the dispersal of counter-revolutionary espionage agents would protect France and her recent conquests. Above all, possession of the Alpine passes would guarantee French armies speedy access to the Cisalpine Republic and northern Italy. An offensive and defensive alliance secured this vital communications route for France. A Constitution, loosely based on that of the Year 3, which

---

[1] Bibliography no. 205.

Ochs so admired, was introduced. Tithes and personal feudal obligations were abolished, while taxes on land and movable property laid the foundation for an equitable fiscal system. France annexed part of the bishopric of Basle, the textile town of Mulhouse, and Geneva, which the writings of Rousseau had given a special place in revolutionary political mythology. As a source of financial aid, Switzerland proved disappointing. The Berne Treasury held only six million francs, and all together, Switzerland yielded only fourteen million francs to France. Of these, three million were sent to Bonaparte, and the rest paid for the upkeep of the Army of Helvetia.

On 8 floréal VI, Lecarlier, *commissaire près l'armée d'Helvétie*, was appointed Minister of Police in Paris. His successor, Rapinat, Reubell's brother-in-law, has been associated with arbitrary exactions and the indiscriminate plunder of the Swiss cantons. The unfortunate connotations of his surname should not disguise his serious attempt to control the abuses committed by generals and *fournisseurs*. His relations with the Directory remained ambiguous. When, in prairial VI, he organised a fructidor-style *coup* which brought Ochs and Laharpe into the Helvetic Directory, he was recalled, but immediately reinstated. The success and vigour of his administration contributed to the comparative leniency with which the Helvetic Republic was treated.

The old federation of the cantons was remoulded. The urban centres of Basle, Berne, Fribourg, and Zurich, ruled by their conservative oligarchies, and the more democratic cantons, like Schwytz, Uri, and Unterwalden, lost their autonomy under the centralist Constitution of the Helvetic Republic. This new unitary organisation of Switzerland put the Roman Catholics in an overall minority. The recruitment of novices came to an end, the property of religious congregations was sequestered, and the tithe and ecclesiastical justice were abolished.

The religious and federal issues also compromised the stability of the Batavian Republic. Here, one inhabitant in three was a Catholic, and the disestablishment of the Dutch Reformed Church won support amongst Catholic Jacobins, and the newly-emancipated Jews. The Dutch patriots, drawn mainly from the commercial and professional classes, welcomed French support against the conservative ruling provincial oligarchies and the Orangist masses. They were, however, never as dependent on the

French as were the Swiss Jacobins. The Dutch Revolution had, after all, begun in 1787, and the Dutch Jacobins won control of Amsterdam before the arrival of the French. The Batavian Constitution, loosely based on the thermidorean Constitution, was adapted to local conditions. The United Provinces became departments of the new Republic, but the federal structure of government remained in the administration of finance. Furthermore, the Constitution was submitted to a referendum, in which the population rejected the compromise between federalism and unitarism. While the Jacobins hoped for a fully centralised administration on the French model, the ruling oligarchies favoured federalism, in so far as this preserved their authority in the provinces. Neither party was satisfied with the Batavian Constitution. In pluviôse VI, Delacroix organised a *coup d'état*, which ushered in a centralist Constitution favourable to the democrats. Although, in the summer of the same year, the Batavian Republic was also to have its version of the floréal *coup*, the Constitution of 1798 was preserved.

In Italy, on the contrary, the Directory rejected the solution of a unified state. The Directory was well aware that the creation of a strong, unified state in Italy under French auspices could prove more of an embarrassment than it was worth, and that this would hardly hasten the end of hostilities. Even for Republicans like La Revellière, essential objectives like the destruction of the power of the Pope did not necessarily imply unification. The Directors were aware, too, of the power of the Church in Italy, and in general they judged that the Italians were not ripe for democracy. Indeed, an instinctive chauvinism led them to despise the pretensions of the Italian Jacobins. The French consul at Livorno in prairial IV wrote of the Italians that 'en général ils ne tiennent à l'espèce humaine que par les formes qui la distinguent et par les vices qui la déshonorent'. Faipoult found Italy still too subservient to its nobles and priests. 'Quand ils voudront être libres', he told the Directory, 'ce sera leur affaire.'

In all the sister republics, there was a Jacobin fringe which preferred the social and political ideals of 1793 to those of the Directory. In Italy, this fringe seemed to pose a serious threat to the Directory's policies. The government knew of the links between the Italian Jacobins who gathered in Milan and the Babouvists in France. The Italian patriots were encouraged by Buonarroti, and by the Robespierrist ex-Conventionnel Jullien.

They corresponded with Babouvists like Lepelletier and Antonelle. By conciliating the Italian Jacobins, the Directory would strengthen Jacobinism on its own doorstep.

The Directory was not averse to spreading revolutionary propaganda in neighbouring or neutral countries. The Cisalpine Republic alone was not capable of supporting the army of Italy indefinitely, and financial needs might force France to seek new sources of money and supplies. The Directory, however, wished to dictate expansion at its own pace, and it refused to be compromised by ambitious generals or avaricious *fournisseurs*. Thus Italian Jacobins and their sympathisers became frustrated at the Directory's policy of apparent protection of the monarchies of Piedmont, Tuscany, and Naples. General Lahoz of the Lombard legion was so disgusted by French policy that he went over to the Austrians. After the *coup* of floréal, the Directory was able to instal a more conservative régime in Milan, and to disown the policy of expansion into Piedmont carried out by the hotheaded General Brune and by its diplomatic representatives in Turin (Ginguené), and Genoa (Sotin). Ginguené was dismissed, Sotin sent to the uninviting consulate at Charleston, and in brumaire VII, Brune was posted to Holland.

The temptation to lay hands once again on the fabulous wealth of the Papacy was too strong to resist, and the assassination of General Duphot by a Roman crowd provided the excuse for the French invasion of the Papal States. In pluviôse VI, Berthier proclaimed the installation of the Roman Republic, and the Pope fled to Siena, which was later to offer another pretext for the invasion of Tuscany. The Rome commission of Daunou, Florent, and Monge, soon replaced by Faipoult, fought an uphill struggle against the indiscriminate exactions levied by the military. Almost immediately, the French were faced with a mutiny against the high command, which produced illuminating revelations about the conditions of the army, and the impotence of the Directory to curb financial waste. The army's pay was four and a half months in arrears, and the junior officers resented the extravagant consumption and luxurious living of their superiors. Essentially their protest was for a more equitable share of the booty. They successfully demanded the recall of Masséna, and the government was forced to accept his replacement by St-Cyr.

The Neapolitans' fears about French intentions were soon confirmed, for when they rashly attacked the Roman Republic, a

French force under Championnet immediately invaded the Kingdom of the Two Sicilies. Championnet, like Brune perhaps, wanted to emulate the personal diplomatic successes of Bonaparte, and make the new Parthenopean Republic his private fief. The Directory accepted the occupation of Naples, but it preferred to exploit the kingdom rather than create a sister republic, at the same time excluding the British fleet from Neapolitan ports. Jullien, whom Championnet appointed his secretary-general, urged him to begin a policy of land redistribution, which would have transformed the corrupt and obscurantist monarchy into the most democratic of all the Italian republics. The Directory could not accept this direct provocation of its continental enemies. Nor could it tolerate the arrogant attitude of Championnet, who ignored all attempts by the civil authority to control military requisitions. *Commissaire* Faipoult fought in vain to bring Championnet to account for military requisitions and taxes. The Directory followed its usually ambiguous policy in such disputes when it recalled both Championnet and Faipoult. When, however, the government learnt that Championnet had brusquely ordered the expulsion of Faipoult from Naples, it arrested the general, who was only absolved after prairial VII.

After French expansion into Switzerland and central and southern Italy, the Directory could hardly hope to console Austria. This expansion was not part of a deliberate and concerted plan by the Directory. Provocation of Austria was forced upon France by irresponsible diplomats like Sotin and Ginguené, by reckless military leaders like Brune and Championnet, egged on by the companies of *fournisseurs*.

In Egypt, meanwhile, Bonaparte, having established French rule in lower Egypt after the Battle of the Pyramids, now led an expedition into Syria, hoping to force Turkey into a separate peace. Here he met spirited resistance from Djezzar Pasha, who led a Holy War against the French with the backing of the Ottoman Porte. Although the French took Jaffa in ventôse VII, their advance was held up at St John of Acre by Djezzar and the English navy. In floréal, weakened by an outbreak of bubonic plague, the French began their retreat. Although they routed a Turkish invasion force at Aboukir in thermidor, Egypt had no more to offer Bonaparte, who sailed for France, deserting his army, on 6 fructidor.

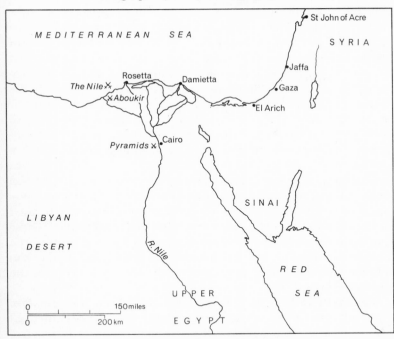

Map 6. The Egyptian campaign

Here, as on the Continent, the French occupation, however brief, brought in its wake important social changes. Equality before the law, a rational judicial procedure, and the abolition of torture were introduced. Tithes were abolished, and religious toleration proclaimed. In the Cisalpine Republic, civil marriage was introduced. National armies were created in the Batavian, Helvetic, and Cisalpine Republics. Switzerland, which had for centuries exported mercenary soldiers to Europe, now learnt that the Revolution had altered the conditions of warfare.

In Italy, important property transfers helped to meet the cost of liberation. Mahcelli suggests that the sales of ecclesiastical property in Bologna amounted to a rapid and violent transfer of wealth.[1] Here the property of thirty-one religious corporations was sold. The property-owning classes needed to sell property quickly, in order to raise cash to pay war taxes and forced loans. Rome had been plunged into financial chaos before the French

[1] Bibliography no. 199.

209

arrived. Not only had the loss of the Legations deprived the Pope of his most productive lands, but the flight of the Papal court removed the Holy City's chief source of income. The property of corporations, hospitals, the university, and vacant benefices went on sale to meet French demands, and to counter the government's deficit. The bulk of alienated property was ceded to the French, who took the most valuable territories: the sulphur mines, the lands of the Pope and his family, and the property of the foreign seminaries. Government contractors like the Company of General Munitions were handsomely paid in *beni nazionali*. A smaller proportion found its way into the hands of individual purchasers, mainly from the rural *bourgeoisie*, who in many cases bought the land they already leased. Among these purchasers were many lawyers, doctors, and priests, who formed the backbone of local support for the Roman Republic. These land transfers, however, were short-lived. According to the Concordat of 1801, the Pope resumed possession of the *beni nazionali*, indemnifying purchasers with only one-quarter of the purchase price.

The most far-reaching consequences of French occupation were perhaps to be seen in the Rhineland, where the seigneurial régime was permanently abolished, and in Egypt. Bonaparte confiscated the property of the Mamelukes, and reorganised local administration under provincial divans of local notables, under the supervision of a French general. He repaired the irrigation network, and was responsible for the introduction of the first western printing press into Egypt. Above all, he installed the flower of the French intelligentsia in the Cairo Institut, and his expedition can be said to have founded the science of Egyptology. The legacy of the French occupation was to inspire the reforms of Mehemet Ali in the 1830s.

The new Constitutions introduced into the sister republics were based on the French thermidorean model, although they took account of indigenous traditions. In the Batavian Republic, for example, the federal structure of the United Provinces was not immediately destroyed, and the Swiss cantons were preserved, at least as administrative units of the Helvetic Republic. In Italy, similarly, the French approach to the religious question was cautious, for the government dared not risk the complete alienation of Catholics and the lower clergy. In the Cisalpine Republic, the separation of Church and State was not put into effect, and the Constitution of the Roman Republic avoided all mention of its relations with the Church.

A two-chamber system was introduced, incorporating the separation of legislative and executive powers, together with an executive, usually of five members. Elections in the Batavian, Helvetic, and Cisalpine Republics were by universal suffrage. Some of the lessons learnt since 1795 were embodied in the new Constitutions. In Switzerland, in Rome, and in Milan, for example, Treasury officials were appointed by the executive. Some elements of the Constitution of the Year 8 were already apparent in the sister republics. In the Roman Republic, the prototype of the consular form of government had emerged. The executive was known as the Consulato, the two chambers as the Senate and the Tribunate, while here, as in Switzerland, the government's local agents were named prefects.

In almost all occupied areas, the introduction of Republicanism and French demands for war contributions provoked serious opposition. With the surprising exception of the Rhineland, all the sister republics had their own version of the Vendée. In Belgium, French anticlericalism and the conscription laws sparked off a peasant rising. The French made the mistake of treating the Belgians as loyal subjects of the Austrian Emperor, although their resistance to Joseph II had proved the contrary. The inhabitants of Le Valais rose in 1798 against the unified Swiss Constitution, the abolition of the tithe, and recruitment, before the French had occupied their territory. In prairial IV, armed peasants marched into Pavia to resist the financial exactions of the French. Those who directly benefited from French occupation feared for their lives when the French departed. This was particularly true of the Jewish communities in Rome and Livorno. All over Europe, the peasant masses resisted new demands for men and money, sudden attacks on hallowed religious traditions, and liberal institutions supported by the wealthy commercial and professional classes, whom they often identified as their oppressors. The sale of Church property, the end of religious holidays, indiscriminate French requisitioning, and the exile of the Pope aroused the hostility of his subjects to the French. The border departments of Trasimene and Circeo were never fully brought under control by the Roman Republic. Cardinal Ruffo's Calabrian *sanfedisti* waged effective guerrilla warfare against the seigneurial system, and against the *bour-*

geoisie who seemed ready to maintain and exploit it. French defeats in the Year 7 encouraged further revolts in the Ionian Isles, and in the region of Arezzo in Tuscany.

In Egypt, Bonaparte's ostentatious respect for Moslem ritual and tradition could not prevent the insurrection which erupted in Cairo in vendémiaire VII. French reliance on the financial expertise of the Christian Copts was not popular, and the policy of collaboration with local notables and religious leaders had only a partial success. Although the insurrection was sparked off by the property tax, it sprang fundamentally from deep-rooted Moslem hostility to the invaders. As long as the tricolor fluttered from the minarets, the French would always be regarded as heathens. Two insurmountable obstacles opposed the assimilation of the occupying forces to Islam: firstly, they were uncircumcised, and secondly they were inveterate wine-drinkers. General Menou, who was converted to Islam, and married a Moslem bride, was inspired by a colonising zeal which was totally unique.

The Directory's foreign policy was, to say the least, equivocal. It professed peace, but continued to extend its influence in Switzerland and Italy. It negotiated with Austria, but at the same time provoked her into war by the establishment of the Helvetic and Italian Republics. The French sword was double-edged; it freed Europe from oppression, but imposed new burdens in order to oil its own war machine, even if, for La Revellière, the idea of invading Switzerland to pay for the Egypt expedition was as futile as collecting the rainwater of Paris to make the Seine navigable. The Directory's opportunist policy continued to fluctuate between exploitation and Republicanisation. It tried to curb the initiatives of its generals, but it needed their political support.

The Directory did not deliberately prolong the war for financial reasons. Rather, it was caught in a circle it could not break. It is true that the French armies were supported by the proceeds of their conquests, but it would be a mistake to assume that the Directory itself drew any direct benefit from the profits of liberation. Godechot estimated the total value of receipts from conquered territories between 1792 and 1799 at about 360 million francs, but little of this found its way back to Paris.[1] Only about one-quarter of the proceeds from Bonaparte's Italian campaign was sent to the Directory. The rest was used to pay the

[1] Bibliography no. 197.

army and the contractors, and to finance expeditions to Egypt, Corsica, and the Ionian Isles. Thus war taxes and other exactions abroad did not bring enormous direct benefits to the government, whose budget in the Year 7 amounted to 600 million francs.

The Directory was not totally to blame for the continuation of the war. In fact, it made serious efforts to bring about a peace, in the Lille negotiations, at Campoformio, and at the conference with Austria at Seltz in the Year 6. At Seltz, however, François de Neufchâteau refused to discuss Kobenzl's demands for Austrian compensation in Italy. The discussions proceeded under the cloud of the international incident provoked by a riot against the French embassy in Vienna, and the departure of Ambassador Bernadotte. This riot, provoked by Bernadotte in the Viennese version, criminally condoned by Austria in the French version, made an agreement even more remote. Both sides were playing for time. France still hoped to secure an alliance with Prussia, although Siéyès' mission to Berlin failed to shake Prussia's solidly neutral stance. Austria, on the other hand, dared not risk a resumption of the offensive until English support was guaranteed and the attitude of the new Tsar Paul became clear. The rupture of the Seltz conference, and the assassination of French representatives at Rastadt, in floréal VII, made peace impossible.

The expedition to Egypt provided the necessary catalyst for the renewal of the Coalition. The Battle of the Nile encouraged Turkey to declare war on France, and England and Russia were both prepared to support the Sultan. England offered the Tsar a subsidy of one million pounds to maintain an army of 50,000 men in Europe. Naples, too, angered by the French expedition to Malta, now supported the alliance against France.

In the campaigns of 1799, therefore, French armies were committed on a wide front against the allied powers, and for the first time, they now faced a Russian army in Italy. Jourdan's advance into southern Germany was repulsed by the Archduke Charles at Stokach in germinal VII, and Masséna's Helvetian army abandoned Zurich. Although MacDonald's Neapolitan army raced north, he was defeated by Suvorov. On 10 floréal, the Russians entered Milan; within a month they were masters of Turin. The French, heavily outnumbered in northern Italy, launched a desperate offensive, but were decisively defeated at Novi on 28 thermidor VII, when General Joubert met his death.

Victory reopened the allied divisions which had paralysed their campaigns in 1792–3. The Russians were unwilling to allow the Austrians to invade Alsace. The Austrians, who also envisaged the reconquest of Belgium, dissuaded Suvorov from taking a similar initiative in Dauphiné. The two prongs of the allied advance, in southern Germany and northern Italy, did not coordinate their efforts. Masséna was able to split their armies by defending the French salient in Switzerland. His success at the second battle of Zurich in the first week of the Year 8 saved France from invasion.

In floréal VII, the moderating influence of Reubell had been removed from the Directory. The defeats of 1799 threatened to resurrect the spectre of foreign invasion, and a return to the stringent measures of 1793. The generals, who blamed the defeats on the activities of the government's civil *commissaires*, were uncontrollable. Championnet, Masséna, and Brune were rehabilitated. In Barras, Lucien Bonaparte, and Siéyès, the generals found a political group sympathetic to the idea of a revision of the Constitution. On 17 vendémiaire VIII, the greatest of them all landed at Fréjus, to embark on a career of imperial expansion, which would far transcend the aims of the Committee of Public Safety of 1793, and Reubell's policy of protecting France's natural frontiers. The lasting peace which had eluded the Directory for five years was now postponed indefinitely.

15

THE *COUPS* OF FLORÉAL
AND PRAIRIAL

The *coup* of fructidor V had shown the Directory that it could use the support of the Jacobins against the Right. The Directory, however, paid a price for this support. Once encouraged, the revival of Jacobinism could not easily be controlled. By the elections of the Year 6, it was apparent that the balance of power had swung too far to the left, and a new purge was necessary to eliminate the Jacobin menace. This was the purpose of the so-called *coup* of floréal VI. For a while, this enabled the post-fructi-dorian Directory to survive, but the respite was only achieved by further undermining the credibility of the Constitution of the Year 3. Soon, two fundamental difficulties were to weaken the government's position. Firstly, its power base was too narrow to prevent violent fluctuations in the balance of power between the two extremes of Right and Left. The propertied middle class alone was not strong enough to hold the delicate balance against both popular Royalism and the danger of social revolution. It survived only with the help of the army, and a series of purges of the legislature. This inevitably provoked a reappraisal of the Constitution itself. Previous supporters of the Directory began to feel that perhaps the Constitution of 1795 was not, after all, the best safeguard against *chouannerie* and *anarchie*.

Secondly, there was always a danger that military reverses would rekindle the glowing embers of political extremism. The threat of invasion was indeed to reactivate the forces of the Counter-Revolution, and to bring about one last resurgence of Jacobinism in the Year 7. This chapter will describe how the Directory tried to steer a tortuous path between the two extremes, and how it eventually succumbed to the threat of defeat abroad and demands for Constitutional revision at home.

After the *coup d'état* of fructidor V, the elections were annulled in forty-nine departments, and all together a total of 195 deputies were excluded from the legislature. The Royalist Director Bar-thélémy was replaced by Merlin de Douai, and the Conseil des

Anciens passed over the claims of Masséna and Augereau, the victor of fructidor, to elect François de Neufchâteau in place of Carnot. Both Merlin and François had held vital ministries – Merlin as Minister of Justice and Police, and François at the Interior. François, who was to play an important part in the economic reconstruction of France, and in the organisation of the *fêtes décadaires*, was at this time principally known as an author and playwright. Merlin de Douai, an ex-Montagnard, had established a solid reputation as a jurist in the Convention, and was reported to work fourteen hours a day. In addition, Cochon, the scourge of the Jacobins, was replaced at the Police Ministry by Lenoir-Laroche.

The government was soon at grips with a new Jacobin offensive in the legislature. In frimaire VI, Siéyès proposed that all ex-nobles should be deprived of their civic rights, and, in the same month, the Jacobins launched a campaign for the indemnification of those acquitted at the trial of the Babouvists. The Conseil des Anciens, which had stood firm against Royalism in the lower chamber in the Year 5, now continued to defend the Directory by vetoing these Jacobin demands.

In the new *Cercles constitutionnels*, the Directorial equivalents of the Jacobin clubs, the Jacobins formulated important criticisms of governmental policies, and built up an organisational base, on which the elections of the Year 6 could be fought. The *Cercles constitutionnels* were prepared to support the Constitution of the Year 3, to defend the government against Royalism, and to encourage observance of the *décadi*. But the Republican consensus achieved in fructidor was nevertheless a fragile one. In asking for added bonuses for army veterans, the Jacobins cultivated the support of the army, attacked profiteering in the war effort, and defended the rights of the small proprietor. They criticised new impositions like the tolls and the proposed salt tax. The Jacobins attributed the government's financial distress not to the lack of tax revenue, but to the greed of the army contractors, and to waste in the administration of the war effort.

In Paris, the *sans-culotte* personnel of the Year 2 were active in the *Cercles constitutionnels*, but in the provinces, the middle-class nature of Directorial Jacobinism was more apparent. In Toulouse, a stronghold of Jacobinism in this period, Jacobinism bore little resemblance to the extremism of the Year 2, and even less to the revolutionary nature of Babouvism. Its leaders were wealthy property-owners, lawyers, doctors, and businessmen. They included men like the Protestant businessman Marie, or the highly respectable landowners the Vaysse brothers, whose capital was estimated at 100,000 francs. Destrem, who was to become a prominent Jacobin deputy in the Conseil des Cinq Cents, had made a fortune of Balzacian proportions selling grain, oil, and groceries to the municipality in the Years 2 and 3. These men subscribed to the moderate claims expressed by one Jacobin orator in the Toulouse *Cercle constitutionnel,* when he stated, 'Je suis républicain, mais j'abhorre tous ces républicains prétendus, qui ne sont que des terroristes, des partisans cachés de la Constitution de 1793, des ennemis du gouvernement actuel.' Jacobinism thrived in Toulouse, as it did elsewhere, on a sense of local solidarity. In a city surrounded by an anti-Republican peasantry, and in which the emasculation of the parliamentary and ecclesiastical hierarchy had left behind many frustrated sympathisers with the Ancien Régime, Jacobinism was an expression of the city's identity in a hostile environment. At the same time, it was, in the circumstances, the only possible form of Republicanism.

The reformist Jacobins concentrated their efforts on winning the elections of the Year 6. They tried to remove the venue of local elections away from many right-wing *chefs-lieux des départements,* and in nivôse VI, Pons de Verdun asked the Conseil des Cinq Cents to allow the enrolment on the electoral register of anyone who had voluntarily paid the government a sum equivalent to the *cens* (the tax payment which qualified Frenchmen to vote). This move, which would have enfranchised many Jacobin subscribers to the patriotic loan for the invasion of England, was defeated in the Conseil des Anciens. In the Sarthe, a Jacobin electoral machine sent propaganda missions to all corners of the department. The Jacobins did have some success. They won their campaign to disenfranchise anyone inculpated in the Vendéan revolt, or in the vendémiaire rising of the Year 4. The Directory, however, would go no further, and made sure that the election of a new Director would be made before the new legislature took its seats. In this way it rectified the mistake which had led to the election of the Royalist Barthélémy in the Year 5.

The government's official pronouncements still suggested that it saw its main threat on the Right. With the replacement of the Jacobin Police Minister Sotin, in pluviôse VI, however, the alliance between the Directorials and the Left seemed to have collapsed. The Directory made a belated attempt to redirect its propaganda efforts against Jacobinism. On 28 pluviôse VI, a message from the Directory warned France of the danger of 'Royalisme à bonnet rouge', arguing for the collusion of Royalism and Jacobinism against the Republican Centre. This echoed the propaganda themes of Robespierre, who had attacked both the '*citras*' and the '*ultras*', and claimed that both right- and left-wing factions were manifestations of the same counter-revolutionary conspiracy. In the Year 2, this thesis presaged 9 thermidor; in the Year 6, it anticipated the *coup* of 22 floréal.

The government had quickly realigned its sights, but its agents in the provinces were slow to absorb the implications of the Directory's message. Merlin de Douai, who devoted himself to the preparation of the elections, tried to bring the departments into line by sending out government agents into the provinces, ostensibly to supervise the erection of the *barrières*, and the collection of the new tolls. They reported that while many of the Directory's *commissaires* were still directing their efforts against the Right, Jacobinism was making alarming progress in, for example, the Ardèche, the Corrèze, and the Dordogne. There was, however, no sign of any alliance between Royalist and Jacobin forces against the Directory.

Through Merlin, the government mounted official pressure to ensure favourable election results. Many *Cercles constitutionnels* were closed in ventôse, and eleven newspapers were suppressed. In electoral assemblies where the Jacobins seemed likely to be in a majority, the supporters of the Directory would organise a *scission*. That is to say, they would secede, to form a rival electoral assembly electing its own deputies. The legislature could then choose which elections it saw fit to ratify. *Scissions* were to occur in twenty-seven departments of metropolitan France.

The electors of the Year 6 had not only to replace the final third of the members of the Convention, but they had also to fill seats left vacant by deaths, resignations, and the purge of fructidor V. In all, 437 deputies had to be elected. The elections confirmed the Directory's worst fears, and testified to the progress of Jacobinism since the *coup* of fructidor. All together 162 ex-Conventionnels were elected, and of these, seventy-one were regicides. The successful candidates included the Abbé Siéyès, the Dantonist

Thuriot, Robert Lindet of the old Committee of Public Safety, and Barère's brother.

Nevertheless, the results were far from a disaster for the government. In forty-three departments, the Directory still had a majority. Although the government had lost seats to the Left, it had to some extent recovered them at the expense of the Right, even in Royalist areas like Brittany. The electoral map of the Year 6 shows the extent of the Jacobin victory. This map, and those for the Years 4 and 5, must be treated with caution. As a guide to the electoral geography of France, their imprecisions would no doubt horrify modern psephologists. Firstly, they only reflect the opinion of the departmental electoral assemblies, not the opinion of all those who voted in the primary assemblies. Secondly, the massive abstention rate meant that some departments experienced wild swings of opinion from one year to the next. Paris and the Bouches-du-Rhône, for example, strongly Royalist in the Year 5, were won by the Jacobins in the Year 6. The maps, however, do give some indication of the electoral allegiance of the voting élite under the Directory, and they suggest that the Jacobin victory of the Year 6 was not on the same scale as the Royalist successes in the Year 5.

The main areas of Jacobin strength were in the South-west, and parts of the Massif Central. The influence of Toulouse made the Haute-Garonne a staunch bastion of Directorial Jacobinism in the South-west, and the supporters of Barère in the Hautes-Pyrénées, of Vadier in the Ariège, and of General Marbot in the Corrèze had been active in the Year 6. The Jacobin oasis in the Haute-Vienne marked the starting-point for a long tradition, which made this department an almost unique socialist stronghold in the early twentieth century. Jacobinism had also made notable advances in Barras's fief of Provence, and claimed substantial support on the fringes of the areas of *chouannerie*, like the Sarthe. The government had hoped that voters in the countryside would neutralise Jacobin strength in the cities. The Directory drew its main support in the Year 6 from the West, and the Republican East. Royalism was still strong in the Gard, where there was a large Protestant population, and in the recently-annexed Belgian departments.

The Jacobins had challenged the government by constitutional means, and won. In the new legislature, however, the Directory could no longer be sure of an overall majority. It

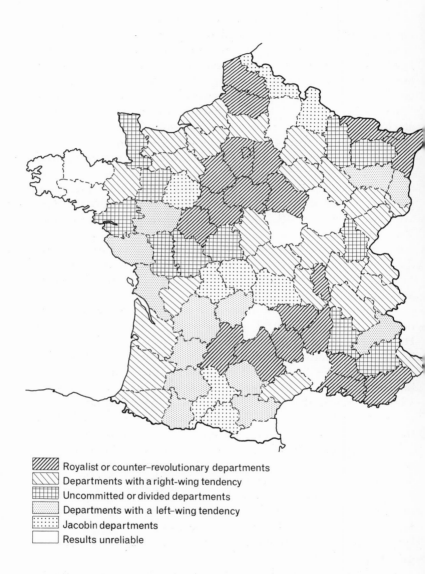

Royalist or counter-revolutionary departments
Departments with a right-wing tendency
Uncommitted or divided departments
Departments with a left-wing tendency
Jacobin departments
Results unreliable

Map 7. Elections of the Year 4 (Source: Bibliography no. 45)

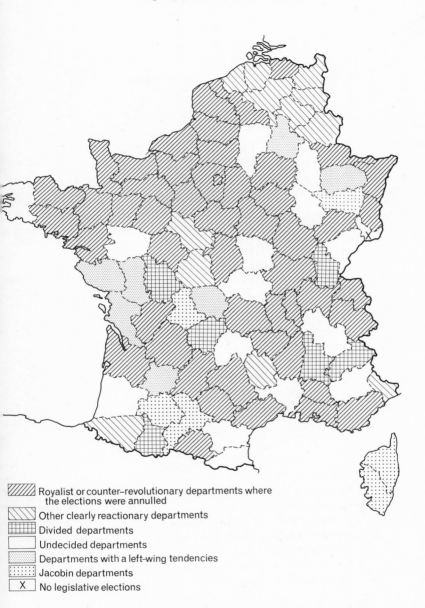

Royalist or counter–revolutionary departments where
the elections were annulled

Other clearly reactionary departments

Divided departments

Undecided departments

Departments with a left-wing tendencies

Jacobin departments

X No legislative elections

Map 8. Elections of the Year 5 (Source: Bibliography no. 64)

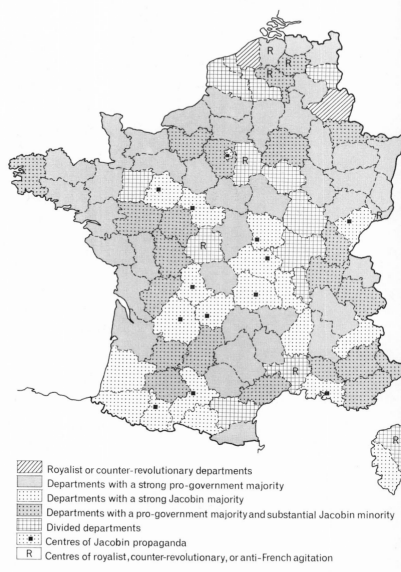

Royalist or counter-revolutionary departments
Departments with a strong pro-government majority
Departments with a strong Jacobin majority
Departments with a pro-government majority and substantial Jacobin minority
Divided departments
Centres of Jacobin propaganda
R Centres of royalist, counter-revolutionary, or anti-French agitation

Map 9. Elections of the Year 6 (Source: Bibliography no. 214)

therefore decided not to tolerate the formation of a constitutional opposition. A propaganda campaign, designed to resuscitate the 'red peril' of the Year 4, anticipated a *coup d'état* against the new deputies. The ponderous Treilhard was elected to the Directory in place of François de Neufchâteau, who reverted to his post as Minister of the Interior. The executive was ready for a brief but intense parliamentary struggle against the Left.

The Conseil des Cinq Cents was urged to ratify as many elections as possible before the powers of the fructidorian legislature lapsed on 1 prairial. So many departmental assemblies had spawned *scissions*, however, that it was very unlikely that the process of ratification would be completed in time. The Directory plied the deputies with lists of 'good' and 'bad' departments, indicating which candidates ought to be admitted, and which excluded, but infuriating delays occurred. A proposal that completely new elections should be held had to be dealt with. The commission reporting on the elections in the Seine department at first proposed the annulment of the proceedings both of the Jacobin electoral assembly, and of the pro-Directorial seceding minority. Time was running out for the Directory. After 1 prairial, the incoming deputies themselves would be responsible for the validation of the electoral returns. Urgent action was required.

On 22 floréal Year 6, the government repeated by law what had been achieved in fructidor Year 5 by armed force. The elections were totally or partially annulled in all but fifty-three departments. Among the casualties were the Lindet brothers, Thuriot, the ex-Police Minister Sotin, and Gohier, Minister of Justice in the Year 2. The most perfunctory excuses were offered for the exclusion of these deputies. The candidates in the Loir-et-Cher, for example, were alleged to have been infected by revolutionary contagion spreading from Vendôme, the site of the Babouvist trial. All together, 127 deputies were deprived of their seats, and the purge ferreted out many of those elected to minor judicial and administrative posts in the departments. Thirty per cent of those elected in the Year 6 were thus eliminated.

Strictly speaking, fructidor had not been repeated. In floréal, for example, the army played no part. Bonaparte was in Egypt, and both Augereau and Jourdan, in the Conseil des Cinq Cents, were no longer sympathetic to the government. Brune and Masséna were openly hostile to the Directory. This time, the purge was carried out by legal methods, and in literal terms it was not unconstitutional. But once again the Directory had reverted to authoritarian means to overrule the expressed wishes of the electorate. The enormous abstention rates in the Years 6 and 7 showed how far successive purges had alienated the mass of the population from the political process. In fructidor, at least, the Directory had been seriously threatened. In floréal, the government had merely wished to preserve its majority against the inroads of a Constitutional opposition.

For Woloch, the historian of Directorial Jacobinism, the floréal *coup* cut short a promising development in French political history – namely, the growth of a party system.[1] The Jacobins, he argues, organised through the *Cercles constitutionnels* and their own press, formed an embryonic opposition party, which was abruptly aborted by the Directorial repression of the Year 6. This remains an open question. It is not clear how influential the important Jacobin newspaper, the *Journal des Hommes Libres*, was outside Paris, or how far it can be considered a truly national party organ. Jacobinism may perhaps be more accurately described in terms of certain departmental lobbies of deputies, or a series of localised pressure groups, centred on individuals or families, like the Barère family in the Hautes-Pyrénées, the Vadier clan in the Ariège, or General Marbot in the Corrèze.

The Directory made the mistake of allowing many Jacobin deputies to slip through its net. The right wing had rallied to the Directory against the Jacobins, but once the menace from the Left had been eliminated, many right-wing deputies now returned to the opposition. The salt tax was only passed in the Conseil des Cinq Cents by a relatively thin majority of forty-six. A nucleus of Jacobins, therefore, remained to challenge the policies of the government.

The renewed outbreak of war and military setbacks in the Year 7 strengthened their hand. The threat of invasion seemed to justify a resurrection of the dictatorial measures of the Terror. The escape of Pichegru from Guiana provoked demands for the confiscation of the property of those deported after the *coup* of fructidor. When deputy Rouchon tried to prevent these fugitive deportees from being assimilated into the list of *émigrés*, he was shouted down by ominous cries of 'À l'Abbaye!' In the months

---

[1]   Bibliography no. 55.

to come, such echoes of the Terrorist past were to reach a last crescendo.

The elections of the Year 7 brought the government no solace. Once again, the government organised the secession of groups of electors sympathetic to the Directory, and *scissions* were particularly frequent in the Midi, the South-west, and the annexed departments. This time, however, the legislature systematically ratified the decisions of the majority.

The Directory's demands for new taxes to finance the war effort made it vulnerable to opposition attacks. The salt tax, which seemed a revival of the odious *gabelle*, was defeated by the Conseil des Anciens, and the Directory was forced simply to double the tax on doors and windows, and increase the other existing taxes. In floréal VII, Génissieux estimated the deficit at 117 million francs, but the Jacobins threw the blame for this on the Directory itself, attacking financial waste, corruption, and fraud by the army contractors. The Jacobins now repeated the criticisms of government finance levelled by Royalist deputies before fructidor V. The War Minister Schérer was a favourite target, and the government's civilian representatives in Italy and Switzerland, like Faipoult and Rapinat, also came under fire. Generals Jourdan, Brune, and Championnet accused the *commissaires aux armées* of squeezing dry the conquered territories, and persuaded a group of deputies, including Lucien Bonaparte, to work for the rehabilitation of the generals. They were soon to have their revenge on the beleaguered and impoverished Directory.

At the end of floréal VII, the Directory lost its powers of resistance, when Reubell left the government to be replaced by Siéyès. The election of Siéyès, who had made no secret of his indifference to the régime, was opposed by all four remaining Directors. His appointment, for La Revellière, was the signal for the destruction of the Constitution of the Year 3, and ultimately, of the Directory itself. The government had lost its firmest pillar of support, and had instead admitted a Trojan horse into its innermost precincts.

The scene was now set for the transformation of the government, which occurred at the end of prairial VII, since then dignified with the name of the '*coup* of prairial'. On 17 prairial, the Conseil des Cinq Cents had invited the Directory to explain the reasons for France's military defeats. Ten days later, no reply had been received. In a permanent session on the night of 28 prairial, Bergasse-Laziroule, prompted by Siéyès, voted the ejection of Treilhard from the Directory, since he had entered the executive before the statutory year had elapsed since his departure from the legislature. Treilhard was replaced by the ex-Jacobin Gohier. Since Barras's loyalty was always unreliable, La Revellière and Merlin de Douai were now in a minority.

On 29 prairial, the Directory replied to the demands of the Cinq Cents, and justified the military reverses by the government's lack of money. The opposition, however, renewed its attacks, and, with the help of the moderates, forced the resignations of La Revellière and Merlin. These last remaining members of the old guard were threatened with a military *coup*, which might declare them outlaws, if they resisted, although La Revellière had enough sense to realise that his resignation would not succeed in saving the régime. Their replacements were the ex-Conventionnel Roger-Ducos, an ally of Siéyès, and the ineffectual General Moulin. Other governmental changes brought Robert Lindet to the Finance Ministry, and Fouché to the Ministry of Police. If the Jacobins expected to benefit from the arrival of this ex-dechristianiser into the government, they were to be cruelly disappointed.

The victims of floréal had taken their revenge on the Directors. In fructidor V and floréal VI, the Directory had acted against hostile deputies in the legislature. Now, in the events of prairial VII, it was the legislature which purged the Directory. With the departure of Reubell, and the resignations of La Revellière and Merlin de Douai, whose staunch Republicanism was never in doubt, the last flicker of hope of saving the régime died. The exponents of Constitutional revision and the generals had taken over the helm. Bernadotte was appointed Minister of War, Joubert commanded the armed forces in Paris, and Championnet, Masséna, and Brune were all rehabilitated. The Directory now went to meet its last crisis.

The advances of the Second Coalition encouraged the victorious *prairialistes* to bring about the last incarnation of Jacobinism. In messidor, a forced loan on the rich was levied to pay for a conscript army, summoned by a new edition of the *levée en masse*. On 24 messidor VII, relatives of *émigrés* and ex-nobles were threatened with detention as hostages in areas of internal subversion and civil war. *Visites domiciliaires* were reintroduced.

The Jacobin club reopened under the title of the 'Réunion des Amis de la Liberté et de l'Égalité', and soon claimed a membership of 3,000, including 250 deputies. Its orators included ex-Babouvists like Drouet and Lepelletier, and ex-Terrorists like Bouchotte, Prieur de la Marne, and Xavier Audouin.

The moderate Centre, however, had only acquiesced to the exclusion of the Directors La Revellière and Merlin on the condition that there would be no reprisals against them. They succeeded in defeating demands for their trial. The Centre was frightened by the resurgence of extreme Jacobinism, and by the emergence of skeletons it preferred to see firmly locked away in the Revolutionary cupboard. The forced loan intimidated property-owners, while the law of hostages appeared as a new law of suspects in disguise. The moderates resisted a return to the dictatorial régime of the Year 2, associated with arbitrary arrest, and the violation of private property. By the end of thermidor they were ready to act. On 26 thermidor, the Directory, supported by Fouché, closed the Jacobin club. On 16 fructidor, Fouché ordered the deportation of sixty-six journalists. The left wing feared another *coup*. The deputy Briot warned, 'Il se prépare un coup d'état, on veut livrer la République à ses ennemis, la renfermer dans ses limites; peut-être les Directeurs des calamités publiques ont-ils un traité de paix dans une poche et une constitution dans l'autre.' The call to declare the 'patrie en danger', which might open the way for a full reconstruction of the Terrorist government, was defeated by a majority of seventy-four. The alliance of prairial had crumbled. The moderates, thoroughly frightened by the Jacobin revival, were now psychologically prepared for the *coup* of brumaire VIII.

During the comparatively calm middle period of the Directory, the government had managed to steer a neutral course between the two extremes of Jacobinism and Royalism. In fructidor V it had drawn on the support of the Left; in floréal VI, the right wing had rallied against Jacobinism. Under the threat of military defeat and economic difficulty, these props were no longer available to the Republican Centre. Political divisions polarised once again. For the military and economic crisis did not only provoke a resurgence of Jacobinism; it also heralded a renewal of Royalist counter-revolutionary activity.

The conscription laws had already brought the Belgian departments to arms. They further encouraged *chouannerie* in Brittany and Normandy. The steady flow of deserters, and of those who avoided conscription, transformed isolated guerrilla bands into new armies of *chouans*. On 23 vendémiaire VIII, they seized Le Mans, and held it for three days. For short periods, *chouan* forces also controlled the towns of Nantes and St-Brieuc. Just as the Jacobin laws of the Year 7 added fuel to Royalist fires, so too the renewal of civil war in the West and elsewhere argued for stronger action from the government.

A greater threat was posed in the South-west, where the network of Royalist conspiracy launched an insurrection in several departments in the late summer of the Year 7. The insurrection was prepared by the *Instituts philanthropiques*, originally set up to campaign for Royalist successes at elections. In the Year 7, with the assistance of British funds, and a handful of returned *émigrés*, they tried to recruit the cadres of a clandestine military organisation. The Instituts were especially strong in Bordeaux and the South-west, which had been ruined by the war, and by the interruption of the Levant trade since the Egypt expedition. Once again, however, the detailed organisation and discipline of an insurrection were beyond the capabilities of the utopian Royalist leadership. They failed to synchronise risings in the South, the Vendée, and Brittany with an allied invasion. Unaccountably, they allowed the insurgents in the Toulousain to act prematurely, and to take up arms early in August, before the Royalist leaders either in Bordeaux or Brittany were ready. Rougé, in command of the insurgents, knew that the capture of the arsenal of Toulouse was vital to his success, and planned to take the city by surprise, before the Jacobin administration had prepared any resistance.

Rougé assembled an army estimated by Destrem at 15,000 strong on the heights of Pech-David, overlooking Toulouse. In his motley band of peasants and deserters, armed mainly with scythes and pitchforks, only one in ten had a rifle. The expected rising in Toulouse, which was intended to open the city to the insurgents, did not materialise. The Toulousain Royalists, true to their tradition of *attentisme*, allowed the Jacobins to take the initiative, arrest a number of hostages, organise arms searches, and mobilise the National Guard. With the assistance of the National Guards of the neighbouring departments of the Lot and the Tarn, the Republicans repulsed the Royalist army, and drove it towards the Pyrenees, and its only escape route, the Spanish frontier. At Montréjeau, on 3 fructidor, the Royalists were routed. Within a fortnight, about 4,000 men lay dead in the departments of the Haute-Garonne and the Ariège. The insurgents uprooted *arbres de liberté*, raided tax offices, destroyed the tax-rolls, and cut down the toll-barriers. Purchasers of *biens nationaux* had their heads shaved. Dire threats were issued against the Protestant communities of the Ariège. Representatives of the government went in fear of their lives, if they did not assist the progress of the insurgent army. The *commissaire du Directoire* in St-Gaudens fled to the woods, and lived there for six days, with his municipal officers and *juge de paix*.

The government had been slow to send regular troops to crush the insurrection, and the Republicans of Toulouse played the major rôle in its defeat. Nevertheless, the government took a lenient view of the uprising. By 20 vendémiaire VIII, a special military court had sentenced only ten men to death, most of them poor peasants who made up the bulk of the Royalist army. They had never enjoyed the leadership they deserved. Landowners like the Villèle family, who had protected the rebels, escaped prosecution. Once again the Directory had scored an important victory over an ill-prepared Royalist insurrection. For the wealthy middle class, and the purchasers of *biens nationaux*, insurrections like these were perhaps more disturbing than the Jacobin forced loan, which in any case proved ineffective. The Directory's clemency, probably designed to dampen Jacobin enthusiasm, may not have reassured them.

Until the second battle of Zurich brought some relief to France, the military setbacks and economic crisis had encouraged the Directory's enemies to right and left. The moderates had defeated these enemies, but there were many former supporters of the Directory who now sensed the inadequacy of the Constitution of the Year 3. A weak executive, and a theoretically liberal régime could not survive a state of emergency. Hence they acquiesced in the expulsion of the Directors in prairial VII. At the same time, however, they did not necessarily accept the Jacobin solution to France's problems. A strong government had to be found to defeat the Coalition, eliminate the deficit, and control political extremism, and such a government could not be allowed to emerge from the ranks of the ex-Terrorists. The search for a new solution had to be directed elsewhere. On 17 vendémiaire VIII, Bonaparte landed at Fréjus. The Directory's nemesis was at hand.

16

THE FIRST REPUBLIC'S LAST
COUP D'ÉTAT

At many different watering-places along the revolutionary road, politicians of very different political allegiance had declared the journey over. First the Feuillants and then the Girondins hoped to bring France the political stability which would make the achievements of the Revolution permanent. For the men of the Year 3, 9 thermidor Year 2 seemed to have ended once and for all the factional strife which had divided the country and prolonged the Revolution. The *coup* of fructidor, however, showed that the struggle was far from over. The crisis of the Year 7 had renewed the struggle and indirectly provoked the *coup* of 18 brumaire Year 8, which again claimed to put the final seal on a decade of revolutionary strife.

By vendémiaire Year 8, the Directory appeared to have weathered the storm. The defeat of the Russians and Austrians at Zurich had dispelled the danger of foreign invasion. The government seemed to have the measure of the Jacobins in the legislature, and the Royalist insurrection in the South-west had been crushed. The crisis, however, had shown that the moderate Republican government of the Directory was no longer capable of guaranteeing political stability. The government maintained its position only by denying liberal demands for a free press and the freedom of association. It was patently unable to face the consequences of annual elections. New assurances were necessary for the purchasers of the *biens nationaux*, and 'tous ceux que la propriété ou l'agriculture attachent au sol de la France: classe nombreuse, utile, respectable, et qui a eu le bonheur de traverser la Révolution avec sagesse', as the President of the Conseil des Anciens described the régime's supporters in the Year 6. The Directory's '*politique de bascule*', which had enabled it to survive for longer than any other revolutionary régime, now seemed inadequate. As Français lamented in the Conseil des Cinq Cents, in fructidor Year 7, 'Je sais qu'on a beaucoup parlé d'un parti neutre et mitoyen, également ennemi de tous les extrêmes et destiné, par sa sagesse, à tenir toujours la balance à la main; mais

ce parti est sans vie, sans couleur, sans mouvement; il se com-
pose, dans toute la France, de quelques Royalistes déguisés, de
beaucoup d'êtres faibles disposés à transiger; dans toutes les
secousses, la balance tombe de leurs mains timides.' A new recipe
for political security was required.

The Constitution, however, made amendments by legal means
extraordinarily difficult. Constitutional revision had to be ratified by the two chambers three times, at intervals of three years.
Even if, after this nine-year period, there was still a majority in
favour of Constitutional revision, this had to be ratified by a
special assembly called for the purpose, as well as by the primary
electoral assemblies. The proponents of revision, like Sièyès,
therefore resorted to a military *coup*.

The model of the 1795 Constitution had already undergone
significant changes, when it had been introduced into the sister
republics. A stronger executive, which controlled the Treasury,
for instance, had been recommended for the Cisalpine Republic. Prefects had been appointed in the Helvetic Republic, and
the Roman Constitution also incorporated at least the nomencla-
ture of future consular institutions. Precedents for the future
were thus already available in the conquered territories.

Siéyès had his own plans for a régime which would institu-
tionalise a rigid separation of powers, and instal a Grand Jury to
guard against violations of the Constitution. Amongst his supporters, the future brumairiens, were disillusioned supporters
of the Directory like Boulay de la Meurthe, moderates like
Rœderer and Cambacérès, intriguers like Talleyrand and
Fouché, and the intellectuals of the Institut like Cabanis, who had
high hopes of Bonaparte. A general was required. The death of
Hoche, and then the unfortunate death of Joubert at Novi in
thermidor Year 7, made Bonaparte the only possible candidate.
With the election of Lucien Bonaparte as President of the
Conseil des Cinq Cents on 1 brumaire, the opportunity for action
now presented itself. In the gardens of the Luxembourg, Siéyès
could be seen taking riding lessons, in preparation for the
fulfilment of his schemes.

Nevertheless, the *coup* was very nearly bungled. On 18 brumaire, on the pretext of an alleged Jacobin conspiracy, Régnier
persuaded the Conseil des Anciens to meet the next day outside
the capital, at St-Cloud. Bonaparte was appointed to command
the armed forces of Paris, which neutralised the opposition of the

War Minister, Dubois-Crancé. In the Cinq Cents, Lucien informed the assembly of the move to St-Cloud, and adjourned the session to cut short any discussion. The conspirators then foolishly rejected advice to arrest prominent Jacobin deputies on the night of the 18th. They hoped instead for a favourable outcome at St-Cloud on 19 brumaire.

Bonaparte occupied the Tuileries gardens, while Moreau 'guarded', or rather imprisoned, the Directory in the Luxembourg. Barras resigned, Moulin escaped, and Gohier was not allowed to leave the Luxembourg until 20 brumaire. Their resignations meant that the Directory had effectively ceased to exist.

At St-Cloud, Bonaparte impetuously demanded that the Conseil des Anciens take urgent measures to defend liberty and equality, asserting that the Constitution had already been irreparably violated by all parties. In the Cinq Cents, his appearance with an escort of armed grenadiers provoked an eruption. Bonaparte himself was physically manhandled, and was greeted with cries of 'À bas le dictateur!' Demands for him to be declared an outlaw echoed in his ears as he was expelled from the chamber. Then, at the very hour of their demise, the deputies defiantly renewed their oath of allegiance to the Constitution of the Year 3.

The course of events had turned against the conspirators. Bonaparte's arrogance, and the tactless display of armed force had angered the deputies. The situation was saved for the brumairiens by the presence of mind of Lucien. In a harangue to the troops, he revealed that the deputies, the despicable *avocats*, had attempted to stab their glorious leader to death. As President of the Cinq Cents, he accordingly ordered them to evacuate the chamber. The deputies were ejected. A rump of the legislature then voted the abolition of the Directory and the establishment of a three-man executive. Sixty-one deputies were formally deprived of their seats, including leading Jacobins like Destrem and General Jourdan. Government now passed into the hands of provisional commissions chosen by both chambers.

Nothing yet suggested that this was any different from any of the previous *coups d'état* of the Directorial period, or that the provisional Consulate of Bonaparte, Siéyès, and Roger-Ducos was anything but a new Directory reduced in size. The intentions of the new régime were shrouded in ambiguity. In Republican centres like Toulouse, the arrest of Destrem seemed to suggest that the *coup* of brumaire was essentially anti-Jacobin. On 7 frimaire, however, the distinguished Terrorist Barère approved of the *coup* in a widely-publicised letter to Bonaparte. Elsewhere, the Royalists drew comfort from events in Paris, anticipating the repeal of the forced loan and of the law of hostages.

The brumairiens cultivated this ambiguity, realising that true success was only possible if all shades of political opinion could find something to support in the new régime. Fouché's assessment of the *coup*, on 20 brumaire, was therefore suitably vague and non-committal. 'Le gouvernement', he claimed, 'était trop faible pour soutenir la gloire de la République contre les ennemis extérieurs et garantir les droits des citoyens contre les factions domestiques: il fallait songer à lui donner de la force et de la grandeur.' The past was not immediately repudiated. Lucien presented 19 brumaire as the continuation of the tradition of fraternal resolve expressed in the Tennis Court Oath of 20 June 1789. Clouds of uncertainty still obscured the breaking of a new dawn.

For Bonaparte, the reactions of Paris would be crucial to the success of the brumaire *coup*. The capital in fact seemed to accept the change with tepid enthusiasm. Since the closure of the Jacobin club, the left wing had no means of exerting pressure, except in the street. Like their successors in 1851, however, the workers of the Faubourg St-Antoine saw no reason to take up arms to defend a Republican régime, which had consistently excluded them from political power. The Stock Exchange gave the brumairiens a warmer welcome. The value of government stock rose from 11 fr. 38 on 17 brumaire to twenty francs a week later.

There was some opposition to the *coup*, however, from the old administrators of the Directory. In the Pas-de-Calais, and the Pyrénées-Orientales, the authorities refused to promulgate the decrees of 19 brumaire. The administration of the Jura even ordered the establishment of an armed force to combat this attack on popular sovereignty. On the whole, however, the *coup* was accepted with apathetic resignation.

The Consulate did eventually give assurances to both sides, by maintaining the *décadi*, by repealing the forced loan and the law of hostages, and by re-admitting many Directorial deputies into the new legislature. For some time, however, there was little to indicate that the *coup* of brumaire Year 8 should not take its place alongside the series of *coups* which punctuated the troubled history of the Directory. The promulgation of the Constitution of the Year 8, however, was intended to give the new régime a rousing start. A new Corps Législatif and a Tribunat were to divide between them the discussion and voting of new laws, while the abolition of the cantonal administrations placed the departments under the tutelage of the new prefectoral system. The Constitution was submitted for approval by plebiscite in pluviôse Year 8.

In spite of optimistic government pronouncements, the plebiscite failed to achieve the desired result. Lucien Bonaparte, now Minister of the Interior, claimed that three million voters had accepted the Constitution, against only 1,562 negative votes. He himself, however, had falsified the result by exaggerating the returns from each department by about 8,000 votes. He further assumed the unanimous approval of the army, which never in fact voted. The truth was that little more than a million and a half voters approved the Constitution: more than had accepted the Constitution of 1795, but less than the vote in favour of the Jacobin Constitution of 1793.

The Consulate, therefore, failed to shake France out of its political apathy. The abstention rate was enormous, especially in the Belgian departments, and in the cities of Toulouse and Marseille. In the Seine department, there were only 32,000 votes in favour of the Constitution. Putting the best face on these meagre results, Rœderer interpreted France's apparent indifference as the tacit approval of the silent majority.

Once again, the brumairiens had mismanaged affairs. The plebiscite was too hastily organised, and, unlike the elections of the Directory, it was held in December, when ice and snow kept many voters away from the polls. The plebiscite thus failed to give the régime the legitimacy it needed. It was clear that the chief cause of the collapse of the Directory was the nation's political apathy. The government's falsification of the returns repeated, in a less open fashion, the Directory's own cynical attitude towards elections. Only two years later, with the plebiscite on the Life Consulate, did Bonaparte succeed in awakening the nation from its soporific indifference to the *coup* of brumaire.

The Directory was not a betrayal of the Revolution, but an attempt to continue its liberal ideals. It was still a revolutionary régime, as anticlerical as previous and (some) future Republican governments, equally anti-Royalist and keen to carry the Revolution to the rest of Europe. The *'politique de bascule'* itself was inherited from the Year 2, foreshadowed by Robespierre's Janus-like proscription of the Indulgents and the Hébertistes.

The strong Centre party, however, whose moderate Republicanism would provide a guarantee of support for a liberal régime, did not emerge. The Directory failed to establish a legitimate form of parliamentary government which could maintain the social gains of the Revolution against Royalist Counter-Revolution, and defend property rights against Jacobin-inspired social democracy. The development of a liberal political system, based on free elections and open discussion, required a period of calm and stability, and a consensus of agreement in favour of a moderate Republican form of government. These conditions were lacking. Economic crisis, and the pressures of war and invasion (in the Year 7) prolonged the emergency situation. It is possible to interpret the Royalist *Instituts philanthropiques* and the Jacobin *Cercles constitutionnels* as the beginnings of nascent political parties, ready to work within the system. The Royalists, however, relied on English financial aid, and the *Instituts philanthropiques* unleashed an armed insurrection in the Year 7. Similarly, the government could not forget that the revolutionary wing of Jacobinism had been responsible for the Babeuf conspiracy and the attack on Grenelle in the Year 4.

The Directory had tried for four years to make a normal parliamentary régime work in abnormal circumstances. In order to defend a liberal system of government, it had resorted to illiberal means, on 18 fructidor Year 5 and 22 floréal Year 6. It had refused to accept the consequences of annual elections, and had overruled the desires of the electorate. Perhaps compromise was possible, with moderate Constitutional Royalists in the Year 5, and with reformist Jacobinism in the Year 6. The Directory never dared risk such a compromise, and it yielded to the temptation to make political capital out of the spectres of Royalism and the 'red peril'. In doing so, it fatally narrowed the basis of its own support.

The dispersal of authority created by the thermidorean Constitution was inadequate to cope with the emergency of war and economic crisis. The political authoritarianism and economic constraints of the Terror were too quickly abandoned in favour of liberalism and a free economy. A revolutionary situation still existed in France, and the memories and divisions of the past decade had not yet been exorcised. Until they were, strong government was required. This was the lesson of fructidor, of floréal, and of brumaire, which all represented the triumph of the executive power over the legislature.

It is easier to describe the Directory's enemies than to define its adherents. It had support in the Conseil des Anciens, among purchasers of the *biens nationaux,* among Republican intellectuals, and, at first, in the army. The Directory's apparent lack of any firm social base has led commentators like Church to portray it simply in political terms, as an attempt to perpetuate the thermidorean political élite in power.[1] It may indeed be too simple to describe the Directory as a *bourgeois* Republic, since, in the last resort, the *bourgeoisie* abandoned the régime. In the Year 5, conservative voters preferred Royalist deputies, and by 1804, they accepted the Empire without regrets.

Yet the aims of the thermidorean Constitution, with its insistence on a free economy, and the protection of property rights, and its denial of universal suffrage, were *bourgeois* aims. During the Directory, the *bourgeois* élite, now enlarged and renewed, reassumed the authority it had temporarily surrendered during the Terror, and was again to surrender to Napoleon. The social bias of the Directorial régime was nothing new. At all stages, the Revolution had enjoyed middle-class leadership, and, adopting an essentially utilitarian attitude towards poverty, remained indifferent to the condition of the lowest classes of society.

For Church, the Directory was merely the 'board of executors of the revolutionary settlement'. If French citizens had agreed on this, then the life of the Directory would have been happier and longer. The vexed question was: which revolutionary settlement? For the left, the régime ought to have been the custodian of the social and egalitarian ideals of 1793; for others, those of the Girondin Convention; and for the moderate right, the programme of the Constitutional Monarchy. The Directory's closest ancestors were probably the men of 1791. It rejected the Jacobin

[1] Bibliography no. 14.

settlement, for a controlled economy and a dictatorial central government seemed odious and dispensable. It rejected the settlement of 1792, for it was dangerous to entrust the fate of the country to a Convention elected by citizens thought unqualified to exercise full political rights. Instead, the Directory hoped to renew the liberalism of the Constituent Assembly. The régime borrowed the idea of a two-chamber system from the repertoire of the anglophile *monarchien* group, but it was not now encumbered by a monarchy whose loyalty to the Revolution had been exposed as a calculated fraud. The Directorials and thermidoreans made the same mistakes as the Constituents – they had an exaggerated distrust of a strong executive – and they paid for such mistakes. But the Directory must take its place in the mainstream of revolutionary liberalism.

The years between 1796 and 1800 were important transitional years. Not only did the period inherit the anticlericalism and revolutionary chauvinism of the Year 2, but it also bequeathed a substantial legacy to its successors – a legacy which Bonapartists were reluctant to acknowledge. The stabilisation of the finances and the reorganisation of the fiscal system were important conditions for Bonaparte's success. Soboul has rightly emphasised the continuity between the Directory and the Consulate, and both he and Sydenham imply that the creation of the Empire was a more decisive break with the past than either 9 thermidor or 18 brumaire.[1]

In educational reform, and in economic life, the Directory achieved a limited reconstruction of the fabric of French life, which had been impossible in the crisis of 1793. New projects and schemes for the transformation of French social institutions had to wait for consideration until the invading armies had been expelled. The Directory was able to put some of these projects into practice, and to elaborate Republican institutions which might replace the Church, the army, the hospitals, and the schools of the Ancien Régime. The régime did not find an alternative to traditional Catholicism, and it left the healing of France's religious schism entirely to its successors. But it tried with mixed success to develop a specifically Republican conception of art, literature, medicine, and science.

The limited reforms carried out by the Directory were vitiated

---

[1] Bibliography nos. 24 and 25.

by lack of funds and the pressures of war. Success was limited by the weakness of the central government and by the 'depoliticisation' of France after the Terror. Banditry and the White Terror could not be controlled, and while popular inertia helped the Directory to survive, it eventually made the régime vulnerable to the sudden *coup* which overthrew it.

Because of these difficulties, the Directory had to improvise, and on many occasions to resign itself to the government's impotence in the provinces. It was above all in its fiscal and administrative reforms that the Directory's successes were most enduring. The régime gave France a remodelled civil service and a new tax structure. In addition, it left posterity the École Polytechnique, the metre, the kilogram, and the franc, smallpox vaccine, and Charenton. In its experimental search for Republican forms of art, education, science, and religion, in its combative spirit of anticlericalism, the Directory represented the final flowering of eighteenth-century humanism.

Nineteenth-century and even twentieth-century French politicians have defined their political stance as 'men of '89', 'men of '92', or 'men of '93', claiming descent from the original Girondins or Jacobins. The Directory of 1796 or 1799 has not enjoyed a surviving political tradition with such compulsive appeal. Its significance may indeed lie as a demonstration of the weakness of the liberal parliamentary tradition in France, or as an indication that a strong executive was necessary in a post-revolutionary France, which remained bitterly divided along social, political, and religious lines. If this is true, then the Directory was not an isolated episode. In 1851, another Republican régime, based on limited suffrage, and with a similar anticlerical bias, failed to find a lasting liberal alternative to a deposed monarchy and the 'red peril' of the June Days. Like the Directory, the Second Republic succumbed to a Bonapartist *coup*. In the early 1870s, a third Republican government tried to renew the experiment, in defiance of a Royalist majority, under the shadow not of the Terror, but of the Paris Commune. On this occasion, too, the Republic survived through the divisions in its opponents' ranks. In the 1870s, however, France was no longer at war, and no Bonaparte arose to put a violent end to its troubled days.

Appendix 1. *Correspondence between the Republican and Gregorian calendars*

	Revolutionary year			
Month	II	III	IV	V
1 vendémiaire	22 Sept. 1793	22 Sept. 1794	23 Sept. 1795	22 Sept. 1796
10	1 Oct. 1793	1 Oct. 1794	2 Oct. 1795	1 Oct. 1796
20	11	11	12	11
1 brumaire	22	22	23	22
10	31	31	1 Nov. 1795	31
20	10 Nov. 1793	10 Nov. 1794	11	10 Nov. 1796
1 frimaire	21	21	22	21
10	30	30	1 Dec. 1795	30
20	10 Dec. 1793	10 Dec. 1794	11	10 Dec. 1796
1 nivôse	21	21	22	21
10	30	30	31	30
20	9 Jan. 1794	9 Jan. 1795	10 Jan. 1796	9 Jan. 1797
1 pluviôse	20	20	21	20
10	29	29	30	29
20	8 Feb. 1794	8 Feb. 1795	9 Feb. 1796	8 Feb. 1797
1 ventôse	19	19	20	19
10	28	28	29	28
20	10 Mar. 1794	10 Mar. 1795	10 Mar. 1796	10 Mar. 1797
1 germinal	21	21	21	21
10	30	30	30	30
20	9 Apr. 1794	9 Apr. 1795	9 Apr. 1796	9 Apr. 1797
1 floréal	20	20	20	20
10	29	29	29	29
20	9 May 1794	9 May 1795	9 May 1796	9 May 1797
1 prairial	20	20	20	20
10	29	29	29	29
20	8 June 1794	8 June 1795	8 June 1796	8 June 1797
1 messidor	19	19	19	19
10	28	28	28	28
20	8 July 1794	8 July 1795	8 July 1796	8 July 1797
1 thermidor	19	19	19	19
10	28	28	28	28
20	7 Aug. 1794	7 Aug. 1795	7 Aug. 1796	7 Aug. 1797
1 fructidor	18	18	18	18
10	27	27	27	27
20	6 Sept. 1794	6 Sept. 1795	6 Sept. 1796	6 Sept. 1797
1er jour complémentaire	17	17	17	17
5e	21	21	21	21
6e		22		

Appendix 1 (*cont.*)

Month	Revolutionary year			
	VI	VII	VIII	IX
1 vendémiaire	22 Sept. 1797	22 Sept. 1798	23 Sept. 1799	23 Sept. 1800
10	1 Oct. 1797	1 Oct. 1798	2 Oct. 1799	2 Oct. 1800
20	11	11	12	12
1 brumaire	22	22	23	23
10	31	31	1 Nov. 1799	1 Nov. 1800
20	10 Nov. 1797	10 Nov. 1798	11	11
1 frimaire	21	21	22	22
10	30	30	1 Dec. 1799	1 Dec. 1800
20	10 Dec. 1797	10 Dec. 1798	11	11
1 nivôse	21	21	22	22
10	30	30	31	31
20	9 Jan. 1798	9 Jan. 1799	10 Jan. 1800	10 Jan. 1801
1 pluviôse	20	20	21	21
10	29	29	30	30
20	8 Feb. 1798	8 Feb. 1799	9 Feb. 1800	9 Feb. 1801
1 ventôse	19	19	20	20
10	28	28	1 Mar. 1800	1 Mar. 1801
20	10 Mar. 1798	10 Mar. 1799	11	11
1 germinal	21	21	22	22
10	30	30	31	31
20	9 Apr. 1798	9 Apr. 1799	10 Apr. 1800	10 Apr. 1801
1 floréal	20	20	21	21
10	29	29	30	30
20	9 May 1798	9 May 1799	10 May 1800	10 May 1801
1 prairial	20	20	21	21
10	29	29	30	30
20	8 June 1798	8 June 1799	9 June 1800	9 June 1801
1 messidor	19	19	20	20
10	28	28	29	29
20	8 July 1798	8 July 1799	9 July 1800	9 July 1801
1 thermidor	19	19	20	20
10	28	28	29	29
20	7 Aug. 1798	7 Aug. 1799	8 Aug. 1800	8 Aug. 1801
1 fructidor	18	18	19	19
10	27	27	28	28
20	6 Sept. 1798	6 Sept. 1799	7 Sept. 1800	7 Sept. 1801
1er jour com-				18
plémentaire	17	17	18	22
5^{e}	21	21	22	
6^{e}		22		

Appendix 2. *Chronological table*

A reference list of the dates of laws, treaties, battles, and other single events mentioned in the text.

1974/Year 2
9–10 therm. (27–8 July)	Overthrow of Robespierre
7 fruct. (24 Aug.)	Law on thermidorean government

Year 3
9 brum. (30 Oct.)	Lakanal law on education
22 brum. (12 Nov.)	Jacobin club of Paris closed
14 frim. (4 Dec.)	Creation of Écoles de Santé
18 frim. (8 Dec.)	Ex-Girondins return to Convention
4 niv. (24 Dec.)	Abolition of the Maximum

1795
1 pluv. (20 Jan.)	French occupy Amsterdam
29 pluv. (17 Feb.)	Vendéan armistice
3 vent. (21 Feb.)	Separation of Church and State
12 vent. (2 Mar.)	Arrest of Barère, Billaud-Varenne, and Collot-d'Herbois
12–13 germ. (1–2 Apr.)	Insurrection in Paris
16 germ. (5 Apr.)	Treaty of Basle, with Prussia
21 germ. (10 Apr.)	Disarmament of Terrorists
27 flor. (16 May)	Franco-Dutch alliance
1–4 prair. (20–3 May)	Insurrection in Paris
3 therm. (21 July)	*Émigrés* defeated at Quiberon Bay
15 fruct. (1 Sept.)	Establishment of École Polytechnique

Year 4
1 vend. (23 Sept.)	Constitution proclaimed
9 vend. (1 Oct.)	Annexation of Belgium
13 vend. (5 Oct.)	Royalist insurrection in Paris
3 brum. (25 Oct.)	Daunou law on education
4 brum. (26 Oct.)	General amnesty for political offences
19 frim. (10 Dec.)	Forced loan

1796
30 pluv. (19 Feb.)	Abolition of *assignats*
6 vent. (25 Feb.)	Execution of Stofflet

28 vent. (18 Mar.)	Creation of *mandats territoriaux*
9 germ. (29 Mar.)	Execution of Charette
2 flor. (21 Apr.)	Battle of Mondovi
9 flor. (28 Apr.)	Armistice of Cherasco, with Piedmont
21 flor. (10 May)	Battle of Lodi. Arrest of Babouvists
4 prair. (23 May)	Rising against French in Pavia
24 prair. (12 June)	French invade Papal Legations
23 fruct. (9 Sept.)	*Affaire* of the camp de Grenelle

Year 5

25 vend. (16 Oct.)	Cispadane Republic proclaimed at Bologna
25–7 brum. (15–17 Nov.)	Battle of Arcole
25 frim. (15 Dec.)	Departure of Irish expedition

1797

25 niv. (14 Jan.)	Battle of Rivoli
11 pluv. (30 Jan.)	Arrest of Brottier
14 pluv. (2 Feb.)	Fall of Mantua
16 pluv. (4 Feb.)	Return to metallic currency
26 pluv. (14 Feb.)	Battle of Cape St Vincent
1 vent. (19 Feb.)	Treaty of Tolentino, with the Pope
29 germ. (18 Apr.)	Preliminaries of Leoben
7 prair. (26 May)	Barthélémy enters Directory
8 prair. (27 May)	Execution of Babeuf and Darthé
18 fruct. (4 Sept.)	*Coup d'état* against Royalists
22 fruct. (8 Sept.)	Merlin de Douai and François de Neufchâteau enter Directory

Year 6

9 vend. (30 Sept.)	Consolidation of the two-thirds
20 vend. (11 Oct.)	Battle of Camperdown
26 vend. (17 Oct.)	Treaty of Campoformio
8 frim. (28 Nov.)	Congress of Rastadt

1798

3 pluv. (22 Jan.)	*Coup d'état* at The Hague
9 pluv. (28 Jan.)	Annexation of Mulhouse
26 pluv. (14 Feb.)	French occupy Berne
27 pluv. (15 Feb.)	Proclamation of the Roman Republic
22 flor. (11 May)	Election of Jacobin deputies annulled
26 flor. (15 May)	Treilhard enters Directory
30 flor. (19 May)	Departure of Egypt expedition
3 therm. (21 July)	Battle of the Pyramids
14 therm. (1 Aug.)	Battle of the Nile
19 fruct. (5 Sept.)	Jourdan law on conscription
23 fruct. (9 Sept.)	Law on *décadi* and *fêtes nationales*

Chronological table of events

Year 7

21 vend. (12 Oct.)	Beginning of insurrection in Belgium
24 vend. (15 Oct.)	First Exposition Nationale
30 vend. (21 Oct.)	Rising against the French in Cairo
4 frim. (24 Nov.)	Creation of tax on doors and windows

1799

7 pluv. (26 Jan.)	Proclamation of the Neapolitan Republic
29 vent. (19 Mar.)	Siege of St John of Acre
5 germ. (25 Mar.)	Battle of Stokach
9 flor. (28 Apr.)	Assassination of French representatives at Rastadt
10 flor. (29 Apr.)	Russians enter Milan
27 flor. (16 May)	Siéyès enters Directory
16 prair. (4 June)	First battle of Zurich
29 prair. (17 June)	Gohier enters Directory
30 prair. (18 June)	*Journée parlementaire.* Resignation of La Revellière and Merlin de Douai
1 mess. (19 June)	Roger-Ducos enters Directory
2 mess. (20 June)	Moulin enters Directory
10 mess. (28 June)	*Levée en masse*
18 mess. (6 July)	Jacobin club re-established
24 mess. (12 July)	Law of Hostages
7 therm. (25 July)	Battle of Aboukir
18 therm. (5 Aug.)	Outbreak of Royalist insurrection in the South-west
28 therm. (15 Aug.)	Battle of Novi

Year 8

3–5 vend. (25–7 Sept.)	Second battle of Zurich
17 vend. (9 Oct.)	Bonaparte disembarks at Fréjus.
18 brum. (10 Oct.)	*Coup d'état.* Resignation of Siéyès, Roger-Ducos, and Barras
19 brum. (11 Oct.)	Formation of a provisional Consulate
24 frim. (15 Dec.)	Publication of new Constitution

1800

18 pluv. (7 Feb.)	Publication of results of plebiscite

BIBLIOGRAPHY

This is not a thorough bibliography, but a selection of those works to which the author has most frequently referred, and which provide a suitable basis for further study. Unless otherwise stated, the works listed were published in Paris.

Abbreviations of periodicals

A.h.R.f.	Annales historiques de la Révolution française
Ann.dém.hist.	Annales de démographie historique
Ann.E.S.C.	Annales – économies, sociétés, civilisations
Ann.hist.écon.soc.	Annales d'histoire économique et sociale
Ann.Midi	Annales du Midi
Ann.Norm.	Annales de Normandie
B.J.R.L.	Bulletin of the John Rylands Library
B.S.H.P.F.	Bulletin de la société de l'histoire du Protestantisme français
F.h.s.	French Historical Studies
J.E.H.	Journal of Economic History
J.M.H.	Journal of Modern History
P. & P.	Past and Present
Pop.	Population
R.h.	Revue historique
Rév.fr.	La Révolution française
Rev.hist.litt.	Revue d'histoire littéraire de la France

Memoirs and published documents

1 A. Aulard, *Paris pendant la réaction thermidorienne et sous le Directoire*, 5 vols., 1899.
2 Barras, *Mémoires*, 1895–6.
3 A. Débidour, *Receuil des Actes du Directoire exécutif*, 4 vols., 1910–17.
4 G. Duval, *Souvenirs thermidoriens*, 1844.
5 *Journal de la Haute Cour de Justice de Vendôme*, ed. P. N. Hésine, ans 4–5.
6 *Journal des Hommes Libres de tous les pays*, ed. R. Vatar, ans 4–5.

Bibliography

7   La Revellière-Lépeaux, *Mémoires*, 1895.

8   Mallet du Pan, *Correspondance avec le cour de Vienne, 1794–8*, 2 vols., 1884.

9   H. Meister, *Souvenirs de mon dernier voyage à Paris, 1795*, 1910.

10 L. S. Mercier, *Le Nouveau Paris*, 1798.

11 *Ré-impression de l'Ancien Moniteur*, 32 vols., 1863.

12 F. Rocquain, *L'État de la France au 18 brumaire*, 1874.

General works and works of reference

13 A. Aulard, *Histoire politique de la Révolution française*, 1926.

14 C. H. Church, 'In search of the Directory', in *French Government and Society, 1500–1850, Essays in Memory of A. Cobban*, ed. J. F. Bosher, London, 1973.

15 R. C. Cobb, *Police and the People, French Popular Protest, 1789–1820*, Oxford, 1970.

16 R. C. Cobb, *Reactions to the French Revolution*, London, 1972.

17 F. Furet and D. Richet, *La Révolution*, vol. 2, 1966.

18 J. Godechot, *Les Institutions de la France sous la Révolution et l'Empire*, 1968.

19 A. Goodwin, 'The French Executive Directory – a re-evaluation', *History*, vol. XXII, no. 87 (1937).

20 A. Kuscinski, *Les Députés au Corps législatif, Conseil des Cinq Cents, Conseil des Anciens, de l'an IV à l'an VIII*, 1905.

21 G. Lefebvre, *Les Thermidoriens*, 1937.

22 G. Lefebvre, *Le Directoire*, 1946.

23 L. Sciout, *Le Directoire*, 4 vols., 1895–7.

24 A. Soboul, *Le Directoire et le Consulat*, 1967.

25 M. J. Sydenham, *The First French Republic, 1792–1804*, London, 1974.

26 D. Woronoff, *La République bourgeoise, 1794–99*, 1972.

Local studies

27 G. Caudrillier, 'Bordeaux sous le Directoire', *Rév.fr.*, vol. 70 (1917).

28 P. Clémendot, *Le Département de la Meurthe à l'époque du Directoire*, 1966.

29 G. Lefebvre, *Les Paysans du Nord*, Lille, 1924.

30 F. L'Huillier, *Recherches sur l'Alsace napoléonienne*, Strasbourg, 1944.

31 R. Marx, *Recherches sur la vie politique de l'Alsace pré-révolutionnaire et révolutionnaire*, Strasbourg, 1966.

32 M. Reinhard, *Le Département de la Sarthe sous le régime directorial*, 1966.

Bibliography

33   J. R. Suratteau, *Le département du Mont-Terrible sous le Directoire*, 1965.

Some biographies

34   P. Bastid, *Siéyès et sa pensée*, 1929.
35   P. Boucher, *Charles Cochon de Lapparent*, 1969.
36   H. Guillemin, *Benjamin Constant, muscadin, 1795–9*, 1958.
37   G. D. Homan, *Jean-François Reubell*, The Hague, 1971.
38   M. Reinhard, *Le Grand Carnot*, 1952.
39   G. Robison, *Revellière-Lépeaux*, New York, 1938.
40   O. Wolff, *Ouvrard*, trans. S. Thomson, London, 1962.

Chapter 1. The thermidorean régime

41   R. C. Cobb and G. Rudé, 'Les journées de germinal et de prairial', *R.h.*, vol. ccxiv (1955).
42   R. Fuoc, *La Réaction thermidorienne à Lyon, 1795*, Lyon, 1957.
43   M. Schlumberger, 'La réaction thermidorienne à Toulouse', *A.h.R.f.*, no. 204 (1971).
44   W. F. Shepherd, *Price control and the Reign of Terror*, Berkeley, 1953.
45   J. R. Suratteau, 'Les élections de l'an 4', *A.h.R.f.*, no. 124 (1951).
46   K. Tonnesson, *La Défaite des sans-culottes*, 1959.
     (See also no. 21.)

Chapter 2. Jacobinism

47   *Babeuf et les Problèmes du Babouvisme*, Colloque international de Stockholm, 1960.
48   F. Buonarroti, *La Conspiration pour l'Égalité, dite de Babeuf*, Brussels, 1828.
49   R. C. Cobb, 'Notes sur la répression contre le personnel sans-culotte, de 1795 à 1801', *A.h.R.f.*, no. 135 (1954).
50   R. B. Rose, 'Tax revolt and popular organisation in Picardy, 1789–91', *P. & P.*, no. 43 (1969).
51   A. Soboul, *Les sans-culottes parisiens en l'an II*, 1958.
52   D. Thomson, *The Babeuf Plot: the making of a Republican legend*, London, 1947.
53   K. Tonnesson, 'The Babouvists: from Utopian to practical socialism', *P. & P.*, no. 22 (1962).
54   J. Tulard, 'Le recrutement de la légion de police de Paris sous la réaction thermidorienne et le Directoire', *A.h.R.f.*, no. 175 (1964).

55   I. Woloch, *Jacobin legacy: the democratic movement under the Directory*, Princeton, 1970.

(See also nos. 5, 6, 41, and 46.)

Chapter 3. Royalism

56   J. Chaumié, *Le réseau de d'Antraigues et la Contre-Révolution*, 1965.
57   W. R. Fryer, *Republic and Restoration in France, 1794–7*, Manchester, 1965.
58   J. Godechot, *La Contre-Révolution, 1789–1804*, 1961.
59   A. Goodwin, 'Counter-Revolution in Brittany: the conspiracy of La Rouërie', *B.J.R.L.*, vol. 39, no. 2 (1957).
60   'Vendée et chouannerie', in C. Mazauric, *Sur la Révolution française*, 1970.
61   H. Mitchell, 'Vendémiaire, a re-evaluation', *J.M.H.*, vol. 30 (1958).
62   H. Mitchell, *The Underground War against Revolutionary France*, Oxford, 1965.
63   G. Rudé, 'Les sans-culottes parisiens et les journées de vendémiaire IV', *A.h.R.f.*, no. 158 (1959).
64   J. R. Suratteau, 'Les élections de l'an V', *A.h.R.f.*, no. 154 (1958).
65   C. Tilly, *The Vendée*, London, 1964.

Chapter 4. 'Les Gros'

66   H. Duveyrier, *Anecdotes historiques*, 1907.
67   J. Godechot, 'Les aventures d'un fournisseur aux armées: Hanet-Cléry', *A.h.R.f.*, no. 73 (1936).
68   'La vente des biens nationaux', in G. Lefebvre, *Études sur la Révolution française*, 1954.
69   J. Sentou, *La fortune immobilière des Toulousains et la Révolution française*, Commission d'hist. écon. et sociale de la Révolution française, mémoires et documents, vol. XXIV (1970).
70   G. Six, *Les Généraux de la Révolution et de l'Empire*, 1947.

(See also nos. 1, 9, 28, 29, 33, and 40.)

Chapter 5. 'Les Maigres'

71   A. Abbiateci *et al.*, 'Crimes et criminalité en France, 17e–18e siècles', *Cahiers des Annales*, no. 33 (1971).
72   J. P. Bardet, 'Enfants abandonnés et enfants assistés à Rouen', in Société de Démographie historique, *Sur la population française au XVIIIe et au XIXe siècles: Hommage à M. Reinhard*, 1973.
73   B. Boutelet, 'Étude par sondage de la criminalité dans le bailliage du Pont-de-l'Arche', *Ann.Norm.*, vol. 12 (1962).
74   L. Chevalier, *Classes laborieuses et classes dangéreuses*, 1958.

75 'Disette et mortalité: la crise de l'an 3 et de l'an 4 à Rouen', in R. C. Cobb, *Terreur et subsistances*, 1965.

76 J. Combes-Monier, 'Population mouvante et criminalité à Versailles à la fin de l'Ancien Régime', in *Hommage à Reinhard* (See no. 72).

77 F. Furet, 'Pour une définition des classes inférieures à l'époque moderne', *Ann.E.S.C.*, vol. 18, no. 3 (1963).

78 P. Galliano, 'La mortalité infantile dans la banlieue sud de Paris à la fin du 18e siècle', *Ann.dém.hist.* (1966).

79 J.-C. Gégot, 'Étude par sondage de la criminalité dans le bailliage de Falaise', *Ann.Norm.*, vol. 16 (1966).

80 H. Hours, 'Émeutes et émotions populaires dans les campagnes du Lyonnais au 18e siècle', *Cahiers d'histoire*, no. 9 (1964).

81 O. Hufton, 'Women in Revolution, 1789–96', *P. & P.*, no. 53 (1971).

82 O. Hufton, 'Towards an understanding of the poor of 18th century France', in *French Government and Society* (see no. 14).

83 J. C. Perrot, 'La population pauvre de Caen d'après les listes de citoyens passifs', *Contributions à l'histoire démographique de la Révolution française, mémoires et documents*, vol. XIV, 1962.

84 J. Sentou, *Fortunes et groupes sociaux à Toulouse sous la Révolution: essai d'histoire statistique*, Toulouse, 1969.

85 M. Vovelle, 'De la mendicité au brigandage: les errants en Beauce sous la Révolution française', *Actes du 86e congrès national des sociétés savantes*, Montpellier, 1961.

86 M. Vovelle, 'Chartres et le pays chartrain: quelques aspects démographiques', *Contributions à l'histoire démographique de la Révolution française, mémoires et documents*, vol. XIV (1962).

87 M. Vovelle, 'Le prolétariat flottant à Marseille sous la Révolution française', *Ann.dém.hist.* (1968).

(See also nos. 1, 10, 12, 15, and 16.)

Chapter 6. Education and social welfare

88 H. C. Barnard, *Education and the French Revolution*, Cambridge, 1969.

89 B. Bois, *La vie scolaire et les créations intellectuelles en Anjou pendant la Révolution française*, 1929.

90 F. Brunot, *Histoire de la langue française des origines à 1900*, vol. 9, 1927.

91 M. Dommanget, 'Le prosélytisme révolutionnaire à Beauvais et dans l'Oise: l'enseignement populaire et civique', *A.h.R.f.*, no. 37 (1930).

92 M. Fleury and P. Valmary, 'Les progrès de l'instruction élémentaire de Louis XIV à Napoléon III', *Pop.*, vol. 12 (1957).

93   M. Gontard, *L'enseignement primaire en France, 1789–1833*, 1958.
94   J. E. Helmreich, 'The establishment of primary schools in France under the Directory', *F.h.s.*, vol. 2 (1961).
95   E. Lamouzèle, 'Une statistique des écoles primaires dans la Haute-Garonne en l'an 7', *Rév.fr.*, vol. 46 (1904).
96   A. Troux, *L'École centrale du Doubs à Besançon*, 1926.
97   G. Vautier, 'L'enseignement secondaire libre à Paris sous le Directoire', *A.h.R.f.*, no. 35 (1929).
98   F. Vial, *Trois siècles d'histoire de l'enseignement secondaire*, 1936.
99   D. Weiner, 'The French Revolution, Napoleon and the nursing profession', *Bulletin of the History of Medicine*, vol. XLVI, no. 3 (1972).

Chapter 7. '*Monsieur Dimanche*' and '*Citoyen Décadi*'

100   J. Boussoulade, 'Le Presbytérianisme dans les Conciles de 1797 et de 1801', *A.h.R.f.*, no. 121 (1951).
101   A. Dansette, *Histoire religieuse de la France contemporaine*, vol. 1, 1948.
102   J. Dupâquier and M. Lachiver, 'Sur les débuts de la contraception en France', *Ann.E.S.C.*, vol. 24, no. 6 (1969).
103   A. Latreille, *L'Église Catholique et la Révolution française*, vol. 1, 1946.
104   J. Leflon, *Monsieur Emery*, vol. 1, 1944.
105   J. Leflon, *Histoire de l'Église: la crise révolutionnaire*, 1949.
106   E. LeRoy Ladurie, 'Démographie et "funestes secrets": le Languedoc, fin 18e–début 19e siècle', *A.h.R.f.*, no. 182 (1965).
107   A. Mathiez, *La Théophilanthropie et le culte décadaire, 1796–1801*, 1904.
108   A. Mathiez, *Contributions à l'histoire religieuse de la Révolution française*, 1907.
109   J. McManners, *The French Revolution and the Church*, London, 1969.
110   R. Patry, *Le régime de la liberté des cultes dans le dépt. du Calvados pendant la première séparation, 1795–1802*, 1921.
111   B. Plongeron, 'Théologie et applications de la Collegialité dans l'église constitutionelle', *A.h.R.f.*, no. 211 (1973).
112   B. C. Poland, *French Protestantism and the French Revolution*, Princeton, 1957.
113   D. Robert, 'Note provisoire sur la situation des Églises Réformés à la fin de la période révolutionnaire', *B.S.H.P.F.*, 105th year (1959).
114   G. and M. Vovelle, 'Vision de la mort et de l'au-delà en Provence', *Cahiers des Annales*, no. 29 (1970).

(See also nos. 7, 28, 29, and 32.)

Chapter 8. Philosophy and science

115   E. H. Ackerknecht, *Medicine at the Paris Hospital, 1794–1848*, Baltimore, 1967.

116   C. H. van Duzer, *Contribution of the Idéologues to French Revolutionary thought*, Baltimore, 1935.

117   J. Fayet, *La Révolution française et la Science, 1789–95*, 1960.

118   G. C. Gillispie, 'Science in the French Revolution', *Behavioral Science*, vol. 4 (1959).

119   J. Godechot, 'L'Aerostation militaire sous le Directoire', *A.h.R.f.*, no. 45 (1931).

120   G. E. Gwynne, *Mme. de Staël et la Révolution française*, 1969.

121   R. Hahn, *The Anatomy of a Scientific Institution: the Paris Academy of Sciences, 1666–1803* (Los Angeles, 1971).

122   P. Huard, *Sciences, Médecine, Pharmacie, de la Révolution à l'Empire*, 1970.

123   J. Kitchin, *Un Journal philosophique: La Décade, 1794–1807*, 1965.

124   Y. Laissus, 'Gaspard Monge et l'expédition d'Egypte', *Revue de Synthèse*, vol. 81 (1960).

125   S. Moravia, *Il Tramonto dell'Illuminismo*, Bari, 1968.

126   F. Picavet, *Les Idéologues*, 1891.

127   M. Régaldo, 'La "Décade" et les philosophes du 18e siècle', *XVIIIe siècle*, no. 2 (1970).

128   W. A. Smeaton, *Fourcroy, Chemist and Revolutionary, 1755–1809*, Cambridge, 1962.

129   D. B. Weiner, 'French Doctors face war, 1792–1815', in C. K. Warner (ed.), *Essays in the History of Modern France, in Honour of S. B. Clough* (New York, 1969).

Chapter 9. Taste

130   C. Bellanger *et al.*, *Histoire générale de la presse française*, vol. 1, 1969.

131   M. Carlson, *The Theatre of the French Revolution*, Ithaca, N.Y., 1966.

132   C. Caubisens-Lasfargues, 'Le Salon de peinture pendant la Révolution', *A.h.R.f.*, no. 164 (1961).

133   D. L. Dowd, 'The French Revolution and the painters', *F.h.s.*, vol. 1, no. 2 (1959).

134   A. Dupront, ed., *Livre et Société dans la France du 18e siècle*, vol. 1, 1965.

135   G. Fleischer, *Annuaire de la Librairie*, 1802.

136   P. Francastel, *Le style Empire: du Directoire à la Restauration*, 1939.

137   W. Friedlaender, *David to Delacroix*, New York, 1968.

138   H. Honour, *Neo-Classicism*, Harmondsworth, 1968.

139   G. Janneau, *Le style directoire: mobilier et décoration*, 1940.

140 P. Lacroix, *Directoire, Consulat, Empire*, 1884.

141 J. A. Leith, *The Idea of Art as Propaganda in France, 1750–99*, Toronto, 1965.

142 R. de Luppé, *Les Idées littéraires de Mme. de Staël, et l'héritage des lumières, 1795–1800*, 1969.

143 A. P. Moore, *The 'Genre Poissard' and the French stage of the 18th century*, New York, 1935.

144 A. Pitou, 'Les origines du mélodrame français à la fin du 18e siècle', *Rev.hist.litt.*, vol. 18, no. 2 (1911).

145 H. Welschinger, *Le Théâtre de la Révolution, 1789–99*, 1880.

(See also no. 92.)

Chapter 10. The army

146 J.-P. Bertaud, *Valmy: la démocratie en armes*, 1970.

147 J.-P. Bertaud, 'Le recrutement et l'avancement des officiers de la Révolution', *A.h.R.f.*, no. 210 (1972).

148 A. and J. Bricard, *Journal du canonnier Bricard, 1792–1802*, 1894.

149 J. P. Charnay, *Société militaire et suffrage politique en France depuis 1789*, 1964.

150 A. Corvisier, *L'Armée française de la fin du 17e siècle au ministère de Choiseul: Le Soldat*, 2 vols., 1964.

151 J. Godechot, 'Les insurrections militaires sous le Directoire', *A.h.R.f.*, no. 56 (1933).

152 L. Lévy-Schneider, *Le Conventionnel Jeanbon St-André, 1749–1813*, 2 vols., 1901.

153 M. Martin, 'Journaux d'armées au temps de la Convention', *A.h.R.f.*, no. 210 (1972).

154 M. Reinhard, *Avec Bonaparte en Italie, d'après les lettres inédites de son a.d.c. Joseph Sulkowski*, 1946.

155 M. Reinhard, 'Nostalgie et service militaire pendant la Révolution', *A.h.R.f.*, no. 150 (1958).

156 M. Reinhard, 'Observations sur le rôle révolutionnaire de l'armée dans la Révolution française', *A.h.R.f.*, no. 168 (1962).

157 S. F. Scott, 'Les officiers de l'infanterie de ligne à la veille de l'amalgame', *A.h.R.f.*, no. 194 (1968).

158 S. F. Scott, 'The Regeneration of the Line Army during the French Revolution', *J.M.H.*, vol. 42 (1970).

159 S. F. Scott, 'Les soldats de l'armée de ligne en 1793', *A.h.R.f.*, no. 210 (1972).

(See also no. 196.)

Chapter 11. Administration

160 C. Bloch, 'Le recrutement du personnel municipal en l'an 4', *Rév.fr.*, vol. 46 (1904).

161 C. H. Church, 'The social basis of the French central bureaucracy under the Directory, 1795–99', *P. & P.*, no. 36 (1967).

162 C. H. Church, 'Bureaucracy, politics and Revolution: the evidence of the Commission des Dix-Sept', *F.h.s.*, vol. 6, no. 4 (1970).

163 A. Mathiez, 'Le personnel gouvernemental du Directoire', *A.h.R.f.*, no. 59 (1933).

164 H. T. Parker, 'Two administrative bureaus under the Directory and Napoleon', *F.h.s.*, vol. 4, no. 2 (1965).

165 O. Festy, 'Les essais de statistique économique pendant le Directoire et le Consulat', *A.h.R.f.*, no. 131 (1953).

166 R. Schnerb, 'De la Constituante à Napoléon; les vicissitudes de l'impôt direct', *Ann.E.S.C.*, vol. 2, no. 1 (1947).

167 G. Vallée, *La conscription dans le département de la Charente, 1798–1807*, 1937.

(See also nos. 13, 15, 18, 20, 28, 31, 32, 33, and 35.)

Chapter 12. Economic life

168 L. Bergeron, 'Profits et risques dans les affaires parisiennes à l'époque du Directoire et du Consulat', *A.h.R.f.*, no. 185 (1966).

169 L. Bergeron, 'À propos des biens nationaux: la signification économique du placement immobilier', *Ann.E.S.C.*, vol. 26 (1971).

170 H. Causse, 'Un industriel toulousain au temps de la Révolution et de l'Empire: F.-B. Boyer-Fonfrède', *Ann.Midi*, vol. 69 (1957).

171 A. Chabert, *Essai sur les mouvements des revenus et de l'activité économique en France de 1798 à 1820*, 1949.

172 F. Crouzet, 'Les origines du sous-développement économique du Sud-Ouest', *Ann.Midi*, vol. 71 (1959).

173 F. Crouzet, 'Les conséquences économiques de la Révolution', *A.h.R.f.*, no. 168 (1962).

174 F. Crouzet, 'Wars, blockade and economic change in Europe 1792–1815', *J.E.H.*, vol. XXIV (1964).

175 F. Crouzet, 'La ruine du grand commerce', in *Bordeaux au 18e siècle*, ed. F. Pariset, Bordeaux, 1968.

176 G. Dejoint, *La politique économique du Directoire*, 1951.

177 F. Evrard, 'Les ouvriers du textile dans la région rouennaise, 1789–1802', *A.h.R.f.*, no. 44 (1931).

178 T. Kemp, *Economic Forces in French History*, London, 1971.

179 G. Lefebvre, 'Les mines de Littry de 1795 à l'an 8', *A.h.R.f.*, no. 14 (1926).

180 G. Lefebvre, 'La place de la Révolution dans l'histoire agraire de la France', *Ann.hist.écon.soc.*, vol. 1 (1929).

181 P. Léon, *La Naissance de la grande industrie en Dauphiné*, part 2, sect. 2, 1954.

182 P. Leuilliot, *L'Alsace au début du 19e siècle*, vol. 2, 1959.

183 J. Marczewski, 'Some aspects of the economic growth of France, 1660–1958', *Economic Development and Cultural Change*, vol. IX, no. 3 (1961).

184 M. Marion, *Histoire financière de la France depuis 1715*, vols. 3 and 4, 1927.

185 M. Reinhard *et al.*, *Contributions à l'histoire démographique de la Révolution française, mémoires et documents*, vol. XVIII, 2nd series (1965).

186 G. Richert, 'Biens communaux et droits d'usage en Haute-Garonne pendant la réaction thermidorienne et sous le Directoire', *A.h.R.f.*, no. 123 (1951).

187 R. Schnerb, 'La dépression économique sous le Directoire après la disparition du papier-monnaie', *A.h.R.f.*, no. 61 (1934).

188 E. Soreau, 'Les ouvriers en l'an 7', *A.h.R.f.*, no. 44 (1931).

189 P. P. Viard, 'Vers l'ajustement des prix dans l'Hérault à la fin de l'an V', *A.h.R.f.*, no. 27 (1928).

Chapters 13 and 14. Foreign policy

190 S. S. Biro, *The German Policy of Revolutionary France*, 2 vols., Cambridge, Mass., 1957.

191 F. Charles-Roux, *Bonaparte: Governor of Egypt*, trans. E. W. Dickes, London, 1937.

192 V. Daline, 'Marc-Antoine Jullien après le 9 thermidor', *A.h.R.f.*, no. 185 (1966).

193 R. Devleeshouwer *et al.*, 'Occupants et occupés, 1792–1815', *Colloque de Bruxelles*, 1968.

194 R. de Felice, 'La vendita dei beni nazionali nella Repubblica Romana del 1798–9', *Storia ed economia*, no. 8 (Rome, 1960).

195 V. E. Giuntella, 'La giacobina repubblica romana, 1798–9: aspetti e momenti', *Archivio della società romana di storia patria*, vol. 73 (Rome, 1950).

196 J. Godechot, *Les commissaires aux armées sous le Directoire*, 2 vols., 1937.

197 J. Godechot, *La Grande Nation: l'expansion révolutionnaire de la France dans le monde de 1789 à 1799*, 1956.

198 R. Guyot, *Le Directoire et la paix de l'Europe*, 1912.

199 U. Marcelli, 'La crisi economica e sociale a Bologna e le prime vendite dei beni ecclesiastici', *Atti e memorie della deputazione di storia patria per le province di Romagna*, n.s., vol. 5 (1953–4).

200 B. Nabonne, *La diplomatie du Directoire et Bonaparte d'après les papiers inédits de Reubell*, 1951.

201 R. R. Palmer, 'Much in little: the Dutch Revolution of 1795', *J.M.H.*, vol. XXVI (1954).

202 A. B. Rodger, *The War of the Second Coalition, 1798–1801: a strategic commentary*, Oxford, 1964.

203 S. T. Ross, 'The military strategy of the Directory: the campaign of 1799', *F.h.s.*, vol. 5 (1967).

204 G. Vaccarino, *I patrioti 'anarchistes' e l'idea dell'unità italiana, 1796–99*, Turin, 1955.

205 C. Zaghi, *Bonaparte e il Direttorio dopo Campoformio*, Naples, 1956.

(See also nos. 7, 37, and 151.)

Chapters 15 and 16. The coups of floréal, prairial, and brumaire

206 'Le lendemain de Dix-Huit Brumaire', in A. Aulard, *Études et leçons sur la Révolution française*, vol. 2, 1898.

207 J. Beyssi, 'Le parti jacobin à Toulouse sous le Directoire', *A.h.R.f.*, no. 117 (1950).

208 G. Caudrillier, *L'Association Royaliste de l'Institut Philanthropique à Bordeaux*, 1908.

209 J. Godechot, 'Le Directoire vu de Londres', *A.h.R.f.*, no. 117 (1950).

210 R. Guyot, 'Du Directoire au Consulat: les transitions', *R.h.*, vol. CXI, no. 1 (1912).

211 Abbé J. Lacouture, *Le Mouvement royaliste dans le sud-ouest, 1797–1800*, Hossegor, 1932.

212 C. Langlois, 'Le plébiscite de l'an 8, ou le coup d'état du 18 pluviôse VIII', *A.h.R.f.*, nos. 207–9 (1972).

213 A. Meynier, *Les coups d'état du Directoire*, 3 vols., 1928.

214 J. R. Suratteau, *Les Élections de l'an VI et le coup d'état du 22 floréal*, 1971.

215 M. Ozouf, 'De thermidor à brumaire: le discours de la Révolution sur elle-même', *R.h.*, vol. CCXLIII, no. 493 (1970).

(See also nos. 2, 7, 11, 13, 34, 55, and 58.)

INDEX